D1611943

War in the Modern Great Power System

War in the Modern Great Power System, 1495-1975

Jack S. Levy

THE UNIVERSITY PRESS OF KENTUCKY

Scholarly publisher for the Commonwealth, serving Bellarmine College, Berea College, Centre College of Kentucky, Eastern Kentucky University, The Filson Club, Georgetown College, Kentucky Historical Society, Kentucky State University, Morehead State University, Murray State University, Northern Kentucky University, Transylvania University, University of Kentucky, University of Louisville, and Western Kentucky University.

Editorial and Sales Offices: Lexington, Kentucky 40506-0024

Library of Congress Cataloging in Publication Data

Levy, Jack S., 1948-
War in the modern great power system, 1495-1975.

Bibliography: p.
Includes index.
1. War. 2. Great powers. 3. Balance of power.
4. World politics. 5. Military history, Modern.
I. Title.
U21.2.L44 1983 355'.02'094 83-10249
ISBN 0-8231-1497-7

To Mom and Dad

Contents

Tables

Figures

Preface

The original idea for this study can be traced to my introduction to balance of power theory as a graduate student over a decade ago. Particularly interesting to me were the numerous theoretical propositions linking international war to various structural characteristics of the international system, including the size of the system, power distributions, alliances, polarity, etc. While recognizing the logical flaws in balance of power theory, I was convinced of the importance of many of the individual propositions associated with it. They deal with theoretically important variables and many have been widely accepted. What disturbed me was that the validity of these propositions is often simply assumed on the basis of a few examples selected from narrow slices of historical experience that are not necessarily representative of international politics in general. I was convinced, therefore, of the importance of subjecting these hypotheses to systematic empirical test. The work of Singer and his colleagues associated with the Correlates of War Project was quite impressive, but I was convinced that many important hypotheses could not be tested with their data. Their temporal domain was too short for many slowly changing systemic variables and included too few major wars. Moreover, the inclusion in most of the early COW studies of small power wars was troublesome because the balance of power framework and its associated propositions were intended primarily as a theory of Great Power behavior. For these reasons I decided to generate a data base for the Great Powers over an extended temporal domain in order to test some of the leading hypotheses associated with balance of power theory.

While driven by the ultimate aim of testing causal hypotheses associated with balance of power theory, this study is confined to more limited objectives. Its purpose is to generate a compilation of war data for the Great Powers for the last five centuries and provide a thorough description of the characteristics, patterns, and trends in war involving the Powers. These are important questions in themselves, particularly given the lack of explicit attention to the Great Powers in earlier studies of war and the relatively short temporal domain for which these questions are normally answered. These questions are also important for our ultimate explanatory objectives, for it is assumed that the explanation of the causes of Great Power war can best be accomplished in the context of a full descriptive analysis of the characteristics, patterns and trends of those wars.

The testing of bivariate and multivariate causal hypotheses will be an even more demanding task, requiring the operationalization and measurement of a host of other variables over an extended temporal domain, and lying beyond the capacities of a single researcher. I do hope that others will see merit in such studies and will seek to use this data base where it serves their purposes. One word of caution should be noted here, however. The data base is in a constant state of revision as subsequent historical research uncovers new information. The present compilation involves numerous changes from the compilation in my earlier doctoral dissertation and further changes will undoubtedly need to be made. Anyone interested in using this data base would be advised to contact me for the most recent alterations. Needless to say, I welcome any and all notifications of errors and suggestions of additional changes in the data base.

The successful completion of this study would not have been possible without the help of many people and I would like to express my appreciation at this time. The initial stages of this project were conducted under the guidance of David Tarr and Bernard Cohen, and the basic design of the project owes much to their criticisms, suggestions, and encouragement. The Helen Dwight Reid Award of the American Political Science Association for 1975 and 1976 provided further encouragement, and convinced me of the value of the project and the utility of undertaking a major reworking of the study for the purposes of publication. Many others have contributed to the final product. Bruce Russett provided many valuable suggestions and helped in numerous ways, and I am very grateful. An earlier version of the manuscript was also read in its entirety by Theodore Ropp, Richard Rosecrance, and Richard Merritt, each of whom provided very useful comments. Others have helped through their comments and criticisms of separate papers that have since been incorporated into this book. They include J. David Singer, Randolph Siverson, Michael P. Sullivan, Stuart Bremer, Harrison Wagner, Karl Schmitt, Terry Sullivan, David Furlow, Neil Richardson, and Jim Austin. I owe special thanks to Cliff Morgan, my research assistant and colleague, who has been involved in every stage of the project over the last several years. He has helped not only with the data analysis and interpretation, but also by offering valuable theoretical and methodological suggestions and generally serving as an indispensible sounding board for my ideas. I have relied a great deal upon his good judgement, and this study is much better because of his contribution.

I would also like to express my appreciation to William S. Livingston and The University of Texas Research Institute for their partial financial support of the project over the last four years. Chuck Cnudde and the Government Department have also been supportive. Elizabeth Manning helped expedite the completion of the manuscript and Betty McEuen did a fine job of typing the final copy. James Pinedo created the computer graphics. I'd also like to express my appreciation to Barbara Sarles, who helped with some of the preliminary editing, assisted with the graphs, and provided the moral support which has meant so much.

Some parts of this study have previously appeared in print elsewhere. I would like to thank Sage Publications for granting their permission to reprint parts of my "Historical Trends in Great Power War, 1495-1975" from *International Studies Quarterly* 26 (June 1982): 278-300, and "World System Analysis: A Great Power Framework" from *World System Analysis: Competing Perspectives* edited by William R. Thompson, 1983. I would also like to thank the University of Texas Press for their permission to reprint parts of "The Contagion of Great Power War Behavior, 1495-1975" from the *American Journal of Political Science* 26 (August 1982): 562-84. I would also like to acknowledge the fact that the conception of this study was strongly influenced by the work of Singer and his colleagues on the Correlates of War Project, and the fact that some of the data for this study have been taken from *The Wages of War* by Singer and Melvin Small (Wiley, 1972).

While I have benefited from the insights and suggestions of others, it is hardly necessary to say that this advice was not always consistent and not always heeded. No one will agree with everything I have written, and I alone should be held accountable for any errors of commission or omission.

1

Introduction: The Empirical Study of War

War has been a pervasive and persistent phenomenon throughout history. It is a major distinguishing characteristic of international politics and probably the most destructive form of human behavior. War is often perceived as a useful and sometimes necessary instrument of policy for the achievement of state political objectives, yet the avoidance of war without the sacrifice of other core values is a primary foreign policy objective of nearly all states. The buildup of national military capabilities is a constant preoccupation of statesmen but one that diverts significant resources from more constructive social pursuits, often contributes little to the security toward which it is directed, and may be a leading cause of the war it aims to avoid. For these and other reasons, the study of war has been a central concern of philosophers, historians, and social scientists since the beginning of recorded history.

In spite of the importance of war and the enormous human and economic resources devoted to its many aspects, our understanding of war remains at an elementary level. No widely accepted theory of the causes of war exists and little agreement has emerged on the methodology through which these causes might be discovered. Instead, the literature is characterized by a proliferation of competing and often contradictory theories. There have been relatively few efforts to subject these theories to rigorous and systematic empirical testing in an attempt to resolve their contradictions and contribute to the accumulation of scientific knowledge about international war. More emphasis has been placed on generating plausible theoretical arguments concerning why certain relationships ought to be true than on verifying empirically whether in fact they are true. An assumption underlying this study is that further progress toward understanding international conflict requires not only the careful specification of theoretical relationships but also the rigorous and systematic testing of these theories to ascertain their validity.

In the last two decades, however, there has been a proliferation of empirically based studies of international conflict.[1] Among the most rigorous and systematic are those based on the war data compiled by Quincy Wright, Lewis F. Richardson, and J. David Singer and Melvin Small.[2] The Singer-Small data and the associated Correlates of War Project have had an especially profound impact on recent conflict research. The data set published in *The Wages of War, 1816–1965,* is unparalleled and has served as the foundation for the statistical analysis of a wide range of important hypotheses regarding international conflict.[3] The studies by Singer and Small as well as those based on Richardson's data, however, are limited in that most of them focus on war behavior in general and fail to differentiate the Great Powers from the hundred or so other states in the international system.[4] Consequently, their findings are not necessarily applicable to the Great Powers.

Few would doubt the importance of war involving the Great Powers. The Great Powers have traditionally been distinguished from other states and viewed as the dominant actors in international politics, particularly with respect to security-related issues. Statesmen have always been most concerned with security threats deriving from the Powers and have devoted disproportionate attention and resources to dealing with these threats. The uniqueness of the Great Powers has also been recognized in international law. They were differentiated from the lesser powers at the Congress of Vienna, for example, and were given a distinct set of rights and responsibilities.[5] Scholars also have recognized the leading role of the great powers. Leopold Von Ranke conceived of the international history of Europe as a history of Great Power relations, and A. J. P. Taylor argues that "the relations of the Great Powers have determined the history of Europe."[6] Many of our theories of international politics are essentially theories of Great Power behavior. Balance-of-power theory, for example, was for years the dominant paradigm in international relations. Its central assumptions of anarchy, the absence of an external authority, and self-help are less valid when applied to lesser states living in the shadows of the Powers. Its concern with balances, the avoidance of war, and the independence of states clearly refers to the Great Powers rather than to states in general.[7] Kenneth N. Waltz argues that any general theory of international politics must necessarily be based on the Great Powers, for in any system the leading actors essentially define the context for others as well as for themselves.[8]

Most important for the purposes of this study is the fact that the Great Powers have participated in a disproportionately high percentage of history's wars. Quincy Wright finds that during the last five centuries four states have each participated in over 20 percent of European wars and that France alone participated in about 47 percent of the 2,600 battles involving European states.[9] Even more compelling is the fact that approximately 70 percent of the wars Wright examines involve at least one of the Great Powers. Moreover, these states had a higher rate of war involvement during the years when they were Great Powers than when they were not.[10] Similarly, Frederick Adams Woods and Alexander Baltzly, focusing on the proportion of years states have been at war since 1700, find that the strongest nations have devoted the most time to war.[11] The same pattern is true for more recent times, though to a slightly lesser extent. In Singer and Small's compilation of all wars since 1816, 60 percent of the interstate wars and 75 percent of the "extra-systemic" wars involve a Great Power.[12] The wars of the Great Powers also account for most of the losses of life from war, with a significant fraction of these losses occurring in a small number of "general wars," defined by the participation of nearly all of the Great Powers. These general wars have been major turning points in international history, marking the rise and fall of hegemonial powers and serving as the primary vehicle for fundamental transformations of the international system. Perhaps George Modelski exaggerates when he concludes that "war is primarily a Great Power activity," that war occurs "because there are Great Powers," and that "the Great Power system exists because there is war,"[13] but the importance of the Great Powers for war and war for the Great Powers is undeniable.

Wars in which the Great Powers participate should be analyzed apart from wars in general because of the importance of the Great Powers and the distinctiveness of their behavior, including their war behavior. If Great Power wars are not analyzed separately, significant patterns of Great Power behavior may be obscured by noise generated by smaller states operating in more restricted regional systems. But analyses of the Great Power wars selected from the Singer-Small compilation would fail to produce meaningful statistical results because the compilation includes fewer than thirty interstate wars involving the Great Powers and fewer than ten wars between the Powers. To test hypotheses of Great Power war behavior by a methodology of aggregate data analysis, it is necessary to consider a longer time span.

Extension of the temporal domain is necessary for other reasons as well. Although the 1816-1980 period is adequate for the testing of many important hypotheses, its utility is limited for application to other theoretical questions. Some important variables—including structural characteristics of the international system that are central to balance-of-power theory and theories of systemic transformation—have changed little over the last century and a half; a meaningful analysis of the impact of these variables on war requires an examination of historical periods in which they fluctuated more widely. The nineteenth and twentieth centuries alone do not provide the variety and richness of data that can be obtained from a more extended period. For example, an analysis of the relative stability of bipolar and multipolar systems should not be restricted to an era characterized by only one period of bipolarity, especially when that period coincides with the development of nuclear technology, the confounding effects of which preclude the generation of any causal inferences. Similarly, an analysis of the impact of technology on the incidence of warfare is best served by incorporating preindustrial periods characterized by less advanced technology and lower rates of change. In addition to increasing both the number of cases and the range of the variables, the extension of the time span facilitates scientific analysis by incorporating additional control variables and by increasing the randomization of extraneous variables and hence minimizing their impact on the relationship under consideration.

Two other sets of questions also call for study of a more extended period. One is the question of long-term trends in war. Not only is the last century and a half too short for effective analysis, but the fact that the nineteenth century was the most peaceful of modern history introduces an upward bias into the secular trends. A more important set of theoretical questions is raised by the recent world system paradigms. Both the capitalist world economy paradigm of Immanuel Wallerstein and Christopher Chase-Dunn and the global political economy of George Modelski and William R. Thompson challenge the traditional realist theories based on power politics.[14] These hypotheses involve processes spanning the entire five centuries of the modern period and can only be tested against realist propositions by using a more extended temporal domain than that employed by Singer and Small.

War data covering a broader historical scope have been compiled by Wright, Pitirim A. Sorokin, and Woods and Baltzly.[15] Each of these compilations has serious limitations. None is specifically a study of the Great Powers, for all include some lesser states. Nor are any of their data bases alone sufficient for the purposes of this study. Neither Sorokin nor Woods and Baltzly provides explicit and rigorous criteria for the inclusion and exclusion of wars, and Wright's criteria are excessively legalistic. These problems, which will be further discussed in Chapter 2, preclude a truly systematic study of the nature, causes, and consequences of war.

This brief survey of existing compilations of war data is not meant to detract from the enormous intellectual accomplishments that these works represent. The studies by Sorokin, Wright, Richardson, and Singer and Small are all critical landmarks in the evolution of modern scientific analysis of war. Each has made a significant contribution to our understanding of international conflict and the methodology by which we analyze it, and each has generated sophisticated theoretical and methodological approaches. But none of these studies deals adequately with the specific question of Great Power war behavior. For this purpose a separate analysis, based on a new set of data and drawing upon the efforts of these earlier scholars, is needed.

Such an analysis cannot be undertaken in the absence of a conceptual and historical examination of the Great Powers. Although the central role of the Great Powers has been widely recognized in the traditional literature, the concept has never been refined for systematic empirical research. As we shall see in Chapter 2, there have been several thorough analytical treatments of the Great Power concept and a few attempts to determine the identity of the Powers in historical systems.[16] The latter, however, are seldom related to the former. Attempts to identify the Powers historically are generally conducted in the absence of any nominal or operational definition of the Great Power concept, which raises serious questions about the validity of these systems of Powers and their utility for systematic empirical research. In addition, there have been few attempts to specify the theoretical assumptions underlying the concept of a Great Power system. These tasks must be completed if theoretical generalizations about the Great Powers and their wars are to be possible.

The basic aims of this study, then, are to define and identify the modern Great Powers; to define, identify, and measure their wars; and to analyze the characteristics, patterns, and historical trends in these wars. In Chapter 2 the assumptions underlying the concept of the modern Great Power system are specified. After an extensive review of previous analytical treatments of the Great Powers, that concept is defined and the relevant empirical referents of Great Power rank are suggested. The origins of the Great Power system are established, and a historical analysis to determine the identity of the Great Powers over time is undertaken. In Chapter 3 we turn to the definition and identification of war. Considerable attention is given to the problem of inclusion and exclusion—the criteria used either to include specific wars or exclude them from the compilation. On the basis of these criteria, a list of interstate wars involving the Great Powers is generated and then compared with previous compilations. After conceptualizing war on a variety of levels, dimensions, and units of analysis, wars are measured in Chapter 4. The war data are presented graphically and analyzed statistically beginning in Chapter 5. The characteristics of the individual wars and of the yearly amount of war are examined. Empirical relationships among the various dimensions of war are determined and interpreted in light of a number of hypotheses in the literature. In Chapter 6 linear and cyclical trends in war are examined and a comparison of different historical eras is undertaken. Finally, the relationship between the amounts of war in successive periods is considered in Chapter 6 in order to deal with the question of whether war is "contagious." Finally, a summary and conclusions are presented.

This is a univariate study of war in the modern Great Power system, and for this reason no effort will be made to analyze the causes of war or its consequences (other than its impact on subsequent war). The premise is that the Great Powers and their wars must be defined, identified, and measured before causes and consequences can be systematically analyzed. This study is designed to lay the groundwork for subsequent testing of key theoretical propositions relating to the causes and consequences of war in the modern Great Power system.

2

The Modern Great Power System

Before the Great Powers can be defined and identified it is necessary to specify the assumptions underlying the concept of a Great Power system. The Great Power framework and the realist paradigm from which it derives is only one of several possible approaches to the study of international relations. Other frameworks are based on a different set of assumptions and concepts, identify another set of leading actors, and offer alternative explanations for war, change, and other phenomena in world politics.[1] If these competing paradigms are to be compared and their constrasting propositions subjected to a critical test, the assumptions upon which they are based must be clearly specified.

Assumptions of the Great Power Framework

The Great Power framework shares the basic assumptions of the realist paradigm of international politics but focuses explicitly on the small number of leading actors in the system.[2] It is assumed that in any anarchic international system there exists a hierarchy of actors determined on the basis of power. In the modern system since 1500 the dominant actors have been dynastic/territorial states and nation-states; in the international system of ancient Greece and Renaissance Italy the dominant actors were city-states. The more powerful states —the Great Powers—determine the structure, major processes, and general evolution of the system.[3] Therefore, the actions and interactions of the Great Powers are of primary interest. Secondary states and other actors have an impact on the system largely to the extent that they affect the behavior of the Great Powers. This hierarchy of actors is intimately related to a hierarchy of issues dominated by military security. It is assumed that issues overlap and that the currency of military power is applicable to and effective in the resolution of other issues. The concept of a Great Power system is based on the traditional assumption, shared by realists since Thucydides, that world politics is dominated by security issues and the struggle for power.[4]

The priority of military security derives from the perception of a high-threat environment, which in turn derives primarily from the anarchic structure of the international system.[5] In this context, it is the Great Powers, because of their military capability and ability to project it, that generally can do most to affect the national interests of others and are therefore perceived as the most serious security threats. Consequently, the Powers direct their primary attention toward each other. A relatively high proportion of their alliance commitments and war behavior is with each other, and they tend to perceive much of international relations as dependent upon and revolving around their own interrelationships. The general level of interactions among the Great Powers tends to be higher than for other states, whose interests are narrower and who interact primarily in more restricted regional settings. Thus the Great Powers constitute an interdependent system of power and security relations, which will be called here the Great Power system.[6]

This is an open rather than a closed system, for it is affected to some extent by the larger world system of which it is a part. The primary influences on the Great Powers, however, derive from within the Great Power system, and their patterns of interaction can be explained largely by the internal dynamics of that system. Because they recognize the interdependence of security relations, the Great Powers play a major role in the management and order maintenance of the larger international system.[7] They participate in a high proportion of the wars in the international system and largely determine the outcome of the peace settlements that follow. In this way the Great Powers play the major role in the transformation of the international system and the structuring of international order. The Great Power system may be a subsystem of the larger international system, but in fundamental respects it is a dominant subsystem.[8]

The basic argument is that any anarchic international system is dominated by a few Great Powers. Great Power systems operated within the international systems of ancient Greece, ancient China, and Renaissance Italy, as well as modern Europe.[9] The concern of this study is with the modern Great Power system, which originated in Europe about five centuries ago and gradually expanded into the contemporary global system. The Eurocentric bias of this study is deliberate. The system centered in Europe is of greatest historical interest to most Western scholars, and most theories of international behavior and war have been derived from it. Most of the wars of the last five centuries have involved European powers and have centered in Europe. Finally, the contemporary world represents a continuing evolution of the Western state system, so the most valid lessons for the future presumably can be learned from this system.

Definition of the Great Power Concept

The widespread recognition of the importance of the Great Powers is not matched by analytical precision in the use of the concept. Scholars have either not attempted to define the concept or made no effort to translate vague definitions into meaningful operational criteria. As we shall see, many historians identify specific dates or events as marking a state's rise to or decline from Great Power status, but they take for granted the meaning of the concept. This is true of modern social scientists as well. Singer and Small, for example, resort to "intercoder agreement" as the sole criterion for the identification of their major power system.[10] Robert L. Rothstein suggests that this absence of definitional precision may be traced to the fairly widespread belief that the distinction between Great Powers and other states is self-evident, particularly for the eighteenth and nineteenth centuries, for which the indicators of military power are said to be unambiguous.[11] It is true that for any historical period the identity of some of the Great Powers is self-evident, but frequently the status of one or two states is uncertain (for example, eighteenth-century Spain or nineteenth-century Italy). Consequently, the precise identity of all of the Great Powers has never been as self-evident as many scholars have presumed, even for the eighteenth and nineteenth centuries. This ambiguity is demonstrated by the numerous contradictions in the literature. In addition, historical developments since World War II have further blurred the distinction between Great Powers and others. It is this very difficulty of defining the Great Power concept and devising operational indicators valid over a range of diverse historical conditions that has inhibited many scholars from undertaking such a systematic analysis.

Nearly all definitions of Great Powers focus primarily on military might. Taylor, for example, asserts that "the test of a Great Power is then the test of strength for war." Modelski claims that a Great Power "must be capable of fighting a major war." Singer and Thomas Cusack insist that the most obvious attribute of a major power is the "ability to wage war frequently and to win most of those wars." The classic definition from which many others are clearly derived was provided by Ranke: a Great Power "must be able to maintain itself against all others, even when they are united." It is not clear what Ranke meant by "maintain itself against all others," but the criterion of self-sufficiency would appear to be far too demanding. Few states in history have possessed capabilities sufficient to defend against a combination of all others. As Taylor notes in his study of several decades of diplomacy before World War I, "Even the greatest of Powers shrank from fighting alone against a coalition."[12] Revisionist Powers seeking hegemony have invariably been defeated by opposing coalitions. Ranke's definition would exclude too many states from Great Power rank, though it might serve as a useful definition of a more restricted class of Superpowers.[13]

Modifications of Ranke's general conception of the self-sufficiency of a Great Power are provided by Michael Haas, Hedley Bull, Robert L. Rothstein, and Stanley Hoffmann. Haas states that a major power "can be totally defeated in battle by no other single power, but instead by a combination of members (usually including another major power)."[14] By not insisting that a Great Power be able to withstand a coalition of Powers, Haas comes much closer to the conventional but unstated notion of what it means to be a Great Power. Haas, however, fails to provide empirical indicators for his concepts, and it is far from clear how he arrives at his list of major powers in a succession of international subsystems since 1649. In addition, although the notion of avoiding total defeat may be useful conceptually as a minimum standard for Great Power rank, it raises the questions of what constitutes total defeat and whether it is a necessary or sufficient condition for major power status.

It would be too demanding to define total defeat only as permanent extinction as a political entity, for this is relatively rare historically and would leave too many Great Powers. Yet relaxing the standard to include military occupation and temporary loss of sovereign independence would also create problems. The German defeat and occupation of France in 1940 would presumably lead to the exclusion of France (for she regained her sovereignty only with the help of her allies), yet Haas includes Vichy France as a major power during this period. Nor should France be eliminated from Great Power status on the eve of World War II because she was capable of being totally defeated. This example suggests that military occupation is not a sufficient condition for the loss of Great Power rank. In addition, the Ranke and Haas conceptualizations are inappropriate in the nuclear age because all states are potentially vulnerable to nearly total destruction.

Other definitions based on the general notion of self-sufficiency are less restrictive than the notion of total defeat. Martin Wight argues that "a Great Power is one that can afford to take on any other Power whatever in single combat." Similarly, Taylor suggests that even the weakest of the Powers "could make a respectable showing in a general conflict among the Great Powers." Rothstein argues that a Great Power is a state that can rely on its own capabilities to provide for its security. Small powers, on the other hand, must rely on external alliances, aid, or international institutions and therefore do not have direct or primary control over their own destinies. This definition is similar to one criterion suggested by Hoffmann: Great Powers can provide for their security without significantly undermining their independence, whereas smaller states must often make a choice between security and independence.[15] This definition allows for a more reasonable conception of security than avoidance of total defeat and can incorporate the concept of deterrence as well as defense. One weakness, however, is that it tends to underestimate the security threats posed by other Great Powers and the interdependence of nearly all states in maintaining security. Before the nuclear age, at least, in only a few instances was one state self-sufficient against a coalition of others.

The persistent danger posed by Great Powers to each other is recognized in Bull's conceptualization: "Great Powers have been secure against the attacks of small Powers; and have had to fear only other Great Powers, and hostile combinations of Powers."[16] Although an improvement over the definitions considered above, this one shares a common limitation with them. By relying on the Rankian concept of self-sufficiency, these formulations define Great Power interests negatively, as passive security. They minimize the importance of the Great Powers' capabilities and willingness to project their military power beyond their borders to advance their interests and structure the environment. Self-sufficiency with respect to security is a necessary but not sufficient condition for Great Power rank. The Powers have always been concerned not only with minimizing their losses but also with maximizing their gains, and they are willing to take risks in order to do so.[17] A state that cannot be conquered but lacks the capability to threaten others or influence security affairs in the system as a whole (for example, seventeenth-century Russia and perhaps the United States in the nineteenth century) would not normally be considered a Great Power. This idea is recognized in several conceptualizations. Michael Howard states, "A Great Power, almost by definition, is one which has the capacity to control events beyond its own borders; and that is usually based on the ability to use military force." Haas, in an alternative formulation to that expressed earlier, defines major powers as "elite or dominant members of a system whose behavior is capable of upsetting an existing power distribution or placing a power equilibrium in jeopardy."[18]

Thus a Great Power must possess both relative self-sufficiency with respect to security, including invulnerability against secondary states, and the ability to project military power beyond its borders in pursuit of its interests. This formulation does not imply that non-Powers cannot project military power beyond their borders but only that qualitative differences exist between them and the Great Powers. These differences include the total amount of power projected, the logistical ability to sustain it over an extended period, and the ability to affect the overall distribution of power at the systemic level. Of course, not all Great Powers have enormous projection capabilities. In this respect as well as others, however, the differences between the Great Powers and nonpowers are far greater than the differences among the Powers.

The few attempts to provide operational criteria for the identification of the Powers have generally relied on indicators of military capabilities alone. This is clearly the basis for the "self-evident" classification of eighteenth- and nineteenth-century states. As Rothstein notes, "counting the number of available infantrymen sufficed" to differentiate the Great Powers. Modelski suggests the more general formulation that a Great Power is one that holds at least 5 percent of the available military power in the global system. He also uses this criterion in his later conceptualization of global powers in a global system, and Thompson has measured the naval capabilities of the leading global powers. But in the Great Power system as defined here, land armies carry greater weight than naval forces.[19]

Several problems arise in establishing a criterion based on a percentage of available power in the Great Power system. One is determining the appropriate percentage to use. Another is determining the relative weights of different elements of military power, including land-based power versus naval or air power, personnel versus armaments, quantity versus quality of armaments, and combat strength versus logistical support. In addition, many elements are resistant to quantitative measurement, including training, morale, leadership, military intelligence, and other intangibles. The relative importance to be given to existing as compared to potential military capabilities also has to be decided. Potential capabilities include such important nonmilitary factors as the administrative skill that determines the efficiency with which given societal resources are used for military purposes; the political foundations of military power, which determine the availability of a society's resources to the military sector; the diplomatic skill that helps shape the political atmosphere in which military power may have to be exerted; and other factors ranging from military reputation or prestige to national morale.[20] Indicators of state power capabilities that are valid over the variety of political, economic, and technological conditions of the last few centuries must be devised. Different indicators could be used for different historical periods, but it is not clear that any measures would be of sufficient validity to permit an interval-level measurement of power capabilities that this approach would require. The most impressive attempt thus far to measure aggregate power capabilities—that of Singer and his colleagues for the nineteenth and twentieth centuries—recognizes these problems and provides ordinal-level rankings of the most powerful states rather than actual numerical levels and differences.[21] Quantitative measurements from earlier historical periods would present even greater problems of validity.

These analytical and methodological problems might be dismissed if the use of objective indicators met the minimum test of face validity, but there is good reason to believe that they do not. First, since the ability to prevail in war is the ultimate test of military power, we would expect states ranked higher in military capabilities to emerge victorious in any military confrontation. The Arab-Israeli wars are only the most obvious counterexamples.[22] Second, and more important for our purposes, the Singer rank orderings of power capabilities generated by objective indicators of military capabilities deviate from conventional wisdom regarding the Great Powers. Singer's Correlates of War Project uses six equally weighted indices of power capabilities: total population, urban population, iron and steel production, fuel consumption, military personnel, and military expenditures. These indicators appear to reflect adequately the important dimensions of existing military capabilities and both military and industrial potential, yet the resulting rank ordering of states is often counterintuitive. In 1845, for example, both Turkey and the United States rank higher than Prussia on this scale, but most scholars (including Singer and Small) identify only Prussia as a Great Power during this period. In 1913 China outranks France, Austria-Hungary, Italy, and Japan, but the latter four are generally considered Great Powers, and China is not.[23] Military power may be the primary defining characteristics of Great Powers, but alone it is not sufficient and must be supplemented with other criteria.

A Great Power is defined here as a state that plays a major role in international politics with respect to security-related issues. The Great Powers can be differentiated from other states by their military power, their interests, their behavior in general and interactions with other Powers, other Powers' perception of them, and some formal criteria.

Most important, a Great Power possesses a high level of military capabilities relative to other states. At a minimum, it has relative self-sufficiency with respect to military security. Great Powers are basically invulnerable to military threats by non-Powers and need only fear other Great Powers. In addition, Great Powers have the capability to project military power beyond their borders to conduct offensive as well as defensive military operations. They can actively come to the defense of allies, wage an aggressive war against other states (including most of the Powers), and generally use force or the threat of force to help shape their external environment. A state whose security rests on a broad territorial expanse or natural barriers to invasion but that is unable to threaten the security of other states is not a Great Power.

Second, the interests and objectives of Great Powers are different from those of other states. They think of their interests as continental or global rather than local or regional. Their conception of security goes beyond territorial defense or even extended defense to include maintenance of a continental or global balance of power. Great Powers generally define their national interests to include systemic interests and are therefore concerned with order maintenance in the international system.[24] Symbolic interests of national honor and prestige are also given high priority by the Great Powers, for these are perceived as being essential components of national power and necessary for Great Power status.

Third, the Great Powers are distinguished from other states by their general behavior. They defend their interests more aggressively and with a wider range of instrumentalities, including the frequent threat or use of military force. They also interact frequently with other Powers. The Great Powers account for a disproportionate number of alliances and wars in the international system (often fought against each other), particularly those designed to maintain the balance of power and prevent the dominance of any single state. They are also involved in major territorial partitions and compensations (the partitions of Poland in the eighteenth century), guarantees (the Barrier Treaty guaranteeing the Utrecht settlement), and informal international organizations (the Concert of Europe).

Great Powers are further differentiated from other states by others' images and perceptions of them. The Powers are perceived as such by other Powers and treated as relative equals with respect to general attention, respect, protocol, negotiations, alliance agreements, and so forth. Equal perception and treatment of one another are among the most important criteria of Great Power rank, for perceptions determine behavior. This perceptual criterion involves an element of circularity, but is useful operationally, particularly in the absence of a rigid set of objective criteria establishing both necessary and sufficient conditions for Great Power rank. At any given time there always exist one or two states whose rank is unquestionable by virtue of their military strength. These states can be used as definitional anchors to help identify other Great Powers.

Finally, Great Powers are differentiated from others by formal criteria, including identification as a Great Power by an international conference, congress, organization, or treaty, or the granting of such privileges as permanent membership or veto power by an international organization or treaty. The Treaty of Westphalia, for example, named France and Sweden as the guarantors of the peace settlement, and the Congress of Vienna explicitly identified certain states as Great Powers. These formal criteria are neither necessary nor sufficient for Great Power rank and are the least important of any of the characteristics of the Powers, though they are useful as indicators of other states' perceptions of the Powers. The Great Powers are important because of their military power and potential and the interests and behavior that flow from that power. Great Power systems existed long before the Great Power role was institutionalized at the Congress of Vienna and before international law was formally codified at the Peace of Westphalia.

The definition of Great Power outlined above is based on the assumed dominance of security-related issues, and security is defined primarily as military security. Other issue areas and linkages across them exist, but it is possible to make some distinctions. A major role in international trade or finance does not automatically ensure Great Power status. Wealth does not necessarily indicate military strength or generate influence on security issues. The Netherlands, for example, was a commercial power but not a Great Power throughout most of the eighteenth century. Nor is status as a colonial power alone sufficient to qualify as a Great Power. Many Great Powers have sought colonial empires as a means of enhancing their power and wealth but some colonial powers have been effectively isolated from the Great Power security system, participating little if at all in its alliances and wars (sixteenth-century Portugal).

These criteria provide the basis for an analytical historical study to determine the membership of the modern Great Power system. These are admittedly not perfectly objective criteria that can be mechanically applied to identify the Great Powers in any particular historical era. The aim is to minimize rather than eliminate subjectivity by providing theoretical criteria that are operationally useful yet sufficiently flexible to guide an interpretation of a rich body of historical evidence in identifying the Great Powers. The validity of these criteria can be tested in part by ensuring that the results do not deviate significantly from certain well-established conventional wisdoms. For example, the set of Powers must not exclude England, France, Austria, Prussia, and Russia for the eighteenth and nineteenth centuries. Before the Great Powers can be identified, however, it is first necessary to determine the origins of the modern Great Power system.

Origins of the Modern Great Power System

The fundamental assumption upon which the concept of a Great Power system is based is the existence of a collection of sovereign territorial states interacting with considerable frequency in an anarchic international environment. A state here means a political organization commanding a predominance of political power within a given territory and characterized by independence from external hierarchical authority. This concept of the territorial state includes dynastic as well as nation-states; it refers merely to independent territorial aggregates of political power. In determining the origin of the modern Great Power system, the first question is when such a system was first established on a permanent basis.

There is, of course, considerable debate concerning the origins of the modern state system. One extreme view is that of F. H. Hinsley, who dates the beginning of the modern state system in the mid-eighteenth century.[25] The more conventional opinion, shared by most political scientists, is that the state system originated in 1648 with the Treaty of Westphalia. This view is excessively legalistic, however, for Westphalia merely provided formal legal backing for the idea of territorial sovereignty and recognition of a state system that had been in existence for more than a century. For similar reasons we cannot accept the view of Frederick L. Schuman, who characterizes the Western state system by the concept of state sovereignty, principles of international law, and the politics of the balance of power and argues that it originated at the end of the sixteenth century with Jean Bodin, Hugo Grotius, and the development of modern international law.[26] Formal sovereignty appears to have made little obvious difference in actual behavior of the major territorial states of Europe. These states existed, interacted, and practiced *Realpolitik* and "balance-of-power politics" long before Westphalia and the formal development of the concept of territorial sovereignty and modern international law. The wars for supremacy in Italy and in Europe in the early sixteenth century, for example, are in many fundamental respects comparable to the struggle for supremacy in the Balkans and in central Europe nearly four centuries later.

There are limits, however, to how far back the system can be extended. The concept of a Great Power system cannot be applied to medieval Europe. Sovereign states had not yet fully developed, in that states were lacking in both internal centralization of power and external autonomy. Medieval kings did not exert effective political control over semisovereign walled cities, duchies, and feudal lords within their domains and did not possess full independence from the authority of the pope and Holy Roman emperor on political as well as ecclesiastical and moral issues. If France and England can perhaps be considered major territorial states by the end of the Hundred Years' War, the same cannot be said of the Hapsburgs until the union of the Austrian and Burgundian lands with the marriage of Mary of Burgundy to Maximilian of Austria in 1477, or of Spain until the union of Castile and Aragon in 1479 (or even until the expulsion of the Moors in 1492).

In addition, the relationships among the major territorial conglomerates of medieval Europe did not involve the high degree of interaction characterizing those of modern European states. There was no permanent diplomatic machinery (that is, permanent diplomatic residents or ambassadors) outside of Italy until the sixteenth century. More important, there was little sense of an interdependent European security system before the late fifteenth century. Instead, there existed several distinct regional systems that seldom interacted. The Italian city-state system is the most familiar. This system had its own major powers, balance-of-power politics, and permanent diplomatic missions (at least by the fifteenth century),[27] and in many respects serves as a precursor of the modern European system. There were also regional systems in Germany, the Iberian Peninsula, and Scandinavia, as well as rivalries between the English and the French, the English and the Scots, and the Turks and their Christian neighbors. Each of these systems had its wars, but they were generally isolated affairs. Charles Oman has described fifteenth-century warfare as "shut up in many watertight compartments . . . separate stories, having few and infrequent cross-relations with each other."[28] These wars, and the regional dynastic and power political struggles that generated them, were not perceived as threats by monarchs in distant parts of Europe. In addition, there was little concern with the Continental balance of power that has been central to the modern system for the last five centuries. The Hundred Years' War, for example, was basically a bilateral conflict between the English and French kings. It did not generate external involvement comparable to that arising from similar conflicts in later years. It was not until the very end of the fifteenth century that war became pan-European in its impact, that the major states first began to concert their behavior to prevent the territorial expansion and political domination of any one state. Not until this time can we begin to speak of a single interdependent *system* of Great Powers and other states.

Although the modern Great Power system was the product of a gradual process of historical development, its primary characteristics emerged during a narrow period of time. A Great Power system has been defined as consisting of states characterized by the centralization of political power within a given territory, independent from any higher secular authority and interacting in an interdependent system of security relations. The very end of the fifteenth century marked the fusion of these three separate elements and therefore the emergence of the modern Great Power system.

By the middle of the fifteenth century several territorial states were well on their way toward consolidation into centralized organizations with stable frontiers.[29] These new territorial states had become virtually independent of the authority of both the pope and the emperor. The decline of papal power was demonstrated in the diplomacy of the Hundred Years' War, and by the end of the century his claims to temporal authority carried little weight among the major states of

Europe. Sir Charles Petrie argues that in the last decade of the fifteenth century the medieval conception of a universal church under pope and emperor had little basis in fact, and Oman writes that the moral supremacy of the papacy and the legal supremacy of the Holy Roman Empire "reached their lowest pitch of degradation about the year 1492-3." René Albrecht-Carrié writes that "the end of the fifteenth century roughly marks the transition of Europe from a congeries of petty feudal interests under the theoretical rule of the Holy Roman emperor and the pope into a system of competing sovereign nation-states. . . . The medieval concept of a united and stratified Christian Europe ruled from on high by the pope and the Holy Roman emperor gave way to the idea of equal rights."[30] The Franco-Turkish alliances beginning in the 1520s symbolized the end of the idea of a unified Christendom many decades before the end of the Reformation.

To be even more precise, the French invasion of Italy at the end of 1494 and the Treaty of Venice in March of 1495 mark the coalescence of the major European states into a truly interdependent system of behavior. This interpretation draws considerable support from the historical literature. Ludwig Dehio notes that the new state system represented a gradual erosion of the medieval structure but argues that "nevertheless, the new structure came into existence at a quite definite moment, the beginning of the struggle among the Great Powers over Italy in 1494." David J. Hill speaks of "a new Europe" and a "new order of things" and argues that "the expedition of Charles VIII may justly be regarded as the last great medieval adventure and the first military campaign of modern times . . . it may be taken to mark the birth of international politics." Arnold Toynbee argues that "modern Western wars" began in 1494, when "the original constellation of Modern Western Great Powers had crystallized out of a Late Medieval nebula." Finally, Garrett Mattingly argues that the Treaty of Venice marks "the first decisive drawing together of the major states of Europe into a single power system" and "the beginning of modern European diplomacy."[31]

On the military as well as political level the Italian wars are described as initiating the modern era. Charles's Italian campaign is described by Richard A. Preston and Sydney F. Wise as the "beginning of a new military era." Theodore Ropp describes the French and other leading European armies as modern because of three distinguishing characteristics: "(1) They were the political instruments of dynastic monarchies and not of feudal barons, private mercenary captains, or city states. (2) They were *armed,* at least partially, with gunpowder weapons. (3) They were *organized* around a permanent (or 'standing') body of professional infantry." Similarly, Howard describes Charles VIII's force as the "first 'modern' army" and argues that it was "not fundamentally different in composition from that which Napoleon was to lead to the same battlefields three centuries later."[32]

There are other considerations as well. In 1513 Machiavelli wrote *The Prince* and introduced the concept of "raison d'etat" into Western international theory.[33] A truly European and even global economy was emerging, in contrast to the distinct economies in the Mediterranean and in the Baltic/North Sea area in medieval Europe.[34] For Wallerstein this time denotes the emergence of a capitalist world economy and for Modelski and William R. Thompson the emergence of a global political system sustained by sea power.[35] Nearly all historians date the beginnings of the modern world from the end of the fifteenth century. Finally, a fundamental revolution in military technology was occurring. Gunpowder and artillery were becoming decisive in warfare, and even the best of the medieval castles were vulnerable. The new technology in general and mobility of artillery in particular led to major changes in the strategy and tactics of warfare.[36]

Sixteenth-century warfare was fought by armies composed largely of *condottieri* or mercenaries of various nationalities, but this is not sufficient reason to exclude this period from the modern system.[37] Mercenary armies had major limitations, as Machiavelli emphasized. But these armies were paid by a central treasury controlled by the monarch and used for the advancement of his dynastic and territorial interests. The wars for the personal honor, vengeance, and enrichment of kings and nobles in the Middle Ages were increasingly replaced by a "Clausewitzian" conception of the "rational" use of force as a political instrument of dynastic-territorial states.[38] The Italian wars or the Hapsburg/Valois wars of the early sixteenth century, for example, were as concerned with state interests and the balance of power as many of the wars of the last two centuries.

For all these reasons the origins of the modern Great Power system can be traced to the late fifteenth century in general and to the 1494-95 invasion of Italy in particular. That system extends to the present time and for the purposes of this analysis ends in 1975.[39]

Composition of the System

Before examining each of the major states individually in an attempt to identify the Great Powers on the basis of the criteria given above, some general problems that repeatedly occur should be considered. First, even though the attainment or loss of Great Power status is rarely a specific event but rather a general process, it is necessary in an empirical analysis such as this one to identify to the year each state's points of entry into and departure from the system. Other studies of this scope have not been particularly concerned with this problem. Wright refers only to one century or another, while Haas limits his points of entry or departure to the ten or so dates of "system transformation" over the last three centuries.[40] Because the primary criteria of Great Power status include military capabilities and reputation, the end of a decisive war is the most obvious symbol marking the rise of a new Power or decline of an old one and is used as a primary indicator of change in Great Power status.[41] Although in some cases a single battle may be the truly decisive point and more definitive than the final termination of hostilities (for example, the Battle of Poltava between Sweden and Russia in 1709), the real change in a state's role in international politics and the recognition by other states of the change in Great Power status generally does not occur until after a peace has been concluded. A very limited number of exceptions have been made, and these are explicitly noted.[42]

Another problem is whether to exclude a Great Power from the system during a temporary period of weakness or relative international impotence, after which that state makes a full recovery and once again qualifies as a Great Power. Such a condition of weakness may derive from general political, economic, and social conditions, as with France during the Wars of Religion in the late sixteenth century, Spain in the late seventeenth century, or Prussia during the early nineteenth century. It may result from a major defeat in war, as with Prussia and possibly Austria during the Napoleonic period, Russia after the Crimean War, and the Soviet Union and Germany after World War I. It may also be imposed by the occupation of foreign armies, as with France from 1815 to 1818 and 1940 to 1945 and Germany from 1945 to 1952. In such cases, I have not excluded from the Great Power system any state that is temporarily incapacitated, as long as that state once again qualifies for Great Power status within a reasonable period of time. This is a difficult choice and needs some justification.

On theoretical grounds, the international political impact of these relatively short and transient periods of social, economic, or military weakness is usually relatively insignificant. My definition of Great Power status includes not only objective capabilities but also subjective perceptions of these capabilities. There is a historical tendency for states to overestimate the military power of an adversary and to underestimate a decline in that power. Consequently, there is a certain lag time in policy makers' perceptions of the decline of an adversary. In addition, a temporary condition of weakness may be perceived as less important than a state's power potential for the future. After the Napoleonic Wars, for example, a defeated France was perceived as the primary threat to European security, even when she was occupied. And although Singer and Small exclude defeated Germany from their major power system during the half decade after World War I, Germany survived the war as the leading continental Power and was generally perceived as the central threat to European security. It is impossible to understand the nature of Great Power relationships regarding security matters in the early 1920s if Germany is excluded from the Great Power system (or in 1815-18 if France is excluded). Similar questions may be raised concerning Singer and Small's exclusion of the Soviet Union from the system for three years after World War I. Soviet power capabilities ranked ahead of those of Italy and Japan and the Soviets were certainly perceived as a major threat by the West. In none of these cases does it appear that temporary periods of weakness or decline had sufficient impact on international security policy to exclude these states from the Great Power system.

This procedure can be justified on methodological grounds as well. Systematic empirical analysis requires that if any of these cases are excluded all comparable cases must be excluded. To do so would require an explicit definition of the criteria for inclusion or exclusion and their rigorous and systematic application to all cases over the last five centuries that might conceivably qualify. To exclude only a few of the more well-known cases is to risk the introduction of a nonrandom bias into the analysis. Why exclude Russia in 1918-21 but not during the period after the Crimean War? Why not exclude France during her occupation after Vienna?

The problem, of course, is that the specification of explicit criteria and their application on a case-by-case basis would be prohibitive in time and resources, and in the end it might make very little difference. It is historically rare that a major state in such a weakened condition is involved quickly in another war, so the compilation of war data would not be affected greatly. Moreover, the time spans involved are short, and in a study of this historical scope the exclusion (or inclusion) of a few states for a few extra years would make little difference in the results of the analysis. For all of these reasons it is better to ignore cases of temporary weakness and to assume continuity in the Great Power system.

Another set of problems has been generated by revolutionary changes in military technology since 1945, particularly the development of nuclear warheads and long-range delivery systems. These technological developments have not only been a primary source of the widening power differentials between the two leading nuclear powers and the other major industrial states, clouding the categories of powers by creating a new class of "Superpowers," but they have also profoundly altered the concept of security in international politics. Has the emergence of the Superpowers effectively eliminated the traditional category of Great Power, leaving only two Powers in the world? Or should a stratification of the international system conceive of the Superpowers as simply an elite within a broader class of Great Powers, leaving the possibility of including such states as Britain, France, West Germany, China, and Japan in the Great Power system? This latter conceptualization is preferable.[43] There are significant power differentials between the Superpowers and these other states, but the gap between these major industrial states and others is significant. Comparable cases of significant power differentials have existed in the past, when the military capabilities of one or two Powers rose far above the rest (for example, France under Louis XIV and Napoleon or the Hapsburgs and Valois in the early sixteenth century), yet their rivals were still recognized as Great Powers. Moreover, there are other dimensions of Great Power rank besides military capabilities, though the latter are clearly the most important. The perceptions of the Superpowers are particularly significant. There is little doubt that for a quarter century Russia has perceived a grave security threat from West Germany and China and the United States from China. Britain, France, and China not only have a veto power in the U.N. Security Council, but they also have the capability for nuclear strikes against major Soviet cities. Britain and France have interests beyond Europe and are no more confined to being regional powers than was Prussia until late in the nineteenth century. An attempt to understand Soviet and American behavior and the security system of which they are a part without including certain other Powers would be as futile as an analysis of the early sixteenth-century Hapsburg-Valois rivalry without considering the Turks and England.

For these reasons, the non-Superpowers should not be automatically excluded from Great Power status. The definition of Great Power and the operational criteria developed earlier can be used to determine which of the major industrial states qualify for inclusion in the system.

Admittedly, the revolutionary changes in the world system since 1945 raise new and serious questions regarding the concept of a Great

Power system and its assumptions of the dominance of military security issues. The questions of the continued validity of the Great Power system and the meaning of the Great Power concept are of enormous theoretical significance, but their implications for this study are too limited to justify a major new theoretical analysis. The period in question covers only 30 years of a 480-year system and involves so few wars that its overall impact is limited. Different conceptualizations, including ones that exclude all but the Superpowers from the system or exclude the entire post-1945 period, would have only a marginal impact on the analysis of war during the last five centuries of the modern Great Power system. Hence the continued existence of the modern Great Power system is adopted as a working hypothesis, derived from the assumption that any anarchic political system contains a Great Power system.

Another problem concerns the identity and continuity of a given Great Power over time. Shall Germany be considered a continuation of Prussia in 1871, or shall that date mark the end of one Great Power and the emergence of another? This kind of problem arises, for example, concerning the Hapsburgs in 1519 and Russia in 1917. In this analysis the continuity of a Great Power's identity over time is generally assumed for a number of reasons. First, the primary focus here is on the war behavior of the system as a whole, rather than the behavior of individual states, and for a systemic-level analysis a Great Power role is of greater concern than the identity of the particular Powers. The enormous conceptual and methodological problems involved in the definition and operational identification of any fundamental discontinuities in national political systems would render such an effort more costly in time and resources than can be justified. In most cases the new regime occupied the same core territory as the old, commanded the same basic power capabilities, and was characterized by a continuity of the military establishment. Finally, the data generated in this analysis are presented in such a way that they can easily be disaggregated and reconstructed should another analyst wish to emphasize these fundamental discontinuities.

Having considered these general problems, let us now apply the general criteria developed earlier to a historical analysis in order to determine the membership of the modern Great Power system at each point over the last five centuries. An effort will be made to indicate the degree of confidence in each entry and exit point. In the process, other attempts in the historical literature to classify the Great Power status of particular states will be noted. It should be emphasized, however, that most of these previous efforts were unguided by explicit analytical criteria and are therefore less important than the historical evidence fitting the theoretical criteria developed here. In the following analysis the most difficult cases receive the greatest attention, and less controversial cases are dealt with only briefly.

France (1495-1975). The status of France as a member of the Great Power system from its inception in 1495 until the German occupation in 1940 is unquestioned. She was one of the two leading European powers at the end of the fifteenth century and the leading power for the half century after 1659 and during her revolutionary period at the turn of the nineteenth century. France's status becomes questionable only in the period after World War II. On the basis of the criteria developed earlier, it can be argued that France should be included as a Great Power though clearly subordinate to the Superpowers. She played a central role in NATO until the mid-1960s and in the Continental military calculations of both Superpowers after that. She has a veto power in the United Nations Security Council and has security interests that extend beyond Europe to Indochina, the Middle East, and Africa. France has ranked around sixth on the Singer scale of military capabilities[44] and possesses an independent nuclear capability. For these reasons, France is included as a continuous member of the modern Great Power system from its inception until the present time.[45]

England/Great Britain (1495-1975). There has been considerable debate about the status of England during the early years of the modern Great Power system. One view is that England did not become a Great Power until the defeat of the Spanish Armada in 1588. Petrie argues that given her declining international prestige after the failure of her bid for European supremacy during the Hundred Years' War and her inferiority to France and Spain in population and material resources, England should not be considered a Great Power at the end of the sixteenth century.[46] A careful examination of the first century of the system reveals that England satisfied most of the criteria for Great Power rank. She lagged behind France, Spain, and the Hapsburg Empire in wealth and population, but her insular position provided considerable freedom of diplomatic maneuver as well as security, both of which England exploited in the pursuit of her interests on the Continent. She played a significant role in early Great Power diplomacy, being much sought after as an ally by the enemies of France in the Italian wars. Though not a part of the League of Venice in 1495, England did join the Holy League in 1511. She played a key balancing role in the bipolar struggle between Charles V and Francis I until mid-century and was later described by Montesquieu as "*la puissance mediatrice de l'Europe*" during this period.[47] She had treaties of alliance with both sovereigns, participated in the wars of the 1520s to limit the hegemony of Charles V, fought two wars with France in the 1540s, and was one of three signatories (with Spain and France) to the Treaty of Cateau-Cambrésis in 1559, ending the Italian wars. As the leading Protestant state, England intervened in the Wars of Religion in France in support of the Huguenots beginning in 1562 and in support of the rebellion against Spain in the Netherlands. Furthermore, England was an important maritime power located along one of Europe's most important sea routes. For these reasons England should be considered a Great Power from the beginning of the modern system. This view is supported by several prominent authorities. Hill, Mattingly, and Dehio all identify England as one of four major powers at the end of the fifteenth century.[48] There is no doubt that England's Great Power status continued until the mid-twentieth century.

Like France, Britain must also be considered a Great Power in the post-1945 period in spite of the gap separating her from the Superpowers. Her military capabilities are not insignificant, ranking fourth on Singer's scale (for 1960), and she has an independent nuclear deterrent force. Britain is an important member of NATO, particularly as a naval power, and has actively defended her security interests in the Middle East and South Atlantic. Her formal status is enhanced by her U.N. veto power. For these reasons she qualifies as a Great Power during the last three decades in spite of her disengagement from her overseas empire and her internal economic problems.[49]

The Hapsburg Dynasty (1495-1519; 1519-1556; 1556-1918). Few would argue against including the Hapsburg dynasty from the very beginning of the modern Great Power system.[50] Its position was firmly established with the passing of the bulk of the Burgundian inheritance to Maximilian of Austria in 1477. The imperial crown of the Holy Roman Empire, elective in principle, was the continuous possession of the House of Hapsburg from 1438 to 1740 and from 1745 to the dissolution of the empire in 1806. The personal power of the emperor, however, derived not from the resources within the Germanic empire but from the Hapsburg family possessions in central Europe, including Upper and Lower Austria, Syria, Carinthia and Tyrol, Bohemia, Moravia, Silesia, and Hungary. References to the emperor in this study are to his role as the head of the Hapsburg dynasty.

The emperor was deeply involved in the international politics of early sixteenth-century Europe. He participated in the Italian wars as a member of the League of Venice, the League of Cambrai, and the Holy League and was also involved in the continuous struggle against the Turks. The territorial and material resources of the Hapsburgs were enormously increased in the early sixteenth century, first with the inheritance of the Spanish dominions under Charles V in 1519 and then with the permanent annexation of Bohemia, Transylvania, and Hungary in 1526. With the death of Charles V in 1556, the dynasty was divided into Austrian and Spanish branches.

The accession of Charles V presents a serious conceptual problem. The election of Emperor Charles V in 1519 brought the territories and resources of two Great Powers, the eastern Hapsburgs and Spain, under the rule of a single sovereign. The question is whether these

Hapsburg domains should be treated as a single Great Power or two distinct Powers for the purposes of this analysis.

In many respects the eastern and western Hapsburg lands continued as distinct political entities. Their economic systems remained separate, and the ties between the two domains derived more from the personal authority of Charles V than from any institutionalized linkages. In international politics, however, which is the central consideration here, the Hapsburgs under Charles V constituted a single actor with a highly centralized foreign policy.[51] For the first decade he had a single foreign minister in Gattinara, and thereafter Charles assumed personal control of the external affairs of all of his lands. He delegated some power to governors and viceroys but reserved the ultimate control over policy and administration to himself.

Distinctive Spanish and Austrian-Burgundian dimensions of the foreign policy of Charles V can be identified. His policies regarding Italy, North Africa, and the Mediterranean area clearly derived from traditional Aragonese interests and policies, while his relations with the German princes were associated with the traditional concerns of the emperor. The point is, however, that these policies were pursued by a single sovereign and were backed by the entire resources at his disposal. The Austrian-Burgundian lands cannot be treated as an independent Power in the diplomacy of the period, for Charles acquired much of his wealth, resources, and military manpower from Spain. Yet Spain cannot realistically be treated as an independent Great Power during this period because her territory and resources were considerably different from those of Ferdinand or Philip II, and Charles's preoccupation with central Europe was a considerable departure from traditional Spanish policies focusing on the New World and the Mediterranean. For these reasons the Hapsburg lands under Charles V have generally been treated as a single Power in many of the diplomatic histories of the period[52] and are so treated here. They were unquestionably one of the two leading Great Powers until mid-century, at which point Spain emerged as the dominant European power for a century.

To avoid any semantic confusion, the Hapsburg Powers are labeled as follows: the reign of Charles V, from 1519 to 1556, is referred to as the United Hapsburgs; the Spanish Hapsburgs are referred to as Spain after 1556. The eastern branch of the Hapsburgs, from 1495 to 1519 and 1556 to 1918, is referred to as the Austrian Hapsburgs. This delineation is partially for practical reasons, to distinguish this political unit from both the United Hapsburgs and the Hapsburg line in Spain after 1556. It also reflects the fact that although Austria was only one of the many eastern Hapsburg dominions, it was the most important. These territories are commonly referred to as Austria in the eighteenth and nineteenth centuries, up to the Ausgleich of Austria-Hungary in 1867.

The Spanish and Austrian states had dynastic ties after 1556, but this alone is not sufficient to deny them independent status as Great Powers. They were distinct not only in their territory, power base, and economic systems but also in their foreign policies.[53] In most significant respects the Spanish and Austrian Hapsburgs after Charles were no less independent than Germany and Austria-Hungary at the turn of the twentieth century or the United States and Britain after World War II. Consequently, the separate Hapsburg lines must be treated as independent Great Powers after 1556. Both continued to be important for several centuries. Few scholars would dispute the exit from the Great Power system of the Austro-Hungarian Empire after its collapse in 1918.

Spain (1495-1519; 1556-1808). There is no question regarding the inclusion of Spain in the modern Great Power system from its beginning.[54] The emergence of Spain as a major force in Europe began with the union of Aragon and Castile in 1479 under King Ferdinand and Queen Isabella and was completed by the conquest of Granada and the expulsion of the Moors in 1492. The lands of the Catholic Kings included Sardinia and Sicily, with the rights to the Kingdom of Naples, and their power base in Europe was greatly strengthened by a thriving overseas empire. Spain intervened to block French expansion in Italy and successfully competed with France for supremacy in Italy.

With the union of the Spanish and Burgundian–Austrian Hapsburgs under Charles V in 1519 Spain is treated as part of a single

United Hapsburg entity until the death of Charles V and the breakup of the Hapsburgs in 1556. At that point Spain is considered a separate Great Power under Philip II. She was the leading European (and world) power until supplanted by France a century later.

Much more difficult is the question of when Spain ceased to be a Great Power. The fluctuations in Spanish military power, economic strength, and diplomatic influence in the century and a half after the Peace of the Pyrenees in 1659 were as dramatic as those for any Power during the five-century span of the modern system. Spain had maintained her supremacy in Europe until 1659 and was the greatest imperial power for years after that. Although Spanish economic and military power suffered an abrupt decline in the half century after the Peace of the Pyrenees, Spain was a major participant in the European coalitions against Louis XIV and in the peace congresses of Nymwegen (1678-79) and Ryswick (1697). Spain was humiliated and her empire dismembered after the War of the Spanish Succession, but political successions and the dynastic inheritances associated with them were perfectly legitimate in the political theory of the time, so the loss of much of Spain's empire cannot be attributed solely to the limitations of her power.[55] In fact, the war resulted in a unified Spanish state, and there was a marked resurgence in Spanish power in the next two decades. Spain pursued an expansionist policy under Alberoni after Utrecht and regained her position of dominance in southern Italy. The other Great Powers felt sufficient fear of Spain after Utrecht that they formed a Quadruple Alliance against her to guarantee the peace settlement, and it took a European Congress at Cambrai in 1724 to settle her dispute with Austria. Spain attended the Congress of Soissons in 1728 and was involved in the diplomacy of the Polish Succession a half decade later. She put up a good fight against Britain in the War of Jenkins' Ear, and her position in Italy was strengthened at Aix-la-Chapelle (1748). Thus many authorities consider Spain a Great Power during the first half of the eighteenth century.[56]

Spanish strength continued to decline, however. She played a minimal role in the Seven Years' War and made many concessions at the

Peace of Paris (although she did gain Louisiana from France). She made a major economic recovery in the last half of the eighteenth century and was allied against England in the American Revolution. Spain was also important in the French Revolutionary and Napoleonic Wars until her major naval defeat at Trafalgar. At this point the Spanish people revolted against the disastrous Francophile policies and were helpless against the French invasions of 1808. Spain contributed little to the defeat of Napoleonic France, was not a major participant at the Congress of Vienna, and was not a part of the Quadruple Alliance. In the next decade Spain lost her American empire. For these reasons Spain departed from the modern Great Power system in 1808. For at least the last half century of her membership, however, Spain's role was subordinate to that of the other Powers.

Ottoman Empire (1495-1699). No treatment of European diplomacy and war in the fifteenth, sixteenth and seventeenth centuries is complete without the inclusion of the Ottoman Empire, which reached the peak of its strength in the century after the capture of Constantinople in 1453.[57] The sultan had a larger standing army than most European monarchs. It was permanent, well-trained, disciplined, and thoroughly professional.[58] It was also respected and envied by the Europeans. Paolo Giovio wrote in 1530 that "their military discipline has such justice and severity as easily to surpass the ancient Greeks and Romans. . . . The Turks surpass our own soldiers."[59] Although the Turks were outside the formal diplomatic community of Europe, their impact on European military affairs, alliances, and the balance of power was considerable, particularly after their wars with Venice and the Persians in the late fifteenth and very early sixteenth centuries. The Turkish invasions of Europe and the Franco-Turkish alliances beginning in 1526 were vital in preventing the further hegemony of Charles V. The alliance between Francis I and Suleyman I is described by Petrie as initiating "one of the most continuous threads in the fabric of European diplomacy for more than three hundred years." Dehio compares the role of Turkey as "balancer" of the

European security system with the classic English role in subsequent balance-of-power systems.[60] The Turks conquered much of southeastern Europe, held most of Hungary, and twice were at the gates of Vienna. By the middle of the sixteenth century the Turkish navy had gained supremacy over the Mediterranean and controlled two-thirds of its shores.[61]

The exit of the Ottoman Empire from the Great Power system is difficult to pinpoint. The Turks suffered a major naval defeat at Lepanto in 1571 but recovered rapidly and continued to ravage the western Mediterranean coasts. Despite growing internal decay and the gradual decline of the Janissary corps (the elite infantry), the Ottoman Empire continued to expand, extending its frontiers to the Caucasus and the Caspian Sea, and by 1683 into the Ukraine and as far north as Vienna. A series of wars with Persia, Venice, Austria, Poland, and finally Russia eroded Turkish power, and by the late seventeenth century they had lost nearly half of their former territory in Europe, including Transylvania, Hungary, and most of Croatia and Slavonia. Their navy had long been weak,[62] and their army was declining in effectiveness. Their weapons and techniques were technically inferior to those of Europe, and the Janissaries prevented modernization of the army. The Turks' traditional logistical problems in supporting a distant war (they always had trouble fighting a two-front war) were becoming more serious. Economically, the Ottoman Empire was declining relative to Europe. Its industries were primitive, its population and political unity were declining further, and its administrative system was weak and decentralized.[63]

This decline was symbolized by the Peace of Carlowitz (1699) after the defeat of the Turks by the Austrians and other European Powers. The Ottoman Empire was forced to make enormous territorial concessions that left it in a vulnerable strategic position. Carlowitz marked the Turks' "transition from the offensive to the defensive" and the beginning of their withdrawal from Europe. Hill argues that "the Peace of Carlowitz disclosed an immense decline in the force of the Ottoman Empire. . . . It marked the end of the period during which the Turkish power seriously threatened Christendom." Petrie asserts that "for the future the Eastern Problem was to be changed, and the question was no longer how to protect Christendom from the Turk, but who was to take his place as the dominant Power in the Near East."[64]

The Ottoman Empire continued to battle the Austrians and Russians in southeastern Europe but in the eighteenth century was no longer taking a major role in Great Power politics. It participated in none of the major multilateral wars or peace congresses of that period and was no longer considered as a major factor in the military calculations of the Powers. For these reasons, Ottoman membership in the Great Power system ceased with Carlowitz in 1699.[65]

The Netherlands (1609-1713). Although the Union of Utrecht, incorporating the seven northern provinces, was formed in 1579, the United Provinces did not achieve effective independence from Spain for another thirty years. The Twelve Years' Truce of 1609 marks the entry of the Dutch into the Great Power system. The independence of the Republic of the United Provinces (as distinct from the Spanish Netherlands) was not formally recognized until Westphalia in 1648, but the diplomatic and military role of the Dutch in the Thirty Years' War is evidence that they had achieved Great Power rank at an earlier date. Although decentralized politically and small in size and population, the Netherlands drew strength from her wealth, central role in European finance and commerce, colonial empire, and naval power.[66] On these grounds, both Wallerstein and Modelski identify the Netherlands as the hegemonic global power in the world system in the seventeenth century.[67] In addition, the Netherlands was deeply involved in the alliance system of late seventeenth-century Europe and participated in most of the major wars of that period, including the three general wars involving Louis XIV.

Although in 1689 William became a sovereign of both England and the Netherlands, the two states are treated as independent powers during this period, as is done in the literature. Their foreign policies were distinct and were supported by distinct political, economic, and military resources, and they signed separate peace treaties (for example, Ryswick in 1697). Dutch power began to wane with the death of William III in 1702 and the costly War of the Spanish Succession. After the Treaty of Utrecht, the Netherlands "ceased to have a great sea power" according to Alfred T. Mahan,[68] and this loss of her major strength began a general Dutch decline in international influence over European security matters. The Dutch were of some importance at Utrecht and in the Quadruple Alliance, but they were involved only minimally in the great wars of the middle of the eighteenth century, which involved nearly all the Powers. They abstained from the War of the Polish Succession and Seven Years' War and played no role in the major postwar conferences at Aix-la-Chapelle (1748) and Paris (1763). The Dutch continued to be important in international trade and finance, but this is not sufficient to qualify them for Great Power status. Thus the Netherlands cannot be considered a Great Power after 1713.[69]

Sweden (1617-1721). No list of Great Powers in the seventeenth century would be complete without Sweden. After a miserable performance in the War of Kalmar (1611-13) against Denmark, Sweden made a remarkable recovery. She defeated Russia in a decade-long war and emerged as the dominant power in the Baltic. At the Treaty of Stolbova in 1617, she forced the tsar to make concessions that cut Russia off from the Baltic and delayed her rise to Great Power rank for a century. Stolbova marks Sweden's entry into the Great Power system.[70] Four years later, when she captured the great trading city and fortress of Riga from the Poles, Sweden's strength further impressed the Powers of Europe.

Under Gustavus Adolphus Sweden was a leading participant in the Thirty Years' War and was largely responsible for checking the expansion of the Hapsburgs and effectively deciding the fate of northern Europe.[71] In spite of her economic and demographic weakness, Sweden had a first-rate army under brilliant military leadership and was respected throughout Europe. Sweden reached the peak of her power by mid-century. She was formally recognized as a Great Power at Westphalia and together with France was named as guarantor of the peace settlement. Sweden was important in the first coalition against

Louis XIV, profitably rewarded by Louis for her abstention from the second, and sought as an ally by both sides during the War of the Spanish Succession. In the Second Northern War Sweden attempted to defend her dominant position in the Baltic against a coalition consisting of Russia, Poland, Saxony, Denmark, England, and Prussia. The Russian victory over Sweden at the Battle of Poltava in 1709 marked the beginning of the end of Swedish military greatness. As a result of the war and major Swedish concessions at the treaties of Stockholm and Nystadt in 1721, Russia replaced Sweden as the dominant influence in the Baltic and ended Sweden's role as a Great Power.[72] Sweden was relatively insignificant in the power politics and wars of the eighteenth century.

Russia/Soviet Union (1721-1975). The precise point at which Russia entered the Great Power system is a matter of debate. During the seventeenth century, she counted for little in the power calculations of the great European states. She was noted more for her military and administrative weaknesses than for her military potential.[73] She played no role in the general wars to maintain the balance of power against Louis XIV and was slaughtered by a Swedish army no more than one-fifth her size at Narva in 1700. She was poor, underdeveloped, and lacking in capital, skilled labor, and a good communication system. By the turn of the eighteenth century, however, Peter the Great had begun his opening toward the West. He was highly impressed with Western technology, expertise, and organizational efficiency during his diplomatic tour (the "great embassy") of 1697 and returned determined to initiate revolutionary reforms in Russia.[74] Peter's Westernization included reorganization of the army and a major shipbuilding program as well as social and administrative changes and the centralization of the bureaucracy.[75] The effectiveness of these changes was demonstrated by Russia's crushing defeat of the Swedes at Poltava, yet two years later she was humiliated by the Turks, then a second-rate Power, at the Pruth River.

With the Treaty of Nystadt in 1721, which gained Russia major territorial concessions from Sweden and a "window" on the Baltic, she replaced Sweden as the dominant state in the north and gradually became involved in European politics. Following Nystadt Russia can be considered a Great Power.[76] By this time she had also established permanent diplomatic relations with West European states. Russia played an important role in the diplomacy and wars of the eighteenth century, including the Wars of the Polish and Austrian Successions and the Seven Years' War. There is no question regarding the continuation of her Great Power status until the present day.[77]

Prussia/Germany/West Germany (1740-1975). Despite Prussia's diplomatic and military involvement in European politics in the early eighteenth century, she cannot be considered a Great Power until her occupation of Silesia in 1740. At the time of Utrecht (1713), Brandenburg-Prussia had not yet risen to predominance among the states within Germany. Her scattered possessions were a main source of weakness. And Saxony was the wealthiest and perceived as the most important politically of the German states.[78] In the decades following Utrecht Frederick William I laid the foundations of power for the Prussian state and, some argue, German militarism.[79] He imposed rigid economizing measures and Spartan discipline and built a formidable army consisting of 3 percent of the population and consuming 80 percent of Prussian revenues.[80] The occupation of Silesia in 1740 solidified Frederick II's military reputation and Prussia's position as a leading Continental Power. This date marks the entry of Prussia into the Great Power system.[81] The continuation of Great Power status for Prussia and then Germany is not in doubt until Hitler's defeat in 1945.

In spite of her present non-nuclear status and her lack of a U.N. veto, the Federal Republic of Germany cannot be excluded from the Great Power system in the post-World War II period.[82] Even during the period of foreign occupation and economic recovery, Germany was a central focus of Great Power diplomacy. Germany's future was the central issue of contention between the United States and the Soviet Union, and their failure to resolve it was a primary reason for the origins and escalation of the Cold War.[83] A primary Soviet diplomatic objective has been to prevent the rise of an independent and unified Germany and the resurgence of German military power (and particularly nuclear power).[84] Some argue that French policy has been motivated as much by a fear of Germany as by a fear of the Soviets. The West German army is the core of NATO's conventional defense in Europe and her industrial strength has made her the economic leader of Europe. For the above reasons, Prussia (1740-1871), Germany (1871-1945), and the Federal Republic of Germany are treated as a continuous member of the Great Power system from 1740 to 1975.[85]

Italy (1861-1943). The case of Italy is a difficult one. Certainly she cannot be considered a Great Power before her unification; her military weaknesses were evident in the failure of the 1848-49 revolution. Even after her unification, Italy never equaled the other Powers and at no time ranks higher than eighth on Singer's scale of power capabilities. Yet because of her strong navy and strategic position in the Mediterranean, Italy was important in Great Power diplomacy during the half century before World War I. She was allied with Prussia in the Austro-Prussian War and received Venetia in compensation for her efforts. She was deeply involved in the Bismarckian system of alliances and was actively sought as an ally by both the Alliance and Entente in the diplomacy leading up to World War I. Moreover, Italy was formally treated as a Great Power by the other Powers, as evidenced by her role at the Congress of Berlin and other diplomatic protocol. For these reasons, Italy is traditionally treated as a Great Power during this period,[86] and she is similarly treated here. Italian membership in the Great Power system began in 1861 with the proclamation of the Kingdom of Italy after the Italo-Roman and Italo-Sicilian Wars of 1860-61, which effectively completed the unification of Italy.[87] Italy left the Great Power system in 1943, when she was defeated by the allies.

United States (1898-1975). Though ranking ahead of Austria-Hungary and Italy in power capabilities by the late nineteenth century, the United States was neither active in international politics nor important in the calculations of the Great Powers. She was not part of Bismarck's complex system of security alliances and was not involved at the Congress of Berlin in 1878. Not until after the defeat of Spain in December 1898 and the acquisition of Guam and the Philippines can the United States be called a Great Power and a world power.[88] The United States ranked first in power capabilities by World War I, and there is no doubt regarding her Great Power rank throughout the twentieth century.

Japan (1905-1945). The timing but not the fact of Japan's entry into the Great Power system is open to question. After being isolated from Great Power politics throughout most of the nineteenth century, Japan initiated a program of rapid industrialization under the Meiji regime beginning in 1868. Her military power was sufficient to defeat China in the Sino-Japanese War of 1894-95. Singer and Small identify that victory in 1895 as the beginning of Japan's role as a major power, but it can be argued that this placement is premature. It was not until her defeat of Russia in the Russo-Japanese War of 1904-5 that Japan was recognized as an important military power. At the beginning of that war she was treated with contempt by all of Europe as well as by Russia, for a European Power had not been defeated by a non-European state in two hundred years. Thus the victory over Russia in 1905 marks Japan's entry into the Great Power system.[89]

The status of Japan after 1945 is more difficult. In spite of her impressive industrial power and leading role in international commerce, Japan has lacked the military power that might provide the basis for a significant role in international security issues. She is constitutionally limited to "self-defense" forces and spends very little money on the military. She ranks eighth, behind India, (for 1960) on Singer's scale of power capabilities, has no power projection capabilities, poses no significant military threat even to medium powers, and is basically dependent upon the United States for her security. Nor does Japan have a veto at the United Nations. Japan could once again join the Great Power system if she builds up her military forces and particularly if she develops a nuclear capability. At the present time, however, her strength as a world economic power is not sufficient to qualify for membership in the Great Power security system, from which she departed in 1945.[90]

China (1949-1975). The People's Republic of China admittedly presents another difficult case, but on the basis of the criteria developed earlier, must be considered a Great Power after the completion of her revolution in 1949. Although China does not match either the United States or the USSR in military capabilities, she does rank third behind them on the Singer scale of power capabilities. Her performance in the Korean War against the American Superpower and in the Sino-Indian War of 1962 demonstrated both her military power and her capability for limited offensive as well as defensive operations. Chinese military power and prestige were enhanced further by her development of nuclear weapons in the mid-1960s. Although in some respects China has pursued a policy of diplomatic isolation, she has played an important role in Great Power politics. She entered into a formal military alliance with the Soviet Union in 1950, but within a decade and a half was competing with her for a position of leadership among international communist movements. She came to be sufficiently perceived by the Soviets as the primary threat to their security interests to justify the deployment of nearly a million Soviet troops along their common border. China was also perceived for two decades as a major threat by the United States. Some U.S. decision makers, for example, gave greater emphasis to the threat of Chinese expansion than to Soviet expansion in the deliberation of American Indochina policy.[91] A decade later China was perceived by the Nixon administration as an integral part of the world balance of power against the Soviet Union. Although China's foreign policy is primarily regional in focus, she has been involved with communist revolutionary movements in Africa, Latin America, and the Middle East as well as Asia. In any case, the importance of China's regionalism must not be exaggerated; Germany and Japan were basically regional powers during the periods of their greatest influence. For all of these reasons the People's Republic of China is a member of the Great Power system from 1949 to 1975.[92]

Exclusions from the System

Other states and political entities have played important roles in international politics over the last five centuries but are excluded from the modern Great Power system. In this section, I shall examine the most significant of these and explain why they do not satisfy my theoretical criteria for Great Power rank.

Holy Roman Empire. It was noted earlier that the emperor's influence in the Great Power system derived from his control of the Hapsburg family possessions rather than his reign over the Holy Roman Empire and that by the late fifteenth century the emperor's influence in Europe had declined markedly from its peak in the Middle Ages. By then he did not even possess true sovereignty within the empire. Sovereign German princes formed leagues among themselves and made informal alliances with external Powers. Henry II of France, for example, assumed the title of Protector of the German Liberties. Because of the absence of centralized political power and sovereignty within its territorial boundaries, as well as its lack of influence within Europe, the Holy Roman Empire does not qualify for Great Power status.

Venice. The Venetian city-state was a regional power in the Italian state system and a commercial power in the Mediterranean but did not qualify for membership in the European Great Power security system. Venice was little more than first among the Italian city-states, none of which were comparable in strength with the Great Powers of Europe, as demonstrated by the course of the Italian wars beginning in 1494. Venice had a minimal involvement in European security affairs. She did not participate in any of the four major wars between the Hapsburgs and Valois for supremacy in Europe or in any of the Ottoman wars between 1503 and 1560. Venice had reached the peak of her power by the end of the fifteenth century and entered into a period of decline in the sixteenth century when Spanish influence increased in Italy and the Mediterranean.[93] Because of her limited military capabilities relative to the European Powers and her limited influence in European diplomatic and strategic issues (as distinct from commercial relations), Venice does not meet the criteria for inclusion in the modern Great Power system.[94]

Swiss Confederation. The Swiss played an important role in European military affairs in the late fifteenth and early sixteenth centuries. They revolutionized military tactics during that period and probably had the best infantry in Europe, as evidenced by their defeat of Charles the Bold of Burgundy in 1476-77.[95] Swiss mercenaries were the most widely sought after in Europe and formed an important part of both the French and Italian armies during the Italian wars. The Swiss Confederation had a limited demographic and territorial base, however, and was not the equal of the five Great Powers of the time. It was further constrained by a highly decentralized political system consisting of a loose union of nearly independent cantons. These were bound by a common hatred of the Hapsburgs, and they fought effectively to defend their integrity against external threats. Beyond this, however, Swiss military power was not used in the pursuit of any coherent national policy. In the words of Lynn Montross, "After their triumph over Burgundy (1477) the Swiss could have challenged any army on the continent. Yet barring a few minor annexations they showed a curious indifference to political or territorial aggrandizement."[96] This behavior stands in sharp contrast to that of nearly all other Great Powers (past and present). The Swiss were driven more by profit than patriotism and were content to sell their services to others rather than join in the pursuit of any distinctive Swiss interests. Thus the Swiss Confederation cannot be considered an independent Great Power.

Portugal. Portugal was a major colonial power in the fifteenth and sixteenth centuries and is even identified by Modelski, with some exaggeration, as the leading global power of the sixteenth century.[97] In spite of her global achievements, however, Portugal does not qualify for membership in the modern Great Power system. The wealth from her colonial empire gave her a role in European commerce, but this did not extend to security affairs. Portugal lacked the military capability to exert political influence on the Continent and was not a major factor in the power calculations of the Great Powers. She did not participate in the Italian wars or in the Hapsburg-Valois wars for supremacy in Europe and in fact fought no war with any European state in the century before her absorption by Spain in 1580. Nor did she participate in any of the alliances or peace conferences. Hence Portugal must be excluded from the modern Great Power system.[98]

Poland. Poland was for a time a Baltic power but never a Great Power. She reached the peak of her strength by the late fifteenth century, just before the emergence of the modern system. Poland fought wars with Sweden and Russia for supremacy in the Baltic, from which she was excluded in 1660, but played no role in the security affairs of the Great Powers. She participated in none of their alliances or wars until her wars against the Turks beginning early in the seventeenth century. By this time Polish decline was well under way, primarily because of internal political weaknesses and the lack of a strong central authority. This process culminated in the partitions of the late eighteenth century and the elimination of Poland as a sovereign state. Poland is rarely identified as a Great Power and is not considered as one here.[99]

Denmark. Denmark, like Poland, was for a time a regional power in the Baltic but never a Great Power. She participated in none of the alliances or wars of the Great Powers until the Thirty Years' War, and by that time she had lost her supremacy in the Baltic to Sweden and had begun to decline in strength. Denmark is rarely identified as a Great Power in the histories of the period and is not included here.

The Modern Great Power System

The membership of the modern Great Power system and the periods of membership for each of the Powers have now been established:

France	1495-1975
England/Great Britain	1495-1975
Austrian Hapsburgs/Austria/ Austria-Hungary	1495-1519; 1556-1918
Spain	1495-1519; 1556-1808
Ottoman Empire	1495-1699
United Hapsburgs	1519-1556
The Netherlands	1609-1713
Sweden	1617-1721
Russia/Soviet Union	1721-1975
Prussia/Germany/West Germany	1740-1975
Italy	1861-1943
United States	1898-1975
Japan	1905-1945
China	1949-1975

The composition of the Great Power system during various time periods is shown in Table 2.1; it should be noted here that the time periods used are not of equal lengths.

The identity of the Great Powers and their points of entry into and departure from the system have been justified by applying my theoretical criteria to the historical evidence. I believe that these are the best decisions, but there is admittedly some margin of error. In the previous sections I have noted uncertainty in categorization of certain Powers and the different decisions of other observers. Now I will summarize these confidence intervals and consider the sensitivity of this study to possible "measurement error" in the identity of the Powers.

First, I am confident that no state has been improperly excluded from the modern Great Power system. Given the theoretical criteria established earlier, none of the exclusions discussed in the previous section present a difficult choice. I am also reasonably confident that no state has been improperly included in the study, though the status of China and perhaps Italy may be questioned by some.[100]

Table 2.1. The Modern Great Power System, 1495–1975

Power	1495–1519	1519–1556	1556–1609	1609–1617	1617–1699	1699–1713	1713–1721	1721–1740	1740–1808	1808–1861	1861–1898	1898–1905	1905–1918	1918–1943	1943–1945	1945–1949	1949–1975
France (Fr)	■	■	■	■	■	■	■	■	■	■	■	■	■	■	■	■	■
England/Great Britain (Eng)	■	■	■	■	■	■	■	■	■	■	■	■	■	■	■	■	■
Austrian Hapsburgs/ Austria (AH)	■		■	■	■	■	■	■	■	■	■	■	■				
Spain (Sp)	■		■	■	■	■	■	■	■								
Ottoman Empire (Tur)	■	■	■	■	■												
United Hapsburgs (UH)		■															
The Netherlands (Net)				■	■	■											
Sweden (Sw)					■	■	■										
Russia/Soviet Union (Rus)								■	■	■	■	■	■	■	■	■	■
Prussia/Germany/ FRG (Ger)									■	■	■	■	■	■	■	■	■
Italy (It)											■	■	■	■			
United States (US)												■	■	■	■	■	■
Japan (Jap)													■	■	■		
China (Ch)																	■

More open to debate are the points of entry into and departure from the system of particular Powers. Some will question the continued membership of France, England, and West Germany and the exclusion of Japan after 1945. These decisions have a minimal impact on the study, however; at most they add two wars. The other most significant cases concern the entry of England and the termination of Spain and the Ottoman Empire. Some might argue that England's entry should be delayed nearly a century (until 1588), that Spain should leave the system up to a century earlier, and that the departure of the Ottoman Empire could be changed several decades in either direction. The latter would have the largest impact on this study because of the existence of several bilateral wars involving Turkey and the other Powers. Changes for any of the other Great Powers would have much less impact, affecting the number of Powers involved in particular wars more than the inclusion or exclusion of the wars themselves. Sweden's entry could be delayed (beginning no later than 1625 or 1630), and Japan's could be moved up to 1895. Russia's entry could conceivably come twelve years earlier (Poltava) or later (beginning of the War of the Polish Succession). The Netherlands could conceivably leave the system seven years later (after the War of the Quadruple Alliance). In all other cases, I believe that the margin of error is negligible. The impact of potential measurement error on my compilation of war data is further discussed in the following two chapters. Now that the Great Powers have been defined and identified, let us turn to their wars.

3

Definition and Identification of the Wars

In previous chapters I established the need for a systematic empirical study of war among the Great Powers over an extended temporal span and suggested that existing compilations of war data are not adequate for this purpose. The aim in this chapter is to define war and suggest operational criteria for the identification of all wars involving the Great Powers in the modern system. A detailed treatment of these criteria of inclusion and exclusion is necessary because in their absence no empirical study of war can be truly systematic. Problems involving the initiation and termination dates of war and the question of the aggregation or disaggregation of multiple wars are also examined. Because no study of this nature can be perfectly objective, it is necessary to acknowledge some of the biases inherent in these data-generation procedures.

Definition of War

Before operational criteria for the identification of wars can be established it is necessary to define war conceptually. One of the most useful definitions is that suggested by Bronislow Malinowski: war is an "armed contest between two independent political units, by means of organized military force, in the pursuit of a tribal or national policy."[1] This definition avoids the serious problems that arise from legalistic definitions of war such as Wright's.[2] It recognizes that the essence of war is armed conflict involving the organized military forces of well-defined political entities. Malinowski's definition, however, does not take into account a minimum threshold of conflict or violence as a prerequisite for war and hence fails to differentiate between wars and uses of force short of war such as border incidents or limited punitive strikes. In addition, the inclusion of the Clausewitzian concept of the pursuit of national policy, unless defined very broadly, would exclude conflicts initiated primarily for domestic political or even personal reasons. War must be defined independently of its motivations or other causes (or consequences), for otherwise hypotheses regarding the causes or consequences of war would be reduced to tautologies and made untestable. Therefore, this study defines war as a substantial armed conflict between the organized military forces of independent political units.[3]

Using this final definition, one criterion for the classification of wars is the nature of the participating actors. The Great Powers constitute a distinctive set of states in the international system; therefore, a distinct set of wars involving the Great Powers can be defined and identified. These wars are a subset of a larger set of interstate wars between sovereign states in the international system. For reasons suggested earlier, the focus in this study is on interstate wars involving the Great Powers. Excluded from this study are the following: (1) any war that does not involve a Great Power (as identified in Chapter 2); (2) civil wars, unless they become internationalized through the intervention of an external state; and (3) imperial or colonial wars, unless they expand through the intervention of another state. Operational criteria to differentiate civil wars and imperial or colonial wars from others will be provided in a later section.

An important subset of the interstate wars involving the Great Powers consists of wars with at least one Great Power on each side of the conflict. These wars, labeled *Great Power wars,* generally involve a greater level of violence and have a greater impact on the international system than do wars involving only one Power. Throughout this study I will differentiate between wars involving the Great Powers and Great Power wars. Another subset consists of wars involving nearly all the Great Powers and particularly high levels of destruction. These *general wars* will be operationally defined at the end of this chapter.

To be useful in empirical research, the definition of war suggested above needs further refinement. War has been defined as "substantial" armed conflict in order to distinguish it from border incidents and other lesser forms of conflict; this minimum threshold must now be operationalized.

Wright suggests a minimum of fifty thousand troops involved in the war, but it is unclear whether he means that these troops must be engaged in actual fighting. If not, two armies engaged in a "war" of maneuver and position with little actual contact or fighting would qualify as a war even if the level of violence was relatively low. This minimum troop level criterion is also of questionable relevance for naval wars, strategic nuclear exchanges, or space wars.

A preferable alternative to the use of troop levels is the number of casualties resulting from the war, a criterion used in a number of studies. Richardson, for example, classifies all "deadly quarrels" according to their magnitude (defined as the logarithmic transformation of the number of battle deaths) and includes all conflicts exceeding 2.5 in magnitude (or 317 casualties). Gaston Bodart defines an "important engagement" as "one in which the combined loss by both antagonists amounted to at least 2,000 men killed, wounded, missing, and prisoners." Singer and Small require a minimum of 1,000 battle fatalities (for all participants combined) before the conflict is considered an interstate war.[4] Thus there is ample precedence for the use of a battle-death criterion to distinguish wars from lesser forms of military conflict. The Singer-Small criterion is used here because it is the most refined and precise and because it results in reasonable decisions on what wars to include and exclude.

In addition to requiring a 1,000 battle-death minimum, Singer and Small include supplementary criteria. To deal with protracted wars with intermittent fighting, they require an annual average of 1,000 battle deaths for a war to qualify. To determine which states should be considered as participants in a given war, they use a minimum threshold of 100 battle deaths. But to avoid excluding a few theoretically important cases in which the combat troops of a given state were involved extensively but did not sustain this minimum number of casualties, Singer and Small provide the alternative criterion of a "minimum of 1,000 armed personnel engaged in active combat within the war theater."[5]

The application of the Singer-Small battle-death criterion to this study raises the question of whether to require 1,000 battle deaths of all participants or only of the Great Powers. For the purposes of replicability and comparability for the post-1815 period, I prefer that this compilation deviate as little as possible from the Singer-Small compilation. Consequently, the 1,000 battle-death minimum is not restricted to the Great Powers but includes all states, even though these other states are not included in the actual measurements of the parameters of the war. In practice, however, the casualty figures for the Great Powers are the primary criterion for the pre-1815 period because usually no figures are available for most of the other states. Use of this criterion might introduce a slight bias against the inclusion of very small wars in the earlier period.

Another problem is whether to apply this constant criterion of 1,000 battle deaths over the entire temporal span of this study, given the increases over time in population, size of armies, and killing power of weapons and the consequent increase in battle casualties. This problem becomes circular, however, for the trends in war over time cannot be determined unless the wars themselves are first identified. Although casualties have increased over time, this trend is not as strong as might be expected. Furthermore, any relation between casualties and army size is an empirical question. For the sake of consistency, therefore, the same criterion is applied to earlier wars because otherwise the upward trend in casualties over time might be eliminated by definition. For similar reasons, the criteria of an annual average of 1,000 battle deaths and 100 battle casualties for a state to qualify is constant over time.

Existing Compilations of Wars

If any of the existing compilations of wars were adequate, the problem of identifying the wars would be solved. What is needed is a list of wars determined by criteria at least as broad as those used here, from which to exclude wars that do not meet these criteria. Unfortunately, no such compilation exists. The most recent compilation of international wars is Singer and Small's *The Wages of War, 1816-1965: A Statistical Handbook.* This is a superb piece of social science research and has had a profound impact on the study of international conflict. It is characterized by a precision of operational definition and measurement and the rigorous application of definitional criteria to the selection of data. Its emphasis on the explicit specification of the empirical system under study and the meticulous concern with the problem of inclusion and exclusion is a model to be emulated. Singer and Small first define the international system and apply strict criteria to determine the membership of that system. On the basis of these criteria Singer and Small identify fifty interstate wars and forty-three extrasystemic wars over the period 1816-1965. They then define a number of dimensions of war, including duration, magnitude, severity, and intensity. Empirical indicators for each are operationally defined, and data are collected describing these various parameters for each war. Thus they end up with a list of wars and a quantitative description of the dimensions of each war. The remainder of their study involves various statistical analyses of the nature of war over time, including linear and cyclical trends, seasonal concentrations, and the amount of war categorized by nation, dyad, and region.

Unfortunately, the Singer-Small war data are not fully adequate for my purposes, for their time span is too restrictive. The period 1816-1965 covers only about one-third of the span of the modern Great Power system. Consequently, if the Singer-Small compilation of wars is to be used here it must be supplemented with other sources.

For the same reasons, the data set compiled by Richardson in *Statistics of Deadly Quarrels,* which covers the period 1820-1949, is not useful for my purposes. In addition to the limited temporal span of the study, Richardson is not as concerned as Singer and Small with the problem of inclusion and exclusion, and consequently there is considerable uncertainty as to whether the biases in the data have been reduced to a minimum. His operational criteria are not as refined as those of Singer and Small and his estimates of battle casualties probably not as accurate.[6] Furthermore, Richardson's conceptual categories are slightly different from those used here. For these reasons, Singer and Small's data set rather than Richardson's is used for the most recent 150-year period.

One compilation that extends further back in time is Pitirim Sorokin's *Social and Cultural Dynamics,* volume 3: *Fluctuation of Social Relationships, War, and Revolution.* Sorokin's list includes "almost all the known wars" of the most important states of Europe from antiquity to 1925.[7] The states treated include ancient Greece, ancient Rome, France, Russia, England, Austria-Hungary, Germany, Italy, Spain, Holland, and Poland and Lithuania. The basic data are listed by state, and the duration and estimates of army strength and battle casualties for each war are given. On the basis of these data, Sorokin analyzes the fluctuation of war over time for Europe as a whole and for each state.

Sorokin's set of war data covers an exhaustive time period, and its restriction to only the diplomatically most active states is satisfactory for the purposes of this study. Unfortunately, Sorokin's list of most important states is not precisely congruent with mine. He includes the wars for the Ottoman Empire and Sweden only when Sweden or Turkey was the enemy of one of his key states, leaving their wars against minor states unaccounted for. But this problem is not major.

The most serious problem with the Sorokin data is the absence of explicit criteria for inclusion and exclusion. "Almost all the known wars" is not a sufficient criterion. Although Sorokin's intent to pursue scientifically acceptable procedures cannot be questioned (his discussion of methodological difficulties involved in the quantitative study of war is excellent), this particular limitation hinders replication of the study and leaves the reader uncertain regarding the nature and magnitude of the biases in the basic data set. Thus once again the question arises of precisely to what set of empirical phenomena any resulting generalizations can be applied. There are other problems, of course, but these are not unique to Sorokin and shall be treated later in the proper context.

Another compilation of war data which covers the temporal span of the Great Power system is contained in Quincy Wright's classic *Study of War.* Wright lists more than three hundred wars for the period 1480-1964. For each war he includes the dates of initiation and termination, a list of participants and their dates of entry, the number of important battles, and the type of war. Wright demonstrates a greater concern than Sorokin with the inclusion/exclusion problem, though his criteria are not as sophisticated as Singer and Small's. He aims to include "all hostilities involving members of the family of nations, whether international, civil, colonial, or imperial, which were recognized as states of war in the legal sense or which involved over 50,000 troops." He includes additional hostilities of lesser magnitude and of nonlegal standing which led to "important legal results."[8] As argued earlier in this chapter, these criteria are ambiguous, and they are not entirely congruent with those listed in this study. They do provide, however, a satisfactory set of standards by which a given conflict can be accepted into or rejected from a compilation of wars.

Still another list of wars can be found in Woods and Baltzly's *Is War Diminishing?* They construct lists of wars from 1450 to 1900 for the following states: Austria, Denmark, England, France, Holland, Poland, Prussia, Russia, Spain, Sweden, and Turkey. They also attempt to analyze trends in war over time on the basis of the duration of wars. Woods and Baltzly include the Great Powers as defined in this study, but they fail to provide the specific operational criteria by which the wars are identified. For this reason their compilation alone is not sufficient as a basic source of data.

Two other attempts at a more scientific study of war are Gaston Bodart's *Losses of Life in Modern Wars* and Samuel Dumas and K. O. Vedel-Peterson's *Losses of Life Caused by War.* Both are more concerned with accurately determining the army strength and battle casualties for the major wars of a few key states than with systematically identifying the basic set of wars. Bodart examines the wars of Austria-Hungary from 1618 to 1913 and France from 1614 to 1913. Dumas and Vedel-Peterson look at "important" (but otherwise undefined) wars from 1756 to 1918. These studies provide useful battle casualty data but cannot be used for the systematic identification of the wars themselves.

The unreliability of the selection criteria used in these various studies, and therefore the inadequacy of any one of them for my purposes, is further demonstrated by a brief comparison of the list of wars generated by each. We find considerable disagreement concerning the identity of the wars and even greater variation in their dates of initiation and termination. A comparison of the Wright and Sorokin lists, for example, shows that of the roughly 125 wars included in one set or the other, only about two-thirds appear in both. Nor are these inconsistencies restricted to minor wars. The Wright, Sorokin, and Woods-Baltzly data sets disagree on the existence of a number of Great Power wars, including the Austro-Turkish War of 1576-83, English-Spanish War of 1656-59, and the British-Spanish War of 1726-29. There are also significant disagreements on dates and the combination of simultaneous or sequential wars, which will be discussed later. Because of the discrepancies, it is impossible to rely on any single compilation of wars, but they can be combined to help generate a more complete set and to serve as mutual validity checks.

Criteria for Inclusion and Exclusion

Since the Singer-Small criteria are nearly congruent with those established here, their set of wars (excluding the wars not involving the Great Powers) are used, with minor modifications, for the post-Vienna period. The Singer-Small criteria can easily be applied to the wars since 1965 in order to extend the data set.

For the 1495-1815 period, the Wright, Sorokin, and Woods-Baltzly compilations have been combined to generate a complete set of wars satisfying my criteria. The simple union of the three sets (including any war identified at least once) is unsatisfactory, however, for it fails to eliminate wars erroneously identified by only one source.[9] Nor would the intersection of the three sets (taking only those wars appearing in all three sets) be satisfacory, for a number of important wars erroneously excluded by one source (for example, the British-

Spanish War of 1726-29) would therefore be excluded. Given the observed discrepancies and the ambiguous or unknown selection criteria of each of these sources, it is best not to rely on the inclusion or exclusion of any war by one source without the concurrence of at least one other source. Wars are included in this compilation, therefore, only if they are identified in any two of the Wright, Sorokin, or Woods-Baltzly sets.[10]

This tentative list of wars must be further refined, however. Any war not involving at least one Great Power is excluded from the final compilation. Furthermore, any war not satisfying the battle-death criterion is excluded. The latter condition is simple in most cases, for Sorokin provides a reasonably reliable set of data on war casualties. Missing, however, are casualty data for Turkey and Sweden and for any war not included by Sorokin, so that some other procedures must be followed to determine whether the 1,000 battle-death minimum is satisfied. This material is available in Bodart's *Losses of Life in Modern Wars,* Dumas and Vedel-Peterson's *Losses of Life Caused by War,* and (since any battle exceeding 1,000 casualties is sufficient to qualify the conflict as a war) Thomas Harbottle's *Dictionary of Battles*.[11] For the few remaining cases, reasonable approximations must be made based on informed judgments from diplomatic histories.[12]

The other classes of conflicts that must be excluded from my war set are civil and imperial or colonial wars. Although Wright attempts to distinguish civil and imperial wars from balance-of-power wars his criteria are not adequate for my purposes. (Imperial wars, for example, are defined as those attempting to "expand modern civilization at the expense of another culture."[13] and therefore all wars involving the Ottoman Empire are classified as imperial.) Nor is Sorokin's classification of "internal disturbances" fully adequate. Since the distinction between interstate wars (which are the focus of this study) and noninterstate wars is sometimes unclear, it is necessary to consider the question in greater detail.

If interstate wars are defined literally as war between states, the problem concerns the ambiguity of what constitutes a state and its defining characteristic of sovereign independence. For example, were the wars within the Holy Roman Empire civil wars or interstate wars? Were the Russo-Persian wars interstate or imperial?

Singer and Small have developed criteria to resolve similar questions for the more recent period. They independently define membership in the international system as requiring a population of 500,000 and diplomatic recognition by Britain and France (after 1920 this legitimizing role of Britain and France is replaced by diplomatic recognition by any two Great Powers or membership in the League of Nations or United Nations). All wars with system members on both sides are classified as interstate; all others are either civil or extrasystemic (imperial).[14] These criteria cannot be applied to the pre-1815 period, however. Population data are not available, and the historical research to determine diplomatic recognition (or its functional equivalent because diplomatic practice has changed over time) would be too time-consuming to consider here. Since the number of ambiguous cases is not great, it is better to make the most reasonable decisions possible on a case-by-case basis.

Regarding the Holy Roman Empire, the main consideration is that sixteenth- and seventeenth-century Germany was a decentralized collection of principalities and other small political units which cannot realistically be treated as sovereign states, for the emperor exerted a considerable degree of moral and political influence within Germany. Given this absence of true sovereignty, wars between the emperor and smaller German polities are classified as civil rather than interstate. (Wars between the smaller polities are of no interest here because no Great Powers were involved.) Another set of cases involves several conflicts between England and Scotland. The political relationship between these two changed in 1707 with the Union of England and Scotland. For the purposes of this study all armed conflicts before that date are treated as interstate wars (the last such war occurred in 1650-51), and all subsequent conflicts are classified as civil wars. On the other hand, all armed conflicts between England and Ireland are treated as civil wars. Most of the other cases are less ambiguous.

Civil wars that became internationalized through the military intervention of an outside state are of interest for this study. Here we can distinguish between those cases in which the outside state intervenes on the side of the insurgents against the existing regime and those in which the external state provides active military support to the regime against the insurgents. Only the former constitutes an interstate war (provided it meets the battle-death criterion) and is included here. Interventions in behalf of an existing regime against insurgents are excluded because the latter cannot qualify as sovereign territorial states. These wars are included, however, if they generate a counterintervention against the existing regime or its supporter.[15]

Some internationalized civil wars are easily identified. The sixteenth- and seventeenth-century Huguenot wars frequently generated English intervention against the French regime and thus became internationalized civil wars. In the War of the Three Henries (1589-98) Spain intervened in France as part of the succession struggle. Other cases are more difficult, especially with regard to the question of when a civil war becomes internationalized. The recent case of the Indochinese wars provides a good example. The French intervention is excluded for that can be classified as a continuation of a colonial war. Also excluded are the Cambodian and two Laotian phases of the war, for there the United States intervened on behalf of the existing regime against the insurgents. It was not an internationalized civil war until a state (North Vietnam) intervened on the side of the insurgents against an existing regime and its Great Power supporter. This was a gradual process, but a definite time must be established for the purposes of analysis. Here I follow Singer and Small and accept February 7, 1965 (the beginning of sustained U.S. bombardment of North Vietnam) as the beginning of the interstate phase.

The two cases that present the most serious problems are the Russian and Spanish Civil Wars. Singer and Small exclude both, and in the case of the former it is questionable whether they rigorously adhere to their own well-defined criteria of inclusion and exclusion. They admit that most of their criteria are satisfied yet claim that the Russian civil war is "something very different."[16] But this is not a sufficient basis for exclusion, given their basic methodological assumptions and their concern for a systematic and unbiased population of wars. The interstate dimension of the war involved five Great Powers (Russia, Japan, Britain, France, and the United States), lasted at least two years (Singer and Small say three), and resulted in more than 2,000 allied fatalities and presumably at least as many Russians (the total Russian fatalities from the civil war were about a half million).[17] This case must be identified as an internationalized civil war and included in this study.[18]

The Spanish case, excluded by both Singer and Small and Richardson, is even more difficult, largely because of the enormous measurement and coding problems and the absence of data to determine whether the battle-death criterion has been satisfied and for which participants. The military involvement of the Great Powers was very limited: the Russian contingents were small, the Germans contributed mainly an aerial squadron, and the Italians were involved primarily in the air and submarine war, all of which tend to limit their casualties. Several of the unofficial and volunteer international brigades were financed, organized, and commanded by Communists, but it is questionable whether they ought to be considered Russian troops. Thus it is questionable whether there were sufficient battle deaths to qualify. Furthermore, on the substantive level, it would be misleading to represent this as a war in which Spain and Russia were arrayed against Germany, Italy, and Portugal. For these reasons, this conflict has been excluded from my population of interstate wars.[19]

Imperial and colonial wars present an even more complex set of conceptual and operational problems. Part of the difficulty in identifying imperial wars is the ambiguity of the concept, which has been ideologically contaminated and has assumed a diversity of meanings. The concept of colonial war is more easily defined and more manageable, but it is too restrictive for my theoretical purposes. Colonies can be defined legally and identified by the presence of formal charters. Colonial wars could then be defined as all wars involving a colony and meeting certain other criteria (for example, battle deaths). But this process would exclude the phenomenon of "informal imperialism,"[20] in which conflicts arise because of economic, political, or military expansion into areas where a formal administrative system is not established and a colonial charter not formally granted (for example Russian expansion in Asia).

Singer and Small appear to avoid this problem by operationally defining imperial and colonial wars (which they fail to distinguish theoretically) as extrasystemic wars (those involving a system member against a nonmember). But this concept incorporates a variety of wars, including those arraying system members against small European states (for example, Polish wars of 1831 and 1863-64 and the Hungarian war of 1848-49) as well as those in which European Powers fought against weaker non-European political entities (Franco-Indochinese wars of 1882-84 and 1945-54). But these wars are sufficiently different that they should not be classified together as imperial wars. It is preferable to adopt the more traditional conception and consider imperial wars to be those in which a major European state (not necessarily a Great Power) fought a relatively weak non-European entity. In applying these criteria to the post-1815 period, therefore, the Singer-Small extrasystemic wars involving weaker European states are not classified as imperial wars. (Instead, most can be classified as civil wars, for they involved semisovereign dependencies of the Powers. In any case, they are excluded from this compilation.) Wars involving non-European entities who qualify as members of the international system are classified as interstate wars.

The Singer-Small system membership criteria can also be applied to the pre-1815 period. No non-European state (other than Turkey and the United States) qualified as an international system member as early as 1816, however, so all wars between the Great Powers and non-European states (except for the War of 1812 and the wars with Turkey) are classified as imperial wars.

This decision reveals the Eurocentric bias in my procedures. Whereas expansionist wars of the Great Powers in Europe are classified as interstate, those involving Russia or the Ottoman Empire in Asia are classified as imperial (for example, Russo-Persian wars), even though these wars may be comparable in many respects and may have served similar purposes for the Powers involved. The classification of some Asian wars (for example, the Persian wars) as interstate wars would create serious problems for this analysis. First, to be systematic it would be necessary to consider other Asian wars besides those involving Persia and to develop general criteria to determine which were interstate and which were imperial. Even more critical is the absence of war data for these states. Wright includes Persia only after 1750 and (along with Woods and Baltzly) identifies only two Russo-Persian wars before 1815 (1795-96 and 1804-13) and none of the Ottoman-Persian wars. Sorokin excludes Turkey as well as Persia. In the absence of an ambitious and systematic effort to generate new and original data, it would be impossible to know what wars to include in the study (other than the two mentioned above). Therefore, I have followed the Singer-Small membership criteria and the Europe/non-Europe distinction (which are equivalent for the pre-1815 period), recognizing the resulting bias.

To summarize, the operational criteria by which wars are included in or excluded from this compilation are as follows. First, a tentative list of wars is generated. For the 1495-1815 period, the Wright, Sorokin, and Woods-Baltzly compilations were consulted and any war included in at least two of these sources is included here.[21] For the 1816-1965 period the Singer-Small list of wars is used, and the Singer-Small criteria are applied to the 1965-75 period to generate a list of wars. From this tentative set of wars I have excluded wars not including a Great Power, imperial wars, civil wars, internationalized civil wars in which the outside states intervene militarily on the side of the existing regime (but include those in which the intervention is against the government), and wars that do not satisfy the battle-death criteria of a minimum of 1,000 battle deaths and a minimum annual average of 1,000 battle deaths for protracted wars. Participation in a war by an individual Power is determined by use of a minimum of 100 battle fatalities or the involvement of 1,000 armed personnel actively engaged in combat.

Initiation, Termination, and Aggregation of War

Adding to the difficulties discussed above are problems in the definition of the beginning and end of a war and in the aggregation or disaggregation of sequential or simultaneous wars. The seriousness of these problems is indicated by the number of discrepancies in the literature. Wright, Sorokin, and Woods and Baltzly often disagree about the dates of initiation and termination of hostilities, if only by a few years. This problem is important because the duration of war is one of its dimensions which is measured and used in the analysis. Wright recognizes this problem and notes that "wars have seldom been separated from peace by a clearly marked line."[22]

One solution is to use the date of the formal declaration of war, but these have been rare and often preceded by serious fighting, as Wright notes. He therefore defines the beginning of a war as the "first important hostilities," which he fails to define explicitly. Wright defines the end of a war as the effective date of the peace treaty, if there was one. Otherwise, he refers to the date of "armistice, capitulation, or actual ending of active hostilities."[23] Richardson also notes the deficiencies in a purely legalistic definition of the temporal bounds of a given war. He refers to "provocative incidents prior to the main outbreak," the outbreak of hostilities without any declaration of war, armistices and other pauses, continuation of guerrilla warfare after the main defeat, and the informal cessation of hostilities without a formal treaty. He ultimately accepts the "conventional date" if authorities are agreed. In the absence of consensus, he prefers "common sense to legalism . . . I have been guided by actual warlike alertness rather than by formal declarations of war or peace."[24] Singer and Small define the beginning of a war to coincide with the formal declaration (if there was one) but "only if it is followed immediately by sustained military combat." If there is no formal declaration or if hostilities precede any such declaration, the first day of combat is used. In dating the termination of war, Singer and Small follow Richardson rather than Wright and give priority to military rather than legal criteria. When the date of the peace treaty differs from that of the actual cessation of military activity, the end of the war is defined as "the day which most clearly demarcates the close of sustained military conflict."[25] Sorokin gives little attention to this problem.

For the 1816-1975 period, the Singer-Small criteria are used. For the earlier period, however, the absence of complete data precludes the direct application of these criteria and approximations must be made. The Wright, Sorokin, and Woods and Baltzly dates are used if they agree. Wright is given slightly more weight if there are minor discrepancies because of his specification of operational criteria. In the case of major disagreements, Langer, R. Ernest Dupuy and Trevor N. Dupuy,[26] and other secondary sources are consulted. Given the nature of my theoretical purposes, the years of initiation and termination (rather than the month and day, as in Singer and Small) are of sufficient precision.

A related but considerably more difficult question concerns the aggregation of wars. The basic problem is how to draw a line around a single war, both temporally and spatially. When are a series of wars over time to be aggregated or compounded into one larger war? Should there be a single War of the Austrian Succession, for example, or of the First, Second, and Third Silesian Wars? Similarly, was there a single Italian War of 1495–1504 or (as Sorokin suggests) distinct Italian War (1495-97), First War of Louis XII for Milan (1499-1500), and Second War of Louis XII for Naples (1501-4)? This problem of temporal aggregation is particularly difficult for the wars involving the Ottoman Empire (or contemporary wars of national liberation), which were fought continuously but intermittently over long periods of time. (Wright, for example, identifies distinct Ottoman Wars of 1521-31, 1532-34, 1537-47, and 1551-68, all involving the Hapsburgs.)

With regard to the spatial dimension, when are a number of simultaneous bilateral wars to be aggregated into a larger multilateral war? Should the Sino-Japanese, Japanese-American, Russo-Finnish, and central European wars of the late 1930s and 1940s be identified as distinct wars or aggregated into a single World War II? Should the War of Jenkins' Ear be defined as distinct from the War of the Austrian Succession? For some wars both temporal and spatial aggregation must be considered (for example, the Thirty Years' War). This problem of the aggregation of wars is of considerable importance for this study because a number of the parameters by which wars are to be measured (including frequency and duration) are highly sensitive to the procedures by which wars are aggregated or disaggregated.

Unfortunately, there is little guidance in the literature on this problem. Neither Sorokin nor Woods and Baltzly appears to give it much thought, though their procedure of organizing the wars by states rather than chronologically for the system imposes a strong bias toward disaggregation. Wright prefers to "group compound wars under a single name, as has usually been done by historians." Wright notes, however, that "makers of lists of wars have often treated hostilities between each pair of states as a distinct war."[27] Singer and Small do not appear to be concerned with this problem. They note a "wide divergence as to whether a given sequence of hostilities is best treated as a single war or as a number of separate ones"[28] but fail to develop any line of argument. It is not clear why some of their wars are considered distinct (for example, the Italian Unification, Italo-Roman, and Italo-Sicilian wars, all falling within the period 1859-61) and others as part of a whole (for example, the Japanese-American war as part of World War II).

One approach would be the legalistic one of distinguishing wars on the basis of the peace treaty (or treaties) terminating the hostilities. For a series of wars over time, each conflict ending in a separate peace treaty would be defined as a distinct war. For wars that end with a formal treaty of peace (and not just a temporary truce or cease-fire), this is a satisfactory means of defining the temporal boundaries of the conflict. But, not all wars end with formal settlements. Many are relatively continuous over time and consist of a series of distinct battles separated by periods of minimal combat—for example, the protracted sieges of the sixteenth and seventeenth centuries, particularly those involving the Ottoman Empire. For these cases, criteria for defining the end of war might include the existence of a significant period of peace (and not simply a temporary cease-fire or tractical withdrawal) separating intense military conflicts, or a reversal in the military alliances that generate a new conflict (for example, the change in alliances after the War of the Cambrian League that led to the War of the Holy League). These criteria are not absolute but should serve as a guide for judgment in particular cases.

Reliance on formal peace settlements is less satisfactory, however, for dealing with multilateral wars that often are formally ended by series of bilateral treaties rather than a single multilateral treaty. The French Revolutionary and Napoleonic Wars, for example, were ended by at least ten separate treaties and World War I by five distinct treaties. To disaggregate wars of this nature and treat them all as bilateral wars would not be very useful. It would eliminate the distinction between bilateral and multilateral wars and conceal some of the major differences between them, including the processes of escalation and termination and the nature of wartime diplomacy. It would fail to give appropriate emphasis to the critical regional and international context within which the war is conducted and would preclude the testing of numerous important hypotheses, particularly at the systemic level. Thus it is important to differentiate between a genuine bilateral war restricted to a pair of states and a multilateral war involving several states.

Not all simultaneous wars are interrelated. Conflicts with different participants (for example the Hungarian and Suez wars of 1956) or totally unrelated issues (for example the Napoleonic Wars and the Russo-Turkish War of 1806-12) should not be compounded. Wars involving coordinated military planning (for example, the European and Asian theaters of World War II) should be aggregated. In this compilation, ambiguous cases are compounded into a single war unless there are compelling reasons to do otherwise. Let us now examine some of the more important cases involving the question of aggregation.

For the Italian wars of 1495-1504, I have followed Sorokin and Woods and Baltzly (rather than Wright) and identified three distinct wars (1495-97, 1499-1500, 1501-4) because well-defined periods of peace occurred between the conflicts in Naples, Milan, and Naples again. Similarly, the War of the Cambrian League, War of the Holy League, and Second Milanese War are considered separately here because of the defection of the other Powers from the French in 1511 and the settlements in 1514-15.

One of the more difficult problems of aggregation involves the Thirty Years' War, 1618-48. To consider it a single war would be misleading because it was not continuous over time. Only two Great Powers (Spain and the Austrian Hapsburgs) were involved over the full span of the war. Nor was there a single set of issues for the entire thirty years. At first it was merely a revolt of the Bohemians against the Austrian Hapsburgs. Within two years it had been transformed into a German war, but it did not become a general European war until later. Before 1630 religious issues predominated, whereas after that time power considerations were the primary motivating force; France and Sweden were dominant in this latter period but participated little in the earlier phases of the struggle. On the other hand, it would be equally misleading to follow Wright and identify thirteen "distinct but overlapping wars."[29]

Historians usually divide the Thirty Years' War into four distinct periods or phases: (1) Bohemian Period, 1618-25; (2) Danish Period, 1625-30; (3) Swedish Period, 1630-35; and (4) Swedish-French Period, 1635-48.[30] There is little disagreement among historians on this periodization, for these four phases were separated by periods of relatively little fighting. Rather than choose either complete aggregation or disaggregation, I have decided to consider each of the four periods as a distinct war.

A similar case is that of the wars of the French revolutionary and Napoleonic periods. These should not be considered a single war because they were broken up by at least ten distinct peace treaties, involving different states and providing a temporary settlement for various phases of the war. Thus Wright identifies thirteen distinct wars (five French Revolutionary Wars and eight Napoleonic Wars). Sorokin also lists thirteen wars, although these are not congruent with Wright's.[31] The basic issues changed very little over the course of the war(s), however, and the fighting was relatively continuous over time. It is conventional to make a distinction between the French Revolutionary Wars (1792-1802) and the Napoleonic Wars (1803-15). Between these two wars all states except France and Britain experienced nearly three years of peace. Furthermore, the issues during these two periods were in many respects fundamentally different. The French Revolutionary Wars were concerned primarily with the consolidation of the revolution and the new regime in France, whereas the Napoleonic Wars were more concerned with European expansion and hegemony. Only the latter period, furthermore, is characterized by the "French Imperial System" and the "Continental System." For these reasons the French Revolutionary Wars and the Napoleonic Wars are considered as distinct in this study.

Potential Biases in the Selection Procedures

There may be some concern that the use of two different selection procedures for the generation of the war data (a combination of the Wright, Sorokin, and Woods-Baltzly compilations for the pre-Vienna period and the Singer-Small data for the post-Vienna period) might introduce bias into the resulting data set. The list of wars generated by the Singer-Small criteria can be compared to a list that would have been generated by the application of the pre-1815 selection procedures to the 1816-1915 period (the end of the Woods-Baltzly set). Of the twenty Singer-Small wars, only one (the Anglo-Persian War of 1856-57) would have been excluded from the combined Wright/Sorokin/Woods-Baltzly list. Nor would this combined list have added a single war to the Singer-Small compilation, with the possible exception of the Mexican Revolution (an internationalized civil war involving the United States, which probably would have been excluded on the basis of the battle-death criterion). These results are encouraging because they suggest that the method of combining the Wright, Sorokin, and Woods-Baltzly compilations results in a very close approximation to the more refined Singer-Small inclusion-exclusion criteria and that therefore any bias deriving from the use of these two different methods is relatively unimportant.

Another potential source of bias concerns the application of the battle-death criterion. Since for small wars Sorokin's casualty figures are sometimes slightly higher than those of Singer and Small,[32] there may be a slight tendency to include a few additional wars on the basis of the 1,000 battle-death criterion. This effect would seem to be balanced, however, by the fact that Sorokin's casualty figures might be slightly lower because the fatalities of lesser states are not included. Still another source of measurement error in the identification of the

Table 3.1. Interstate Wars Involving the Great Powers, 1495–1975

War	*Denotes Great Power war.	Dates	Fr	Eng	Sp	AH	Tur	UH	Net	Sw	Rus	Ger	It	US	Jap	Ch
1	*War of the League of Venice	1495–1497	■		■	■										
2	Polish-Turkish War	1497–1498					■									
3	Venetian-Turkish War	1499–1503					■									
4	First Milanese War	1499–1500	■													
5	*Neapolitan War	1501–1504	■		■											
6	War of the Cambrian League	1508–1509	■		■	■										
7	*War of the Holy League	1511–1514	■	■	■	■										
8	*Austro-Turkish War	1512–1519				■	■									
9	Scottish War	1513–1515		■												
10	*Second Milanese War	1515–1515	■		■	■										
11	*First War of Charles V	1521–1526	■	■				■								
12	*Ottoman War	1521–1531					■	■								
13	Scottish War	1522–1523		■												
14	*Second War of Charles V	1526–1529	■	■				■								
15	*Ottoman War	1532–1535					■	■								
16	Scottish War	1532–1534		■												
17	*Third War of Charles V	1536–1538	■					■								
18	*Ottoman War	1537–1547					■	■								
19	Scottish War	1542–1550		■												
20	*Fourth War of Charles V	1542–1544	■					■								
21	*Siege of Boulogne	1544–1546	■	■												
22	*Arundel's Rebellion	1549–1550	■	■												
23	*Ottoman War	1551–1556					■	■								
24	*Fifth War of Charles V	1552–1556	■					■								
25	*Austro-Turkish War	1556–1562				■	■									
26	*Franco-Spanish War	1556–1559	■	■	■											
27	*Scottish War	1559–1560	■	■												
28	*Spanish-Turkish War	1559–1564			■		■									
29	*First Huguenot War	1562–1564	■	■												

War	Dates	Fr	Eng	Sp	AH	Tur	UH	Net	Sw	Rus	Ger	It	US	Jap	Ch
30 *Austro-Turkish War	1565–1568				■	■									
31 *Spanish-Turkish War	1569–1580			■		■									
32 *Austro-Turkish War	1576–1583				■	■									
33 Spanish-Portuguese War	1579–1581			■											
34 Polish-Turkish War	1583–1590					■									
35 *War of the Armada	1585–1604		■	■											
36 Austro-Polish War	1587–1588				■										
37 *War of the Three Henries	1589–1598	■		■											
38 *Austro-Turkish War	1593–1606				■	■									
39 Franco-Savoian War	1600–1601	■													
40 *Spanish-Turkish War	1610–1614			■		■									
41 Austro-Venetian War	1615–1618				■										
42 Spanish-Savoian War	1615–1617			■											
43 Spanish-Venetian War	1617–1621			■											
44 *Spanish-Turkish War	1618–1619			■		■									
45 Polish-Turkish War	1618–1621					■									
46 *Thirty Years' War—Bohemian	1618–1625		■	■	■			■							
47 *Thirty Years' War—Danish	1625–1630	■	■	■	■			■	■						
48 *Thirty Years' War—Swedish	1630–1635			■	■			■	■						
49 *Thirty Years' War—Swedish-French	1635–1648	■		■	■			■	■						
50 Spanish-Portuguese War	1642–1668			■											
51 Turkish-Venetian War	1645–1664					■									
52 *Franco-Spanish War	1648–1659	■		■											
53 Scottish War	1650–1651		■												
54 *Anglo-Dutch Naval War	1652–1655		■					■							
55 *Great Northern War	1654–1660				■			■	■						
56 *English-Spanish War	1656–1659		■	■											
57 Dutch-Portuguese War	1657–1661							■							
58 *Ottoman War	1657–1664	■			■	■									
59 Sweden-Bremen War	1665–1666								■						
60 *Anglo-Dutch Naval War	1665–1667	■	■					■							

Table 3.1. Continued

War	*Denotes Great Power war.	Dates	Fr	Eng	Sp	AH	Tur	UH	Net	Sw	Rus	Ger	It	US	Jap	Ch
61	*Devolutionary War	1667–1668	■		■											
62	*Dutch War of Louis XIV	1672–1678	■	■	■	■			■	■						
63	Turkish-Polish War	1672–1676					■									
64	Russo-Turkish War	1677–1681					■									
65	*Ottoman War	1682–1699				■	■									
66	*Franco-Spanish War	1683–1684	■		■											
67	*War of the League of Augsburg	1688–1697	■	■	■	■			■							
68	*Second Northern War	1700–1721		■						■						
69	*War of the Spanish Succession	1701–1713	■	■	■	■			■							
70	Ottoman War	1716–1718				■										
71	*War of the Quadruple Alliance	1718–1720	■	■	■	■										
72	*British-Spanish War	1726–1729		■	■											
73	*War of the Polish Succession	1733–1738	■		■	■					■					
74	Ottoman War	1736–1739				■					■					
75	*War of the Austrian Succession	1739–1748	■	■	■	■					■	■				
76	Russo-Swedish War	1741–1743									■					
77	*Seven Years' War	1755–1763	■	■	■	■					■	■				
78	Russo-Turkish War	1768–1774									■					
79	Confederation of Bar	1768–1772									■					
80	*War of the Bavarian Succession	1778–1779				■						■				
81	*War of the American Revolution	1778–1784	■	■	■											
82	Ottoman War	1787–1792				■					■					
83	Russo-Swedish War	1788–1790									■					
84	*French Revolutionary Wars	1792–1802	■	■	■	■					■	■				
85	*Napoleonic Wars	1803–1815	■	■	■	■					■	■				
86	Russo-Turkish War	1806–1812		■							■					
87	Russo-Swedish War	1808–1809									■					
88	War of 1812	1812–1814		■												
89	Neapolitan War	1815–1815				■										

War		Dates	Fr	Eng	Sp	AH	Tur	UH	Net	Sw	Rus	Ger	It	US	Jap	Ch
90	Franco-Spanish War	1823–1823	■													
91	Navarino Bay	1827–1827	■	■							■					
92	Russo-Turkish War	1828–1829									■					
93	Austro-Sardinian War	1848–1849				■										
94	First Schleswig-Holstein War	1849–1849										■				
95	Roman Republic War	1849–1849	■			■										
96	*Crimean War	1853–1856	■	■							■					
97	Anglo-Persian War	1856–1857		■												
98	*War of Italian Unification	1859–1859	■			■										
99	Franco-Mexican War	1862–1867	■													
100	Second Schleswig-Holstein War	1864–1864				■						■				
101	*Austro-Prussian War	1866–1866				■						■	■			
102	*Franco-Prussian War	1870–1871	■									■				
103	Russo-Turkish War	1877–1878									■					
104	Sino-French War	1884–1885	■													
105	Russo-Japanese War	1904–1905									■					
106	Italo-Turkish War	1911–1912											■			
107	*World War I	1914–1918	■	■		■					■	■	■	■	■	
108	*Russian Civil War	1918–1921	■	■							■			■	■	
109	Manchurian War	1931–1933													■	
110	Italo-Ethiopian War	1935–1936											■			
111	Sino-Japanese War	1937–1941													■	
112	*Russo-Japanese War	1939–1939									■				■	
113	*World War II	1939–1945	■	■							■	■	■	■	■	
114	Russo-Finnish War	1939–1940									■					
115	*Korean War	1950–1953	■	■										■		■
116	Russo-Hungarian War	1956–1956									■					
117	Sinai War	1956–1956	■	■												
118	Sino-Indian War	1962–1962														■
119	Vietnam War	1965–1973												■		

wars derives from the uncertainty in identifying the Great Powers; but since that uncertainty is relatively small, the potential error in the identity of their wars would be small also. The problem is minimized by the fact that the uncertainty in the number of wars is generally inversely proportional to the uncertainty in the points of entry into and exit from the system. The existence of many wars outside the established dates of entry and exit would have been a reason to extend those dates, since wars with other Powers are one key indicator of participation in the Great Power security system. Changes in Great Power status that would generate the largest changes in the frequency of wars are those that are least likely to occur, and those most likely to occur would have the smallest impact. Moreover, most of the changes would not add or subtract a war but would change its classification from a Great Power war to a war involving a Power, or vice versa. Exceptions might be a lengthy delay in England's entry (because of the Scottish wars) and a combined change in Turkish exit and Russian entry (because of their bilateral wars). It was noted earlier that a change regarding the identity of the Great Powers in the post-1945 period could result in a change of at most two wars, as would the exclusion of Italy for the eighty years after her unification.

Overall, there is a high degree of accuracy in this list of interstate wars involving the Great Powers and even more in the compilation of Great Power wars. The most significant uncertainties lie not in the identification of the Powers or of their wars but in the procedures for the aggregation and disaggregation of these wars.

Wars in the Modern Great Power System

Table 3.1 lists all interstate wars involving at least one Great Power for the period 1495-1975 and identifies the Great Powers participating in them. Participation is defined as a minimum of 100 battle deaths or a minimum of 1,000 armed personnel engaged in active combat. The abbreviations for the Powers are those shown in Table 2.1. Great Power wars, which involve at least one Great Power on each side of the conflict, are denoted by asterisks.

Table 3.2. General Wars

War	Dates	Ratio Powers Involved
Thirty Years' War	1618–1648	6/7
Dutch War of Louis XIV	1672–1678	6/7
War of the League of Augsburg	1688–1697	5/7
War of the Spanish Succession	1701–1713	5/6
War of the Austrian Succession	1739–1748	6/6
Seven Years' War	1755–1763	6/6
French Revolutionary and Napoleonic Wars	1792–1815	6/6
World War I	1914–1918	8/8
World War II	1939–1945	7/7

A class of "general wars" was earlier defined as those involving nearly all the Great Powers and resulting in high levels of destruction. Although the primary defining characteristic of general war is that it involve nearly all the Great Powers,[33] a war in which most of the Powers participate but only to a limited degree is not usually considered a general war (the Russian Civil War, for example). The addition of a criterion based on relative human destructiveness ensures exclusion of wars that involve most of the Powers but are serious in no other respect. Relative human destructiveness is defined in the next chapter as "intensity" and measured in battle deaths per million European population. General wars are therefore operationally defined as wars involving at least two-thirds of the Great Powers[34] and an intensity exceeding 1,000 battle deaths per million population. The nine general wars of the modern system are listed in Table 3.2. The four phases of the Thirty Years' War have been merged, as have the French Revolutionary and Napoleonic Wars. The table includes the ratio of the number of participating Powers to the number of Powers in the system.[35] This class of general wars will be used in the analysis of war contagion in Chapter 7.

In this study the Great Power system is the unit of analysis. For some theoretical purposes, however, it is preferable to shift to the national level of analysis and analyze the war behavior of individual Great Powers or the differences between Powers. A separate set of wars for each Great Power can be derived directly from Table 3.1.

Having now generated a compilation of interstate wars involving the Great Powers over the period 1495-1975, we will turn in the next chapter to the task of the measurement of the wars.

4

Measurement of the Wars

It is widely recognized that war is a multidimensional concept. Some wars are longer or more destructive than others, and some countries or historical eras are more warlike than others. If general statements like these are to be meaningful, they must be made more precise, which requires a refined conceptualization of war. The aim of this chapter is to define various dimensions of war, devise corresponding operational indicators and measurement procedures, and measure the values of these indicators for each of the 119 wars since 1495.

Conceptualization of War

War can be conceptualized on a multiplicity of levels, dimensions, and units of analysis. The *level* of war is defined by the type of participating political entities. International war can be distinguished from internal war, which includes civil war, revolutionary war, and other forms of domestic violence.[1] International war includes conflicts between political units transcending national boundaries. A subset of this general class of international war is interstate war, in which at least one sovereign state participates on each side of the conflict. Within this category is the set of interstate wars involving the Great Powers, which may be subdivided further into the set of Great Power wars with Powers on each side of the conflict. This study is concerned only with interstate wars involving the Great Powers and with Great Power wars.

War also has several *dimensions.* Singer and Small, identify magnitude, severity, and intensity as the primary dimensions.[2] I have generally followed their conceptualization but with a few refinements at both the conceptual and operational levels.

Whereas Singer and Small use the single concept of magnitude to represent a joint spatial-temporal dimension, I have included independent spatial and temporal elements. The spatial dimension, which Singer and Small ignore, is defined here as the number of Great Powers participating in the war and is called the *extent* of war. The number of Great Powers is an indicator of both the geographic scope of the war and the overall importance of war. The key concept of a "general war," for example, is defined according to the number or proportion of participating Great Powers.[3] For these reasons, the extent of war must be included as an analytically distinct dimension.[4]

The temporal dimension is reflected by war's length or *duration,* defined as the elapsed time from beginning to end. *Magnitude,* defined as the nation-years of war,[5] incorporates both spatial and temporal dimensions. It includes more information than either the extent or duration indicators and is useful as a compound measure of the seriousness of war.[6] For some theoretical purposes, it may be necessary to refer independently to either the extent or duration of war, and for this reason they have been defined independently.

The *severity* of war, based on the number of lives lost, reflects its human destructiveness. In many respects this dimension is the most important, for it is the best measure of the violence of the conflict.[7] But because of the nearly exponential growth in population over the five centuries encompassed by this study, battle-death figures are not truly comparable. Therefore, I have used an additional dimension reflecting the number of battle deaths compared to the population as a whole.

Singer and Small define such a dimension but create confusion by identifying it as one of three separate measures of the intensity of war. These three measures are the ratio of battle fatalities to (1) the magnitude of war, (2) the total size of the prewar armed forces of all participant system members, and (3) the total prewar population of all participant system members.[8] These three indicators, however, are not simply different measures of the same theoretical concept. The first reflects the concentration of war in space and time; the second reflects the relative costs of the war to the respective military establishments; and the third reflects the relative human costs of the war to the society as a whole. Singer and Small minimize the confusion only by essentially ignoring the first two measures and focusing on the third. This relative human destructiveness is defined here as the *intensity* of war.[9] The second Singer-Small intensity measure is not sufficiently distinct from the third to be included as a separate dimension, for long-term increases in population have been accompanied by comparable increases in the size of military establishments. The first Singer-Small intensity indicator, the ratio of battle deaths to the magnitude of war, is analytically distinct from the others (for it is unaffected by population size). It reflects the *concentration* of war in space and time, and is identified here as a separate dimension.

Whereas the preceding dimensions are conceptualized as characteristics of the wars themselves, the *frequency* of war, or number of wars in a given period, is based on time. Thus the dimensions considered here deal with two different units of analysis—the individual war and time. Each of the dimensions except frequency can be measured using either time or war as the unit of analysis. For example, we can speak not only of the number of battle deaths in a particular war but also of the number of battle deaths in a given period of time or of the average yearly number of battle deaths. Similarly, each of the other war indicators defined above can be aggregated over time to generate a measure of the *amount* of war (along each dimension) per unit of time. None of these units of analysis or sets of indicators is inherently less meaningful than the other. Their relative utility depends on the particular theoretical question under investigation.

Because of the change in units of analysis these aggregated war indicators may have slightly different theoretical interpretations. Frequency and severity are straightforward. Extent is used to refer to the total number of Great Powers involved in war in a given period, each weighted by its number of wars. Similarly, duration refers to the total number of years of war in a given period, with separate wars counted separately. Magnitude refers to the total number of nation-years of war (with separate wars counted separately). The intensity and concentration indicators cannot be simply summed over time because their base measures change. The intensity of war in a given period can be figured as the ratio of the total number of battle deaths to the average population during that period. Similarly, the concentration of war in a given period refers to the ratio of the total number of battle deaths to the total magnitude of war during that period.

The aggregation of war indicators over time introduces another set of categories. As Singer and Small note, the amount of war per period of time (along each dimension) can be conceived as the amount of war beginning, under way, or terminating in that period.[10] The amount of war in these three stages will be equal only if all wars end in the same period in which they begin, which rarely occurs. Which of these three indicators is most appropriate is determined by the question under investigation. If the focus is the *causes* of war, the primary concern will be with the amount of war beginning at a given time. To measure this dimension, the values of each war indicator for the entire period are aggregated into the year in which the war begins. On the other hand, if we wish to view war as an independent rather than a dependent variable and examine its social, political, or economic *consequences,* the amount of war terminating at a particular time might be a more relevant measure. For other questions, the amount of war under way may be more appropriate.

If the amount of war underway is considered, frequency refers to the number of wars under way in a given period, regardless of when they were initiated. Extent refers to the number of Powers involved in war during that period, regardless of the total number of wars each was fighting concurrently. Duration refers to the number of years war occurred in a given period, not counting simultaneous wars separately. If a one-year period of aggregation is used, the duration variable is reduced to a dichotomy of zero or one. Magnitude refers to nation-years of war, counting simultaneous wars separately. Severity refers to the total number of battle deaths during the period. Intensity is the ratio of battle deaths to the average population, and concentration is the ratio of the total number of fatalities to the total nation-years of war.

Difficult methodological problems arise in determining the severity, intensity, and concentration of war under way. Yearly battle-death data are usually unavailable. In the absence of more precise data, I have computed yearly averages by assuming a homogeneous distribution of battle fatalities over the course of a war. This linear model is used for the sake of simplicity, given the absence of alternative models empirically confirmed to be superior. Over the entire five-century span of the modern system, most errors will in all probability cancel out.

To summarize, at each level of war there are several dimensions, and each dimension can be interpreted by using two separate units of analysis. This conceptualization allows for greater theoretical differentiation than do most other frameworks. The failure to make some of these analytical distinctions results in considerable confusion in the literature. Empirical measures for each of these dimensions will now be provided.

Operational Indicators and Measurement Procedures

The *extent* of war is defined as the number of Great Powers participating. This is easily measured, for participation was defined earlier as military involvement requiring at least 100 battle deaths or 1,000 armed forces personnel actively engaged in combat. The Great Powers participating in each war can be read directly from Table 3.1.

Determining the *duration* of war is somewhat more complex than one might expect. In the previous chapter the criteria for establishing the opening and closing dates of the war were discussed. Because the precise dates of the initiation and termination of a war are sometimes difficult to determine, only the year (rather than the month and day) is identified. Thus the duration is measured in years and is calculated by subtracting the beginning date from the ending date. If a war begins and ends in the same year, but the month and day dates cannot be determined, the average length is estimated to be one-half year. For the last 150 years the more precise Singer-Small dates for the beginning and end of hostilities are used, but in no case does the degree of precision exceed .1 year.

Temporary interruptions in war, including formal truces and cease-fires and more informal lapses in the fighting, present an additional problem. Should these temporary interruptions be subtracted from the total duration of the war? If so, precisely how should they be defined and measured? Singer and Small subtract from the total duration of war a time equal to that of all temporary interruptions, which they define as follows: "A cessation of hostilities which endured for less than 30 days is not treated as an interruption of the war, whereas a longer break *is* so treated."[11]

The duration of actual fighting may be a useful measure for some purposes, but with respect to the diplomatic and perhaps domestic impact of the war the elapsed time is probably more important. If the concern is with the degree of violence, battle casualties are a better measure. In addition, the nature of war has changed over time. Wars in the post-Vienna period have been characterized by relatively continuous fighting, but earlier wars were often characterized by distinct battles separated by lengthy periods of minimal contact. This discontinuity complicates the measurement of duration as well as the identification and demarcation of the war. A measure based on the duration of actual fighting would not reflect the protracted nature of earlier wars and would minimize their real lengths. Furthermore, the hypothesis that wars have been getting shorter over the last several centuries can best be tested by using elapsed time to measure duration.

There are also important methodological reasons for using the elapsed-time measure. Serious problems would arise in attempting to identify and measure all interruptions in the 119 wars since 1495. Historians have not tended to view temporary interruptions in war as particularly salient, so the relevant information is often not available. Nor would a historical search to generate such data be worth the enormous investment in time and resources that would be required. Therefore, the duration of war is defined as the elapsed time between beginning and end, regardless of any temporary interruptions, and is not identical to the duration of actual fighting. Thus for the later period my measurements may differ from those of Singer and Small.

The *magnitude* of war is a joint spatial-temporal dimension, combining the extent and duration indicators. It is operationally defined as the sum of the years of war for each participating Great Power and is measured in nation-years. Mathematically, the magnitude of war M can be expressed as

$$M = \sum_{i}^{n} d_i$$

where n = extent of war and d_i = the duration of war for Power i.[12]

The *severity* of war, or its human destructiveness on the battlefield, is operationally defined as the number of battle-connected deaths of military personnel. Civilian casualties are not included. This conceptualization follows Singer and Small's use of battle-connected fatalities rather than Richardson's use of all military and civilian deaths resulting from actual combat, disease, or exposure. Richardson includes the latter because they are "accepted as a risk contingent to planned operations."[13] Civilian casualties are excluded here for both conceptual and methodological reasons. Singer and Small's concern to maximize the comparability of the severity indicator over time by minimizing the effects of technological (and other) changes[14] is even more compelling here, for those changes are more dramatic over a five-century span. The exclusion of civilian casualties removes the bias introduced by (1) changes in military technology that make it easier to kill civilians, (2) changes in the nature of power and the economic system that increase the incentive to kill civilians because of their increased contribution to the war effort, and (3) changes in medical technology that have the opposite effect of reducing the proportion of civilian casualties. The exclusion of civilian casualties would be more problematical in a study that focuses on civil or guerrilla war.

There are also methodological considerations. As Singer and Small note, the variety of situations in which civilians might be killed from wars precludes the construction of reasonable operational criteria, particularly for a study covering a long time span. Additionally, the original fatality estimates were generated by historians on the basis of battle-connected deaths.[15] So many methodological problems arise in estimating these that it is best to avoid the enormous additional problems of attempting to determine civilian casualties. This orientation, however, biases any attempt to use these data to test hypotheses about the changing destructiveness of war.

Richardson attempts to deal with the problem of the unreliability of war estimates by using a logarithmic transformation to collapse the scale and also using accepted scientific notation to indicate the accuracy of the last digit.[16] Minor errors in the original figures are relatively insignificant in the transformed variables. Richardson's data for the last century and a half are inferior to Singer-Small's, however, because the latter employ a more rigorous set of procedures in their data search, although their data are based essentially on estimates. Their final figure was affected by "army size, weapons and medical technology available, number of major battles, other's estimates of the wounded-to-killed ratio . . . , and the historians' appraisal of the war's intensity."[17] In general, however, the Singer-Small casualty data are quite satisfactory and I have used them for all wars since 1815.

Unfortunately, the data on battle casualties for the pre-1815 period are not as good as those for the post-Napoleonic period. Wright does not provide casualty data for individual wars, and other sources (including Bodart and Dumas and Vedel-Peterson) cover only a limited number of the wars identified here. The main source for this study is Sorokin's compilation of war data. Like Singer and Small, he provides estimates rather than hard data. Given the methodological problems involved in determining battle fatalities in all wars over the last five hundred years, Sorokin's estimates cannot be expected to be as accurate as those of Singer-Small for the nineteenth and twentieth centuries, for which data are more accessible. His estimation procedures are reasonable, however, and Sorokin recognizes the limitations in his data: "The figures given for each period are aimed not so much to lay down the actual number of the mobilized or killed and wounded as to obtain a rough measure of the comparative increase or decrease of war from period to period."[18] Given the lengthy historical scope of this study some degree of measurement error is tolerable, and Sorokin's estimates should be adequate.

Sorokin's estimation procedures are as follows. First, the average size of the army for a given war is determined. In some cases relatively hard data are available. Generally, however, the figures are estimated from known army strengths in particular battles, taking into account the average number of fronts in the war (multifront wars were relatively uncommon before the seventeenth century). Then the average casualty rate is estimated on the basis of well-studied battles of that war or of similar wars during the general period. These estimates are calculated by year, and then the approximate number of casualties for the entire duration of the war can be estimated. In some cases, casualty figures are estimated directly from the information available in historical sources. Sorokin's data are given for each state, and the totals for the war as a whole can then be computed. Adjustments must be made in those cases for which Sorokin's temporal boundaries of the war do not correspond with mine, but these are easily estimated from the casualty data by a linear interpolation.

The Sorokin data contain several imperfections. Most serious for my purposes is inclusion of the wounded as well as the dead in his casualty figures.[19] Furthermore, he is not explicit about what classes of casualties he includes (that is, combat-related casualties only, death caused by exposure or disease, and so forth). The resulting expected upward bias in his casualty estimates appears to be confirmed by comparing the Sorokin and Singer-Small data for the 1816-1925 period. The two sets of estimates are not dissimilar for the low-severity wars, but Sorokin's are generally higher for the larger wars. This pattern is not consistent, however, for Sorokin's figures for World War I are less than one-third those of Singer and Small. It is not obvious, therefore, that the overall bias is necessarily serious. Furthermore, because advances in medical technology have occurred relatively recently, a considerably higher percentage of casualties in the earlier wars resulted in death, so that the discrepancy between casualties and battle deaths was smaller than in more recent times.

Another problem concerns exactly who to include in the casualty figures for a given Great Power. One aspect of this problem is the differing definitions of the spatial boundaries of a given state. For example, Sorokin includes the Holy Roman Empire as part of Austira-Hungary before the seventeenth century. In Germany he includes all territory (and hence the armies and casualties) that eventually became part of the German Empire. Consequently, some casualty figures may not technically belong to the Great Powers. This problem is further compounded because before the nineteenth century it was common for relatively large numbers of an army to be mercenary troops from other lands. Should foreign mercenary troops fighting for state A be included in the casualty figures for A? Their inclusion would be reasonable, but unfortunately the data are not sufficiently discriminating to allow precision. The number of foreign mercenaries was generally not well known to the statesmen of the time or to the historians. Sorokin does not deal with this problem explicitly, but his focus on army strength indicates that mercenaries are included in the casualty figures.[20]

Another limitation of the Sorokin war data is that they do not provide a complete set of estimates. Not all of the wars in my compilation are included, and casualty estimates are not provided for either the Ottoman Empire or Sweden. Data are missing for only about 36 out of 263 cases (the total number of Great Powers in all 119 wars). But since the missing data are for wars and states that clearly do not constitute a random sample, they cannot be replaced by a simple statistical average of all wars or temporally proximate wars. Instead, each case or classes of cases is dealt with separately in an attempt to generate the most reasonable estimate possible based on information derived from other cases judged to be similar in nature. The general procedures and specific estimates for missing data are given in the Appendix.

The error in these fatality estimates may be as great as 20-25 percent in some cases. Nevertheless, they are adequate for the present purpose, given the five-century span of this study. A slight systematic bias tending to exaggerate the battle fatalities for the earlier periods is marginal compared to the differences between centuries and the changes over time, two of the important questions of interest here. Similarly, the measurement error is large (25-30 percent) but tolerable in the other fatality-based indicators discussed below.

The *intensity* dimension is designed to reflect the relative human costs of war compared to the population as a whole. Singer and Small operationalize the concept by using the ratio of battle fatalities to prewar population for each state. This indicator cannot be used here, however, because of the absence of accurate population data for each of the Great Powers over the last five centuries. An alternative measure that reflects the casualties from war relative to changing population over time is needed. One such measure is the population of Europe as a whole. The Great Power system has historically been European-based, and for most of the Powers and for most of the temporal span of the system national population growth rates have not deviated significantly from that of Europe as a whole.[21] Thus although the ratio of battle deaths to European population is not equivalent to the intensity of war as defined by Singer and Small, it does provide a means of comparing the relative human costs of war over time.

Of the various estimates of European populations, among the more highly regarded are those generated by Walter F. Wilcox and Alexander M. Carr-Saunders. The estimates used here are based on these and on the more recent United Nations estimates for this century. For the 1450-1900 period, these data at fifty year intervals were compiled by R. R. Kuczynski. For the 1900-1960 period, population data at ten-year intervals are taken from the 1966 United Nations estimates compiled by John V. Grauman.[22] For the purposes of computing the European population for intervening years linear interpolation is used, and extrapolation is used for the 1960-75 period. The value of the battle-death/population indicator for a given year is based on the population for the year in which the war begins and is measured in battle deaths per million population.

The spatial and temporal *concentration* of war is operationally defined as the ratio of the battle fatalities to the nation-years of war, or the ratio of severity to magnitude.

Table 4.1. The War Data

	War	Dates	Duration	Extent	Magnitude	Severity	Intensity	Concentration
1	*War of the League of Venice	1495–1497	2.0	3	6.0	8000	119	1333
2	Polish-Turkish War	1497–1498	1.0	1	1.0	3000	45	3000
3	Venetian-Turkish War	1499–1503	4.0	1	4.0	4000	60	1000
4	First Milanese War	1499–1500	1.0	1	1.0	2000	29	2000
5	*Neapolitan War	1501–1504	3.0	2	5.0	18000	269	3600
6	War of the Cambrian League	1508–1509	1.0	3	3.0	10000	145	3333
7	*War of the Holy League	1511–1514	3.0	4	12.0	18000	261	1500
8	*Austro-Turkish War	1512–1519	7.0	2	14.0	24000	343	1714
9	Scottish War	1513–1515	2.0	1	2.0	4000	57	2000
10	*Second Milanese War	1515–1515	.5	3	1.5	3000	43	2000
11	*First War of Charles V	1521–1526	5.0	3	15.0	30000	420	2000
12	*Ottoman War	1521–1531	10.0	2	20.0	68000	958	3400
13	Scottish War	1522–1523	1.0	1	1.0	3000	41	3000
14	*Second War of Charles V	1526–1529	3.0	3	8.0	18000	249	2250
15	*Ottoman War	1532–1535	3.0	2	6.0	28000	384	4667
16	Scottish War	1532–1534	2.0	1	2.0	4000	55	2000
17	*Third War of Charles V	1536–1538	2.0	2	4.0	32000	438	8000
18	*Ottoman War	1537–1547	10.0	2	20.0	97000	1329	4850
19	Scottish War	1542–1550	8.0	1	8.0	13000	176	1625
20	*Fourth War of Charles V	1542–1544	2.0	2	4.0	47000	629	11750
21	*Siege of Boulogne	1544–1546	2.0	2	4.0	8000	107	2000
22	*Arundel's Rebellion	1549–1550	1.0	2	2.0	6000	79	3000
23	*Ottoman War	1551–1556	5.0	2	10.0	44000	578	4400
24	*Fifth War of Charles V	1552–1556	4.0	2	8.0	51000	668	6375
25	*Austro-Turkish War	1556–1562	6.0	2	12.0	52000	676	4333
26	*Franco-Spanish War	1556–1559	3.0	3	8.0	24000	316	3000
27	*Scottish War	1559–1560	1.0	2	1.5	6000	78	4000
28	*Spanish-Turkish War	1559–1564	5.0	2	10.0	24000	310	2400
29	*First Huguenot War	1562–1564	2.0	2	4.0	6000	77	1500

30	*Austro-Turkish War	1565–1568	3.0	2	6.0	24000	306	4000
31	*Spanish Turkish War	1569–1580	11.0	2	22.0	48000	608	2182
32	*Austro-Turkish War	1576–1583	7.0	2	14.0	48000	600	3429
33	Spanish-Portuguese War	1579–1581	2.0	1	2.0	4000	50	2000
34	Polish-Turkish War	1583–1590	7.0	1	7.0	17000	210	2429
35	*War of the Armada	1585–1604	19.0	2	38.0	48000	588	1263
36	Austro-Polish War	1587–1588	1.0	1	1.0	4000	49	4000
37	*War of the Three Henries	1589–1598	9.0	2	18.0	16000	195	889
38	*Austro-Turkish War	1593–1606	13.0	2	26.0	90000	1086	3462
39	Franco-Savoian War	1600–1601	1.0	1	1.0	2000	24	2000
40	*Spanish-Turkish War	1610–1614	4.0	2	8.0	15000	175	1875
41	Austro-Venetian War	1615–1618	3.0	1	3.0	6000	70	2000
42	Spanish-Savoian War	1615–1617	2.0	1	2.0	2000	23	1000
43	Spanish-Venetian War	1617–1621	4.0	1	4.0	5000	58	1250
44	*Spanish-Turkish War	1618–1619	1.0	2	2.0	6000	69	3000
45	Polish-Turkish War	1618–1621	3.0	1	3.0	15000	173	5000
46	*Thirty Years' War—Bohemian	1618–1625	7.0	4	15.0	304000	3535	20267
47	*Thirty Years' War—Danish	1625–1630	5.0	6	26.0	302000	3432	11615
48	*Thirty Years' War—Swedish	1630–1635	5.0	4	20.0	314000	3568	15700
49	*Thirty Years' War—Swedish-French	1635–1648	13.0	5	65.0	1151000	12933	17708
50	Spanish-Protuguese War	1642–1668	26.0	1	26.0	80000	882	3077
51	Turkish-Venetian War	1645–1664	19.0	1	19.0	72000	791	3790
52	*Franco-Spanish War	1648–1659	11.0	2	22.0	108000	1187	4909
53	Scottish War	1650–1651	1.0	1	1.0	2000	22	2000
54	*Anglo-Dutch Naval War	1652–1655	3.0	2	6.0	26000	282	4333
55	*Great Northern War	1654–1660	6.0	3	12.0	22000	238	1833
56	*English-Spanish War	1656–1659	3.0	2	6.0	15000	161	2500
57	Dutch-Portuguese War	1657–1661	4.0	1	4.0	4000	43	1000
58	*Ottoman War	1657–1664	7.0	3	13.0	109000	1170	8385
59	Sweden-Bremen War	1665–1666	1.0	1	1.0	2000	11	1000
60	*Anglo-Dutch Naval War	1665–1667	2.0	3	6.0	37000	392	6167

Notes: *Denotes Great Power war. The units of measurement are as follows: duration—years; extent—number of Powers; magnitude—nation-years; severity—battle deaths per million European population; concentration—battle deaths per nation-year.

Table 4.1. Continued

War	Dates	Duration	Extent	Magnitude	Severity	Intensity	Concentration
61 *Devolutionary War	1667–1668	1.0	2	2.0	4000	42	2000
62 *Dutch War of Louis XIV	1672–1678	6.0	6	33.0	342000	3580	10364
63 Turkish-Polish War	1672–1676	4.0	1	4.0	5000	52	1250
64 Russo-Turkish War	1677–1681	4.0	1	4.0	12000	125	3000
65 *Ottoman War	1682–1699	17.0	2	34.0	384000	3954	11294
66 *Franco-Spanish War	1683–1684	1.0	2	2.0	5000	51	2500
67 *War of the League of Augsburg	1688–1697	9.0	5	45.0	680000	6939	15111
68 *Second Northern War	1700–1721	21.0	2	27.0	64000	640	2370
69 *War of the Spanish Succession	1701–1713	12.0	5	60.0	1251000	12490	20850
70 Ottoman War	1716–1718	2.0	1	2.0	10000	98	5000
71 *War of the Quadruple Alliance	1718–1720	2.0	4	8.0	25000	245	3125
72 *British-Spanish War	1726–1729	3.0	2	6.0	15000	144	2500
73 *War of the Polish Succession	1733–1738	5.0	4	20.0	88000	836	4400
74 Ottoman War	1736–1739	3.0	2	6.0	38000	359	6333
75 *War of the Austrian Succession	1739–1748	9.0	6	44.0	359000	3379	8159
76 Russo-Swedish War	1741–1743	2.0	1	2.0	10000	94	5000
77 *Seven Years' War	1755–1763	8.0	6	38.0	992000	9118	26105
78 Russo-Turkish War	1768–1774	6.0	1	6.0	14000	127	2333
79 Confederation of Bar	1768–1772	4.0	1	4.0	14000	149	3500
80 *War of the Bavarian Succession	1778–1779	1.0	2	2.0	300	3	150
81 *War of the American Revolution	1778–1784	6.0	3	15.0	34000	304	2267
82 Ottoman War	1787–1792	5.0	2	10.0	192000	1685	19200
83 Russo-Swedish War	1788–1790	2.0	1	2.0	3000	26	1500
84 *French Revolutionary Wars	1792–1802	10.0	6	51.0	663000	5816	13000
85 *Napoleonic Wars	1803–1815	12.0	6	58.0	1869000	16112	32224
86 Russo-Turkish War	1806–1812	6.0	2	7.0	45000	388	6429
87 Russo-Swedish War	1808–1809	1.5	1	1.5	6000	51	4000
88 War of 1812	1812–1814	2.5	1	2.5	4000	34	1600
89 Neapolitan War	1815–1815	.2	1	.2	2000	17	10000

90	Franco-Spanish War	1823–1823	.9	1	.6	400	3	667
91	Navarino Bay	1827–1827	.1	3	.1	180	2	1800
92	Russo-Turkish War	1828–1829	1.4	1	1.4	50000	415	35714
93	Austro-Sardinian War	1848–1849	1.0	1	1.0	5600	45	5600
94	First Schleswig-Holstein War	1849–1849	1.2	1	1.2	2500	20	2083
95	Roman Republic War	1849–1849	.2	2	.4	600	4	1500
96	*Crimean War	1853–1856	2.4	3	6.2	217000	1743	35000
97	Anglo-Persian War	1856–1857	.4	1	.4	500	4	1250
98	*War of Italian Unification	1859–1859	.2	2	.4	20000	159	50000
99	Franco-Mexican War	1862–1867	4.8	1	4.8	8000	64	1667
100	Second Schleswig-Holstein War	1864–1864	.5	2	1.0	1500	12	1500
101	*Austro-Prussian War	1866–1866	.1	3	3.0	34000	270	113333
102	*Franco-Prussian War	1870–1871	.6	2	1.2	180000	1415	150000
103	Russo-Turkish War	1877–1878	.7	1	.7	120000	935	171429
104	Sino-French War	1884–1885	1.0	1	1.0	2100	16	2100
105	Russo-Japanese War	1904–1905	1.6	1	1.6	45000	339	28125
106	Italo-Turkish War	1911–1912	1.1	1	1.1	6000	45	5454
107	*World War I	1914–1918	4.3	8	29.9	7734300	57616	258672
108	*Russian Civil War	1918–1921	3.0	5	13.0	5000	37	385
109	Manchurian War	1931–1933	1.4	1	1.4	10000	73	7143
110	Italo-Ethiopian War	1935–1936	.6	1	.6	4000	29	6667
111	Sino-Japanese War	1937–1941	4.4	1	4.4	250000	1813	56819
112	*Russo-Japanese War	1939–1939	.4	2	.7	16000	116	22857
113	*World War II	1939–1945	6.0	7	28.0	12948300	93665	462439
114	Russo-Finnish War	1939–1940	.3	1	.3	50000	362	166667
115	*Korean War	1950–1953	3.1	4	11.3	954960	6821	84510
116	Russo-Hungarian War	1956–1956	.1	1	.1	7000	50	70000
117	Sinai War	1956–1956	.1	2	.1	30	0	300
118	Sino-Indian War	1962–1962	.1	1	.1	500	1	5000
119	Vietnam War	1965–1973	8.0	1	8.0	56000	90	7000

Notes: *Denotes Great Power war. The units of measurement are as follows: duration—years; extent—number of Powers; magnitude—nation-years; severity—battle deaths per million European population; concentration—battle deaths per nation-year.

The *frequency* of war is defined simply as the number of wars per unit of time. The only question is what unit of time is most appropriate, and that depends on the particular question under investigation. Singer and Small refer most often to a five-year period; Sorokin uses a twenty-five-year period. Both periods are used here, and a one-year period is used in considering some questions involving the amount of war under way. The choice of the unit of temporal aggregation is important both for frequency and for other aggregated indices because the particular unit of time used to group the data can have an important effect on the observed relationship between variables. This is a very complex problem, which is rarely acknowledged by social scientists. Most of the relationships dealt with in this study, however, are not overly sensitive to the aggregation problem (though exceptions will be noted). Moreover, since my concern is with the description of a theoretical universe rather than with making inferences from a sample to a universe, many of the standard problems of temporal aggregation are of no direct concern.[23] Still, the choice of a temporal unit for each analysis must be justified to fit the question under consideration.[24]

The War Data

Each of the 119 wars is measured according to the procedures developed above. The resulting set of data for all interstate wars involving the Great Powers is presented in Table 4.1. All other relevant sets of war data can be derived from this basic data set (including the amount of war per unit of time for various periods of temporal aggregation).

5

Quantitative Description of the Wars

The data in Table 4.1 can now be used in an attempt to answer a variety of questions regarding the nature of war among the Great Powers. (1) What are most wars like? How long do they last, how many Great Powers do they involve, and how destructive are they in loss of life? What are the central tendencies of the various characteristics of war, and how great are the variations? (2) How warlike has the Great Power system been? How frequently does war occur? What is typical yearly amount of war? (3) What is the relationship among the various dimensions of war? Are there generally more casualties in long wars than shorter wars? Is the severity of war inversely related to its frequency? (4) Are there any significant historical trends in war? Are wars becoming more or less frequent, longer or shorter, more or less destructive? Or does the level of war tend to follow a cyclical pattern? (5) Is the amount of war in one period related to the amount of war in previous periods? Does war beget war? Or does war generate a repulsion against conflict and a period of relative peace?

The first three sets of questions concerning the nature of the wars, the warlikeness of the Great Power system as a whole, and the relationship among the various dimensions of war will be examined in this chapter. The questions of historical trends in war and the contagion of Great Power war behavior will be treated in Chapters 6 and 7, respectively. Since the analysis of a given theoretical question may be sensitive to the particular empirical indicators used, it will often be necessary to examine each question from a variety of perspectives, each representing a different operational slant on the general theoretical question. In doing so I hope to resolve a number of ambiguities in the literature deriving from the failure to make these analytical distinctions.

Characteristics of Individual Wars

In this section, the distributions of the war indicators will be examined. What have most wars been like along each of the dimensions defined earlier? What is the value of each indicator for the average war and to what extent do most wars deviate from this average?

This information is presented both graphically and numerically. In Figure 5.1, frequency histograms for each interstate war indicator are displayed. For a given interval on the horizontal axis (listing a range of values of the war indicator in question), the number of wars for which the value of the indicator falls within that interval is plotted on the vertical axis. Additional information about the nature of the wars is provided in Table 5.1, where the mean, median, minimum, maximum, and standard deviation for each indicator are given (rounded to two significant digits). Statistics on Great Power wars as well as interstate wars involving the Powers are given in Table 5.1.

Table 5.1 indicates that the typical (median) interstate war involving the Great Powers lasts about three years and involves about two Great Powers, five nation-years of war, and 17,000 battle deaths (180 fatalities per million European population and 3,400 fatalities per nation-year of war). Many of the wars deviate significantly from these central tendencies, as indicated by the frequency histograms and the minimum, maximum, and standard deviation statistics. This variation is particularly large for the severity, intensity, and concentration indicators, whose distributions are more highly skewed.[1] Figure 5.1d suggests that over 80 percent of the wars involve fewer than 100,000 casualties, in seventeen wars there are between 100,000 and a million casualties, and in five wars over one million fatalities, raising the

Figure 5.1. Histograms of the War Indicators
(Number of wars characterized by a given value or range of values of each indicator)

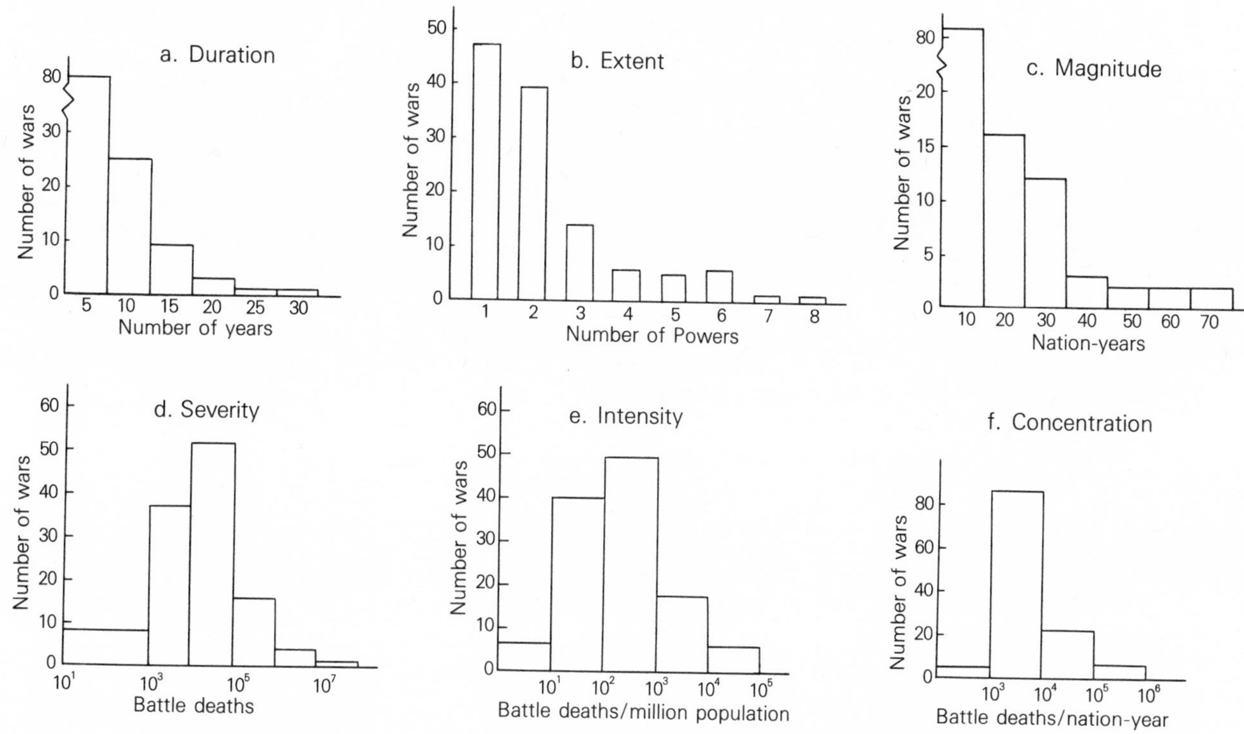

Table 5.1. Characteristics of the Wars

Indicator[a]	Mean	Median	Minimum	Maximum	Standard Deviation
	Interstate Wars Involving the Great Powers				
Duration	4.4	3.0	.1	26	4.7
Extent	2.2	1.8	1.0	8.0	1.5
Magnitude	10	4.8	.1	65	14
Severity	280000	17000	30	13000000	1400000
Intensity	2300	180	.2	94000	10000
Concentration	19000	3400	150	460000	55000
	Great Power Wars				
Duration	5.5	4.0	.1	21	4.6
Extent	3.2	2.5	2.0	8.0	1.6
Magnitude	16	11	.4	65	16
Severity	500000	34000	300	13000000	1900000
Intensity	4100	420	2.7	94000	14000
Concentration	24000	4000	150	460000	69000

[a]The units for the indicators are: duration—years; extent—number of Great Powers; magnitude—nation-years; severity—battle deaths; intensity—battle deaths per million European population; concentration—battle deaths per nation-year.

average (mean) to over a quarter million. The standard deviation is five times larger than the mean. Because of the highly skewed nature of these distributions the median is a better measure of central tendency than is the mean, particularly for the fatality-based indicators. The variation and skewness in the other indicators is somewhat less but still significant. The standard deviation of the magnitude indicator is three times the magnitude of the typical war. Two-thirds of the wars are over within five years, and nearly 90 percent within ten years, but five wars have lasted more than fifteen years. The distributions of the extent and magnitude indicators are similar to those for the duration indicator. The vast majority of the wars (nearly three-fourths) involve two Powers or less, and more than half of these (forty-seven), a single Power. Several wars have involved more Powers, however, and two wars involve seven or eight Powers. The magnitude of half the wars is less than five nation-years, but ten wars exceeding thirty nation-years.

These characteristics can be compared to those for Great Power wars. Slightly over half (sixty-four) of all interstate wars involving a Great Power are Great Power wars. As expected, these are more serious than the larger set, as indicated by their summary statistics. Great Power wars typically (on the median) last a year longer, involve over twice as many nation-years of war and battle deaths, and are more concentrated in space and time. It is not surprising that wars between the Powers, whose military strengths are roughly comparable, last longer than wars between states of unequal military strength and result in greater loss of life. Histograms of the Great Power war indicators would be similar to those for wars in general, except that there are fewer cases ranking low on each of the indicators. Since both sets of distributions are far from being normal or even symmetrical, many of the assumptions underlying most tests of statistical significance are not satisfied by the data generated in this study, and caution must be exercised in the use and interpretation of significance tests.

Yearly Amount of War

In this section the focus shifts from the characteristics of the wars to the frequency and yearly amount of war under way. The number of wars (and Great Power wars) beginning, the number of wars (and Great Power wars) under way, the number of Great Powers at war, the magnitude of war under way, the severity of war under way, and the concentration of war under way are all determined.[2]

Histograms for these indicators are presented in Figure 5.2, and the key summary statistics are given in Table 5.2. There can be no doubt regarding the pervasiveness of interstate war involving the Great Powers. The Powers have been involved in interstate wars for nearly 75 percent of the 481 years of the system, and in 60 percent of these years they have been involved in Great Power war. On average, a new war begins every four years and a Great Power war every seven or

Figure 5.2. Histograms: Yearly Amount of War Under Way
(Number of years characterized by a given value or range of values of each indicator)

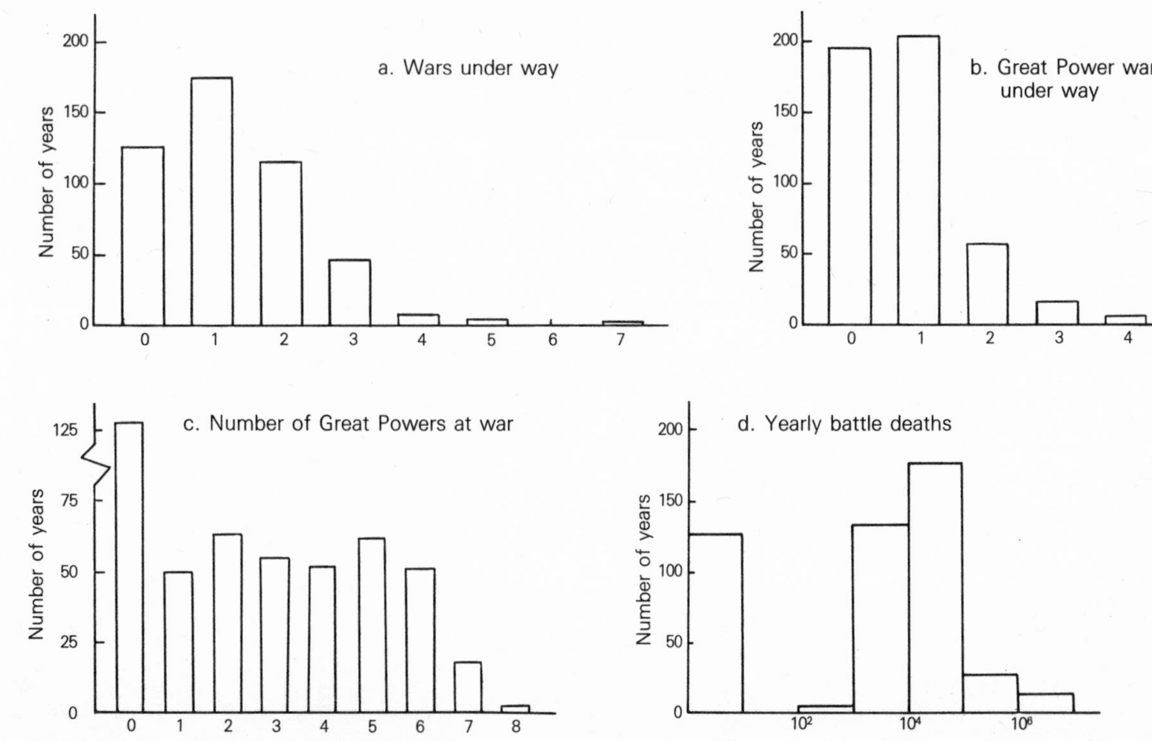

Table 5.2. Yearly Amount of War Under Way: Summary Statistics

Indicator[a]	Mean	Median	Minimum	Maximum	Standard Deviation
Number wars beginning	.25	.13	0	3	.52
Number GP wars beginning	.13	.07	0	2	.36
Number wars under way	1.3	1.1	0	7	1.2
Number GP wars under way	.82	.73	0	4	.83
Number powers at war	2.7	2.5	0	8	2.3
Magnitude	3.2	2.7	0	13	2.8
Severity	69000	6500	0	1900000	270000
Concentration	12000	2300	0	310000	38000

[a] Magnitude is measured in nation-years, severity in battle deaths, and concentration in battle deaths per nation-year.

eight years. In the typical year (and again the median rather than the mean is used because of the skewed nature of some of the distributions), slightly over one war involving the Great Powers and slightly less than one Great Power war is under way, two and a half Great Powers are at war, there are nearly three nation-years of war, and 6,500 battle deaths (or about 2,300 fatalities per Power at war).

Many years do not conform to this typical pattern. Although about one-fourth of the last 481 years have been free of interstate wars involving the Powers, some years as many as seven wars were under way (including four Great Power wars), with a total of eight Great Powers, thirteen nation-years of war, and nearly two million battle deaths. In more than one-sixth of the years two or more Great Power wars were under way, and in over 60 percent of the years two or more Great Powers were at war. There have been more than 1,000 battle deaths in most (75 percent) years, more than 100,000 fatalities in forty years, and over twelve years with more than a million fatalities.[3]

Although this analysis describes the typical year on the basis of certain parameters of conflict, it does not provide a complete description of the frequency and amount of war over time. It would make a difference, for example, if the more conflictual years in the system were concentrated together or dispersed more widely. Therefore, an analysis based on longer time intervals is needed. For these periods it is more appropriate to examine the amount of war beginning than the amount of war under way, for the latter is less meaningful when the duration of many wars falls short of the unit of temporal aggregation. Let us first consider the frequency of war.

Histograms for the frequency of war indicator for five and twenty-five-year periods of aggregation for interstate wars involving the Powers and for Great Power wars are presented in Figures 5.3 and 5.4. As noted earlier, there has been one war every four years and a Great Power war every seven and one-half years over the last five centuries. As we see from the histograms, twenty-eight of the ninety-six five-year periods since 1495 (30 percent) have been characterized by the absence of a new war beginning, and half (fifty) have been spared a Great Power war. Longer periods are rarely free of war: histograms based on ten year intervals would show that in only five of the forty-seven periods have there been no new wars, and Figure 5.4 shows that no twenty-five-year period has been perfectly peaceful. Two twenty-five-year periods have been free of the outbreak of a Great Power war, however. Nor are the wars themselves particularly concentrated in time. Of the sixty-eight five-year periods characterized by war, over half have only one war, and over 80 percent have two or less. All of this information is suggestive, but we shall save for Chapter 6 an analysis of whether war begets war.

Summary statistics for the other dimensions of the amount of war beginning per five-year period are presented in Table 5.3. The distributions are similar to those for the individual war indicators (except for twenty-eight periods in which there were no wars), so the histograms are not presented. The distributions of the indicators for Great Power war are similar to those for interstate wars involving the Powers, so they are not included here.

Table 5.3 indicates that in the typical five-year period there is one new outbreak of war, lasting two and one-half years, involving two Great Powers and four nation-years of war, and resulting in 17,000 battle fatalities. The variation is considerable, however. Twenty-eight

Table 5.3. Characteristics of Aggregated War Data, Five-Year Periods

Indicator[a]	Mean	Median	Minimum	Maximum	Standard Deviation
Frequency	1.2	1.1	0	6	1.2
Duration	5.4	2.4	0	33	7.1
Extent	2.8	2.2	0	12	2.8
Magnitude	13	4.0	0	87	18
Severity	350000	17000	0	13000000	1600000
Intensity	2900	160	0	96000	12000
Concentration	23000	4400	0	720000	81000

[a]Measured in the following units: frequency—number of wars; duration—years; extent—number of Great Powers; magnitude—nation-years; severity—battle deaths; intensity—battle deaths per million European population; concentration—battle deaths per nation-year.

five-year periods have witnessed no new outbreak of war, while many others have seen much higher levels of war. In eight of these five-year periods, wars involving more than forty nation-years of conflict are begun, and in one-quarter of the ninety-six periods there are more than 100,000 fatalities. A large number of periods are also characterized by 10,000-100,000 fatalities. The resulting distributions of the fatality-based indicators are therefore bimodal. The next question concerns the relationships among the war indicators. Are wars that are serious in some respects equally serious in all respects?

Relationships among the War Indicators

A variety of statistical measures of association might be used to determine the empirical relationships among the various war indicators. The best for our purposes is Kendall's tau-*b*, a rank-order measure of association. An ordinal-level correlation coefficient has the advantage of being less sensitive to the highly skewed nature of the distributions of some of these war indicators and thus does not allow a limited number of extreme cases to dominate the analysis. In addi-

Figure 5.3. Histograms: Frequency of War
(Number of periods characterized by a given frequency of war outbreak)

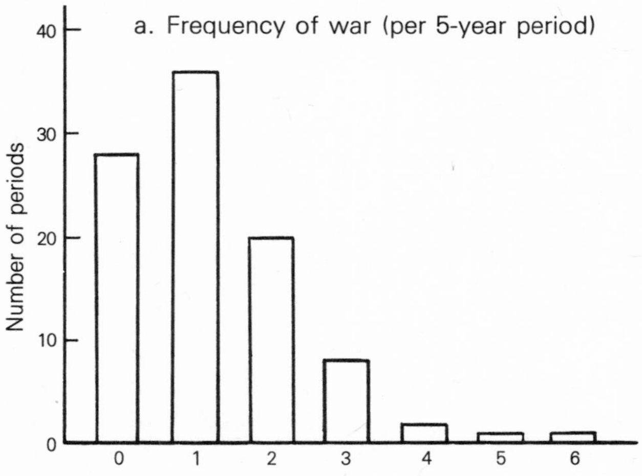

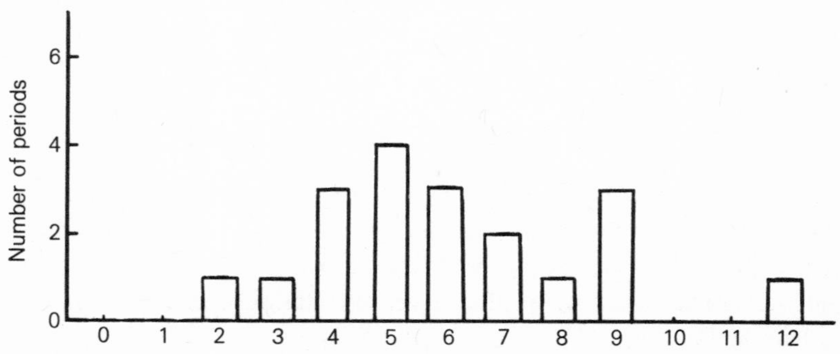

Figure 5.4. Histograms: Frequency of Great Power War (Number of periods characterized by a given frequency of war outbreak)

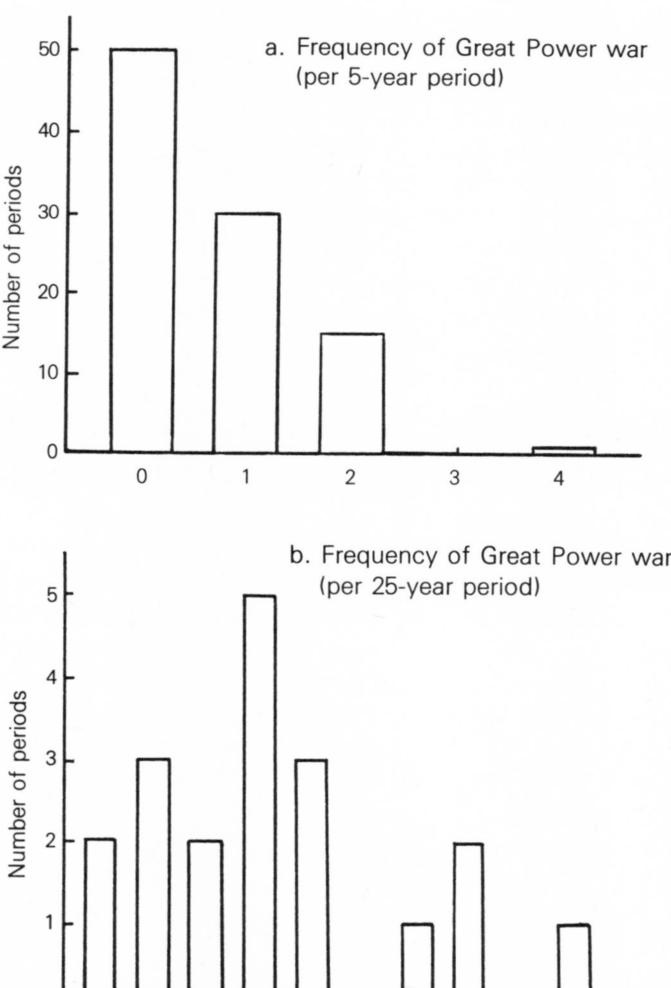

tion, an ordinal measure of association better reflects the inherent uncertainty in some of the war data, in that it is based only on rank order rather than quantitative differences.[4] Some caution must be exercised, in interpreting these statistics, however, for tau-*b* is a measure of the strength of association, not causation. Further research is often necessary to determine the direction of causation and whether the correlation is spurious.

In addition, the magnitude of the test statistics (for example, tau-*b*) is of more concern than their levels of statistical significance. This study deals with the entire universe of interstate wars involving the Great Powers rather than a sample from that universe (or population), and there is considerable debate regarding the relevance of significance tests for populations. Moreover, the distributions of the war indicators are highly skewed so that a number of the assumptions upon which significance tests are based may not be satisfied here. Nevertheless, significance levels provide a standard benchmark for comparison and interpretation in the social sciences. They can also be used to indicate the sensitivity of the analysis to the coding rules for the various indicators. A large number of statistically significant relationships would suggest that a change in coding rules that would generate nonsystematic changes in the data would have only a marginal impact on the resulting analysis.[5] Thus significance levels are generally given in the following analyses, though the emphasis is on the size of the correlation coefficients. For general purposes of interpretation, correlations below .30 in absolute magnitude are defined as low, those exceeding .70 as high, and those between .30 and .70 as moderate.[6]

Characteristics of the Wars

The empirical associations among the various war indicators for the 119 wars involving the Great Powers since 1495 are given in the correlation matrix in Table 5.4.

Many of the correlations are as expected. Several of the high correlations may be deceiving, however, because some of the indicators are mathematically very similar by virtue of their definition. Thus severity

Table 5.4. Correlation Matrix (tau-*b*) of War Indicators

Indicator	Dur	Ext	Mag	Sev	Int	Con
Duration	1.00					
Extent	.25	1.00				
Magnitude	.79	.51	1.00			
Severity	.52	.46	.64	1.00		
Intensity	.53	.47	.65	.92	1.00	
Concentration	.07	.19	.13	.52	.47	1.00

Note: Twelve of the fifteen correlations below the diagonal are statistically significant at the .001 level.

and intensity are highly correlated, as are duration and magnitude. It is perhaps a little surprising that the severity-intensity correlation is as high as tau-*b* = .92 (r = .998), suggesting that the human losses in warfare have generally increased as rapidly as population. The table suggests a moderate relationship between the number of casualties and the duration, extent, and magnitude of war (tau-*b* = .52, .46, and .64, respectively) but a considerably weaker relationship between the duration of war and number of Powers involved (tau-*b* = .25). These figures suggest that wars involving a larger number of Powers do not tend to last much longer than wars involving fewer Powers and, conversely, that longer wars do not generally involve significantly more Powers than do shorter wars. This finding appears to have some relevance for theories of escalation processes, because it suggests that longer wars do not generally tend to draw in additional Powers. The severity of war is moderately associated with its duration, extent, and magnitude. These same general patterns hold true for Great Power wars. Nearly all of the rank-order correlations differ from those in Table 5.4 by less than .05, and in no case do the differences exceed .10.

Thus most of the empirical associations among the war indicators are moderate, indicating that the various theoretical dimensions of war are distinct but not completely independent. This conclusion is consistent with the view that the various dimensions are nonredundant measures of the more general phenomenon of war and that war is a multidimensional concept.

Yearly Amount of War

The relationships among the various measures of the yearly amount of war may be sensitive to the temporal period of aggregation and also to whether the focus is on the amount of war beginning, under way, or ending. The correlation between the number of wars beginning each one-year period and the number of wars under way, for example, is only $r = .27$, suggesting that knowledge of the number of wars beginning tells us very little about the number of wars under way. It will be necessary, therefore, to examine the relationships among the war indicators for both the amount of war under way and the amount of war beginning. For a particular substantive question, of course, one set of indicators may be more appropriate than the others.

In examining relationships among the war indicators (and later in examining historical trends in war), it is not necessary to control for the number of Great Powers in the system. The correlations between the number of Powers in the system and each of the indicators of the yearly amount of war under way are surprisingly low. None of the tau-*b*'s exceed .20. Thus the amount of war in the system (including even the number of Powers at war) is relatively independent of the number of Great Powers.[7]

Let us begin by examining the amount of war under way on a yearly basis and consider the relationships among the number of wars under way, the number of Great Powers at war, and the magnitude, severity, and concentration of war under way. The rank-order (tau-*b*) correlation matrix of the war indicators is presented in Table 5.5. A separate analysis of Great Power wars is not included here, because of the high correlation between the number of wars under way and the number of Great Power wars under way ($r = .76$) and the small differences (generally less than .04) between their respective correlations with the other indicators. All of the correlations are moderate to high, confirming our expectations. One result of some substantive significance is

Table 5.5. Correlation Matrix (tau-*b*) of Indicators for War Under Way per Year

Indicator	Number of Wars	Number of Powers at War	Mag	Sev	Con
Number wars	1.00				
Number powers at war	.67	1.00			
Magnitude	.75	.93	1.00		
Severity	.54	.74	.73	1.00	
Concentration	.42	.59	.56	.84	1.00

Note: All correlation coefficients are significant at the .001 level.

that the number of battle deaths is more closely associated with the number of Powers at war than with the number of wars under way, suggesting that the severity of war is affected more by the number of Great Powers at war (regardless of the number of wars for each) than by the total number of wars under way. This finding is consistent with the earlier argument that general wars involving nearly all the Great Powers account for a disproportionately high number of the total fatalities from war.

Having established the relationships among the measures of the amount of war under way per year, let us now consider longer periods of temporal aggregation. Here it is most useful to focus on the amount of war beginning. These relationships are examined for five-, ten-, and twenty-five year periods. The resulting rank-order correlations are presented in Table 5.6. The items in each cell refer to correlations for the three time intervals. The intensity indicator has been excluded because of its nearly perfect correlations with the other fatality-based indicators (tau-*b* = .96, .98).

The results are surprising: not only do the relationships between the indicators vary over different units of aggregation, but these variations are much greater than anticipated and often substantively significant. The associations between frequency and severity, for example, move

Table 5.6. Correlation Matrices (tau-*b*) of War Indicators for Five-, Ten-, and Twenty-Five-Year Periods

	Freq	Dur	Ext	Mag	Sev	Con
Frequency	1.00					
	1.00					
	1.00					
Duration	.72	1.00				
	.55	1.00				
	.40	1.00				
Extent	.79	.71	1.00			
	.72	.59	1.00			
	.81	.39	1.00			
Magnitude	.66	.86	.78	1.00		
	.46	.83	.65	1.00		
	.25	.77	.34	1.00		
Severity	.60	.72	.73	.80	1.00	
	.41	.55	.64	.67	1.00	
	–.16	.01	.06	.17	1.00	
Concentration	.50	.46	.55	.52	.72	1.00
	.26	.21	.40	.30	.64	1.00
	–.20	–.54	–.39	–.40	.43	1.00

Note: The three items in each cell refer to tau-*b* for five-, ten-, and twenty-five-year periods of temporal aggregation, respectively.

from tau-*b* = .60 at five-year intervals to tau-*b* = – .16 at twenty-five-year intervals. The former implies a fairly strong tendency for periods of frequent wars to be the most costly in the loss of life, whereas the latter implies (if anything) a very slight tendency for periods of frequent wars to be the least costly in loss of life. In nearly all cases, the correlation declines as the length of the period of aggregation increases, reflecting the increased variation generated by the higher number of wars in longer periods. This sensitivity of the correlations to the length of the period of temporal aggregation suggests that we must be extremely careful in interpreting these statistics and making inferences about empirical associations among the war indicators. Many of the theoretical generalizations in the literature are not sufficiently precise because they fail to make a distinction between the short run and the long run.

For five-year periods of aggregation among the indicators for the amount of war, all of the correlations (tau-*b*) are positive and moderate to high (all exceed .45). Thus periods ranking high on one dimension of war behavior tend to rank high on all other dimensions as well. But all of the indicators are positively correlated with the frequency of war, and these other correlations may therefore be spurious. The cumulative amount of war in any period would be expected to increase with the number of wars in that period. On the other hand, a common generalization found in the literature is that there is an inverse relationship between the frequency and seriousness of war; at some times war is frequent but limited—where "limited" is interpreted to refer to low magnitude and severity—and at other times relatively infrequent but more serious. Preston and Wise, for example, characterize eighteenth-century warfare as frequent but limited, whereas Inis L. Claude, Jr., refers to the "frequent" but "localized and limited" wars of the nineteenth century.[8]

This hypothesized inverse relationship between the frequency and seriousness of war cannot be fully tested here, for many "limited" wars have been excluded from this compilation. Wars not involving a Great Power, imperial and colonial wars, civil wars, and wars involving less than 1,000 battle deaths have all been excluded. Nevertheless, it remains an important question whether wars involving the Great Powers are either frequent but limited or infrequent but serious. The evidence here suggests that this particular inverse relationship is not valid. If anything, there may be a slight tendency for interstate wars involving the Great Powers to be most serious when they are most frequent and less serious when they are less frequent, at least in the short term. Over the long-term (twenty-five-year periods of aggregation), however, there may be a slight inverse relationship between the frequency and severity of war.

Table 5.7. Correlations (tau-*b*) between Frequency of War and Characteristics of the Average War

	Tau-*b* (freq, W_i)		
	Unit of Aggregation		
War Indicator (W_i)	5-year	10-year	25-year
Duration	.07	.004	–.04
Extent	–.006	.06	–.12
Magnitude	.02	.08	–.15
Severity	.02	.07	–.41
Concentration	–.08	–.01	–.16

It is not clear, however, whether the "seriousness of war" refers to the total amount of war in a period or to the nature of the average war during that period. The hypothesis based on the latter conceptualization can be tested empirically by computing the correlations between the frequency of interstate war involving the Powers and the characteristics of the average war (W_i) for each period.[9] These rank-order correlations (tau-*b*) for five-, ten-, and twenty-five-year periods of aggregation are given in Table 5.7.

For a five-year period, the statistics in Table 5.7 show no relationship between the number of wars and the nature of the average wars, as indicated by the near-zero correlation for all indicators. Thus the hypothesized inverse relation between the frequency and seriousness of war is not supported by the empirical evidence. This conclusion is valid for ten-year periods as well, as indicated by the statistics in Tables 5.6 and 5.7. Over a twenty-five-year period, however, there is some evidence of a moderate inverse relationship between the frequency of war and the severity of the average war. Moreover, all of the characteristics of the average war, not just severity, demonstrate an inverse relationship (however weak) with frequency.

The relationship between the frequency and seriousness of war varies depending on whether seriousness is defined as the total amount of war or the characteristics of the average war, and depending on whether wars are aggregated over the short term (five to ten years)

or the long term (twenty-five years). It must be emphasized further that these findings are valid only for interstate wars involving the Great Powers (and at least 1,000 fatalities) and therefore do not constitute a valid test of the more general hypothesis that *wars* are either frequent but limited or infrequent but serious.[10]

Relationships between the other indicators of the average amount of war per period can also be determined. All of the correlations are positive and moderate in strength except for those involving the concentration of war (which is related only to the other fatality-based indicators). These relationships are generally not as strong as those for the total amount of war per period (here tau-$b < .55$, except for the duration-magnitude relationship), since the spurious impact of the frequency of war has been removed. These results are only slightly dependent on the particular period of temporal aggregation and are substantively unchanged if only Great Power wars are considered. The relationships between severity and the duration and extent indicators are similar to those for the total amount of war. Although tau-*b* is comparable for the severity-extent and severity-duration relationships, Pearson's *r* suggests that severity is determined more by the number of Powers than by the duration of war.

The next problem to be discussed is the extent to which the patterns of war behavior uncovered in this chapter are consistent over the five-century span of the Great Power system. That is, are there any significant historical trends in war? This question is considered in the following chapter.

6
Historical Trends in War

The twentieth century has been characterized as a particularly warlike era because of the destructiveness of the two world wars, the high level of tension and frequent crises of the Cold War, the persistent madness of the arms race between the two Superpowers, and the seemingly continuous conflicts among lesser states. A counterargument is that the world has not experienced a major war since 1945, that the impression that war is widespread derives more from the expanded role of the media in making war a more immediate and personal experience than from the actuality of war itself, and that war is in fact much less common today than it was centuries ago. A resolution of these contradictory views need not rest on impressions and speculation, however, for the data base generated here has been designed to answer these kinds of questions. The focus here, of course, is not on war in general but on interstate war involving the Great Powers. This chapter is concerned primarily with the question of whether these wars are increasing or decreasing. Cyclical trends in war will be discussed briefly and the respective levels of war for the last five centuries will be compared.

Linear Trends

Several scholarly efforts have addressed the question of whether war has been increasing or decreasing with time. Singer and Small find no significant trend in the frequency, magnitude, severity, or intensity of international war since 1815 for either the international system as a whole or the central European system.[1] Richardson examines the period from 1820 to 1950 and finds a very slight downward trend in the frequency of war, a slight tendency for wars of high severity to become more frequent and those of low severity to become less frequent, and no upward trend in the per capita losses of life from war.[2] Frank H. Denton analyzes the Richardson data and finds that the frequency of war has been relatively constant since the Congress of Vienna, but the size of war (defined as a combination of the other dimensions identified here) has been increasing.[3] These studies of historical trends in war based on the Richardson or Singer-Small data are of limited value because they describe only the last century and a half and provide no basis for generalization to the Great Power system (or the modern state system) as a whole. Their starting point immediately after the Congress of Vienna introduces a serious bias into trend analysis, for this was the most peaceful period in the last five centuries. Richardson recognizes the need to extend the analysis over a broader time span.[4]

Analyses of long-term trends in war have been undertaken by Woods and Baltzly, Wright, and Sorokin. Woods and Baltzly focus on the proportion of years of war during each half century and find that by this measure war has been on the decline over the last five centuries.[5] Sorokin describes a continuous increase in army size and an even faster increase in casualties over the last eight centuries (ending in 1925), except for a definite drop in both variables in the nineteenth century. Sorokin rejects the arguments that war has been either increasing or decreasing steadily over time and concludes that war fluctuates erratically.[6] Wright finds that the frequency of European wars has declined since 1480 and that both the absolute and per capita human and economic costs have increased. Military activity is becoming more concentrated in time, with longer intervals of peace between wars, and also more extended in space.[7]

Clearly, scholars do not agree on the question of whether war is increasing or decreasing over time. By the definitions used here, Wright finds a downward trend in the frequency of war, but Richardson and Singer and Small fail to detect any trend in either direction.

Wright identifies an increase in the severity and intensity of war, but Sorokin, Richardson, and Singer and Small find no trend. It is difficult, however, to make direct comparisons between these diverse and occasionally contradictory findings because each of the studies focuses on different characteristics of the wars under consideration, the operational indicators of the key variables, and the temporal span of the analysis. Woods and Baltzly, for example, focus only on a single indicator (the proportion of years of war per half century) and therefore do not adequately capture the full multidimensional nature of war. The Singer-Small and Richardson studies cover only the period since the Congress of Vienna and include all interstate wars, including those involving smaller states. Although the Woods and Baltzly, Sorokin, and Wright studies cover a longer temporal span and focus on the major European states, none of their major power systems is perfectly congruent with the Great Power system identified here.[8] Furthermore, some states are included in these analyses during periods before they rose to or after they fell from Great Power status. Consequently, these conclusions may not be applicable to the war behavior of the Great Powers as defined here. The finding by Woods and Baltzly, for example, that war is diminishing may simply reflect the lower level of war behavior of medium powers as compared to Great Powers and the fact that many Great Powers have left the system. Their data show a diminishing level of war for states that could no longer claim Great Power status but no such tendency for the continuing Great Powers. The utility of the Woods and Baltzly study is further limited because their historical system ends in 1900, after the most peaceful century in modern history and just before two of the most destructive wars of all time. The following analysis of historical trends in the war behavior of the Great Powers is necessary because of the limitations of these earlier studies.

Methods of Analysis

An analysis of historical trends in war must distinguish between the levels, dimensions, and units of analysis of war conceptualized earlier. This section examines linear trends in the frequency of war, the characteristics of the individual wars, and the aggregate amount of war per period, including both the annual amount of war under way and the amount of war per twenty-five-year period. Both Great Power war and interstate war involving the Powers are analyzed. Discussion of each category begins with a graphical representation of the war data. Increasing or decreasing trends can be identified, and a rough estimate of the strength of these trends can be made. The extremely large variation in the war indicators precludes a high degree of precision in a visual analysis, however, and a statistical analysis of the war data is necessary to permit a quantitative measurement of the change in war over time.

Several quantitative techniques are available for determining the historical trends in the war data. Here a combination of frequency counts and percentages, regression analysis, and rank-order correlation analysis is used. If war indicator W_i is regressed against time (the year in which the war or period begins), the regression coefficient b (or slope) measures the strength of the historical trend by the average yearly change in W_i. To compare the relative magnitude of the trends in two different indicators, the standardized regression coefficients (b^*) can be compared.

If the linear regression model is applied to the fatality-based indicators, the least-squares criterion gives excessive influence to extreme cases, with the result that the two world wars have a disproportionate impact on the trend lines. To eliminate this effect deriving from the method of analysis (rather than from the true importance of the wars), two alternative methods are employed. First, the rank-order correlation coefficients (tau-b) between each indicator and time are provided. These measure whether war indicator W_i is increasing over time but incorporate no information regarding the amount of increase. Second, the logarithms of the severity, intensity, and concentration indicators are regressed against time. These will reveal the same positive or negative trends as for the regular regressions (since a logarithmic transformation is a monotonically increasing function) but the interpretation is equivalent. Since this technique is equivalent to running an exponential curve throughout the raw data, the beta coefficient is equivalent to the percentage increase in the war indicator per unit change in time.[9] Given beta, the doubling time of any indicator can be calculated.[10] Another advantage of both logarithms and rank-order correlations is that they are less sensitive than regression coefficients to measurement errors in the data. Rank-order correlations require only ordinal-level precision, a requirement basically met even by the fatality-based indicators for the pre-1815 period. The use of these multiple methods of analysis minimizes the possibility that the conclusions will be determined by the idiosyncracies of particular techniques.[11]

The Frequency of War

Scattergrams of the frequency of war indicator are presented in Figure 6.1 a–d for interstate wars involving the Great Powers and for Great Power wars. Both five and twenty-five-year periods of aggregation are used. The decline in the frequency of interstate war involving the Great Powers is evident from the scattergrams, particularly for the longer period of aggregation. This trend is confirmed by a regression analysis of frequency against time, based on a one-year unit of aggregation. For interstate wars involving the Powers, $b = -.0049$ and $b^* = -.13$, significant at $p = .004$. The decline amounts to 1.2 fewer wars per five-year period (or six fewer wars per twenty-five-year period) over the five-century span of the system. This declining frequency of war is significant substantively as well as statistically; the average frequency of war is only 1.2 per five-year period. Therefore, the decline in the frequency of war over the five-century span of the system is equal to the average frequency of war, which attests to the strength of this historical trend.

The overall decline in the frequency of Great Power war is even more pronounced, as portrayed by Figure 6.1 b and d. The number of Great Power wars declined continuously from the sixteenth to the nineteenth centuries, with a very slight increase in the twentieth century. Over 75 percent of the Great Power wars occurred in the first half of the 480-year system (before 1735); less than 25 percent occurred in the last 240 years. An examination of the data based on a five-year period of aggregation demonstrates that only 25 percent of the half decades since 1815 have witnessed the initiation of Great Power war, compared to nearly 60 percent in the previous three centuries. The relative absence of Great Power war in the nineteenth century (except for the 1850–75 period) is striking, particularly in contrast with the relatively high frequency of Great Power war in earlier periods (ranging up to nine in one twenty-five-year period in the sixteenth century). Great Power war has been only one-fourth as frequent in the twentieth century as in the sixteenth century.

The strength of this downward trend is confirmed by a correlation and regression analysis. The rank-order correlation between time and frequency of war per five-year period gives tau-b = –.36 (the corresponding statistics for ten- and twenty-five-year periods are –.44 and –.61). The rate of decline can be measured by a linear regression analysis. Regressing frequency against time (using one-year periods) produces a b of –.00053 and a b^* of –.20 (statistically significant at .000). This means that the number of wars per year has been declining by .00053 each year (or .25 wars per year over the last five centuries). In other words, the average decade today is characterized by 2.5 fewer Great Power wars than the average decade 480 years ago. This decline is significant substantively, given that it is roughly two times the average frequency of Great Power war per decade for the entire period (1.3). It is evident from Figure 6.1c that this trend was under way long before the twentieth century and the development of modern military technology.

Characteristics of the Individual Wars

Given that interstate war involving the Powers and particularly Great Power war have been declining in frequency, the next question is whether the individual wars have become more or less serious along the dimensions of duration, extent, magnitude, severity, intensity, and concentration. Interstate wars involving the Great Powers and Great Power wars are analyzed separately because there are significant differences between them.

The scattergrams of the indicators for interstate war involving the Great Powers are presented in Figure 6.2a–f. The fatality-based indicators are plotted on a logarithmic scale.

Figure 6.1. Scattergrams: Frequency of War and Great Power War

a. Frequency of war, 5-year periods

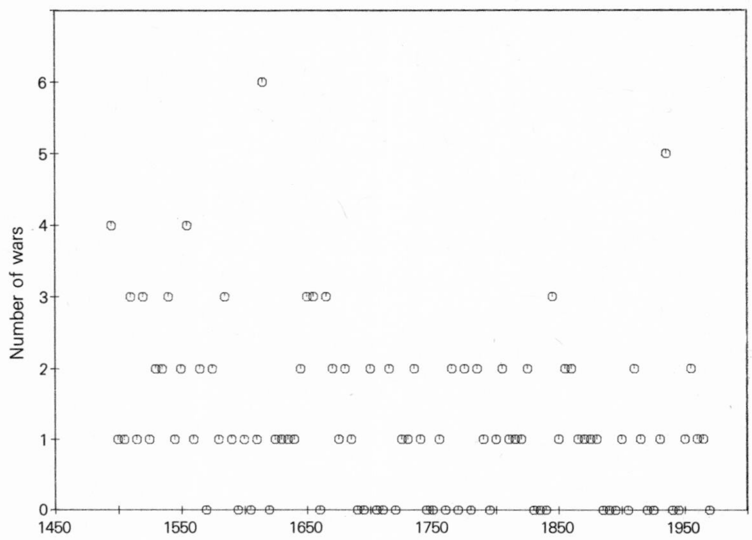

b. Frequency of Great Power war, 5-year periods

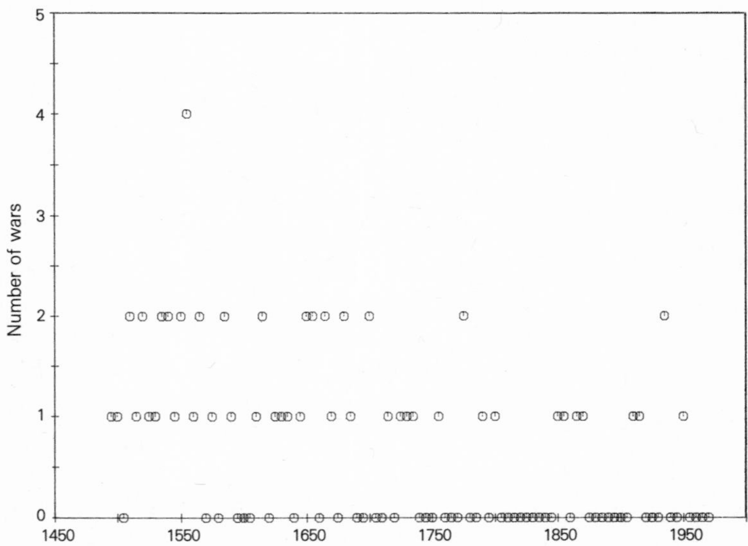

Figure 6.1, continued

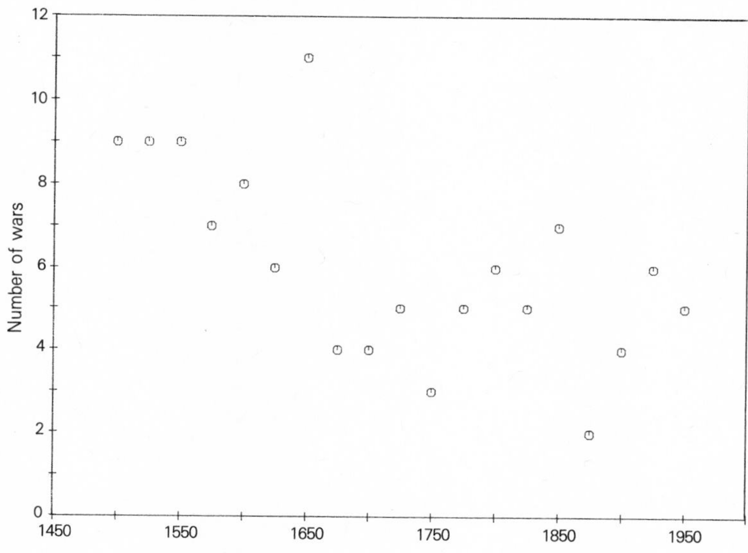

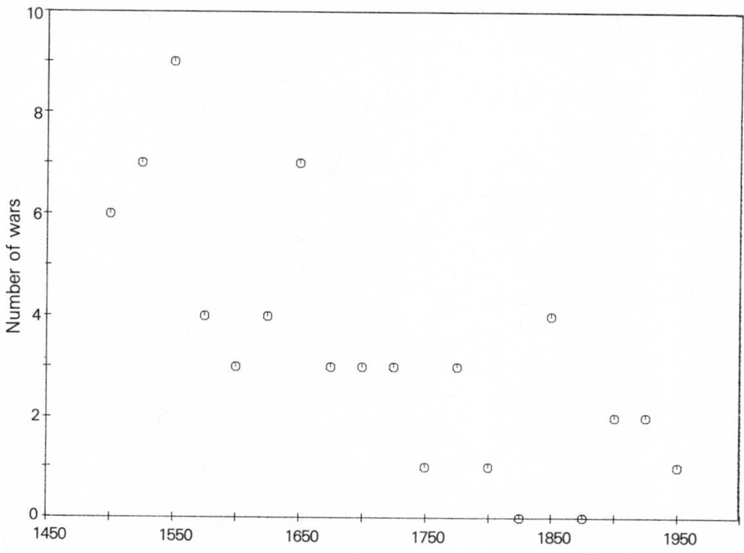

Figure 6.2. Scattergrams: Characteristics of the Wars

a. Duration

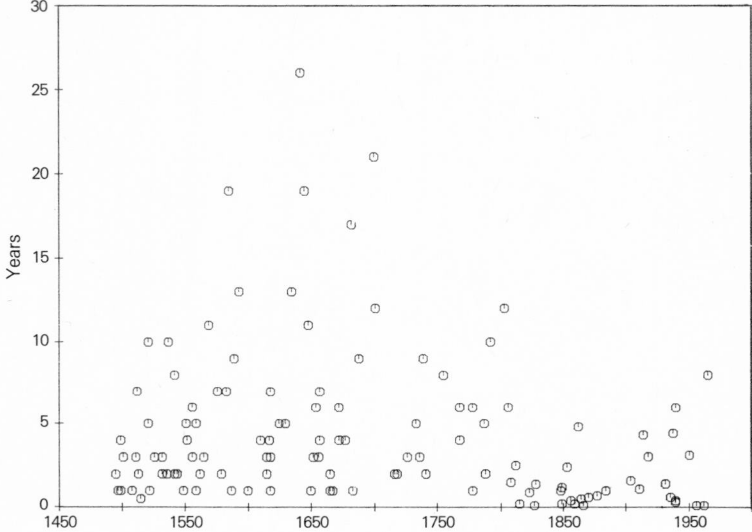

b. Extent

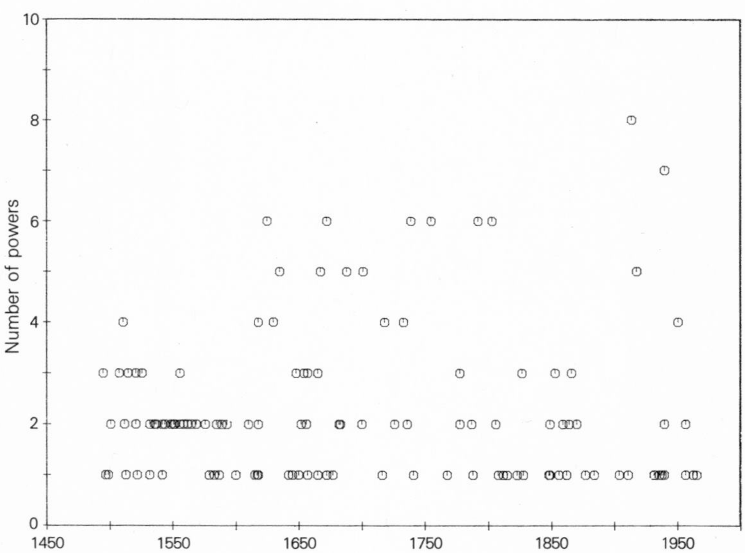

Figure 6.2, continued

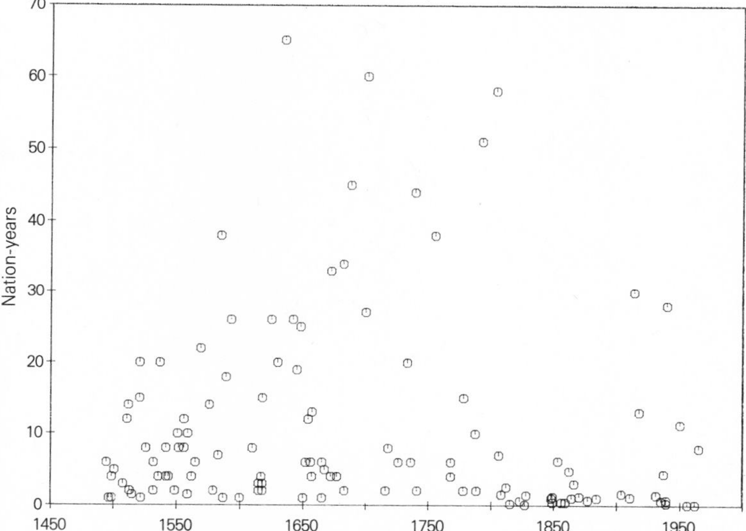

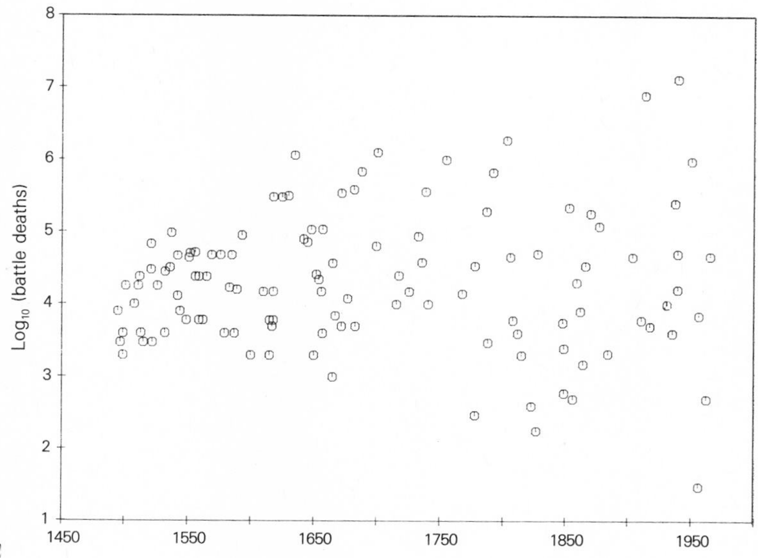

Figure 6.2, continued

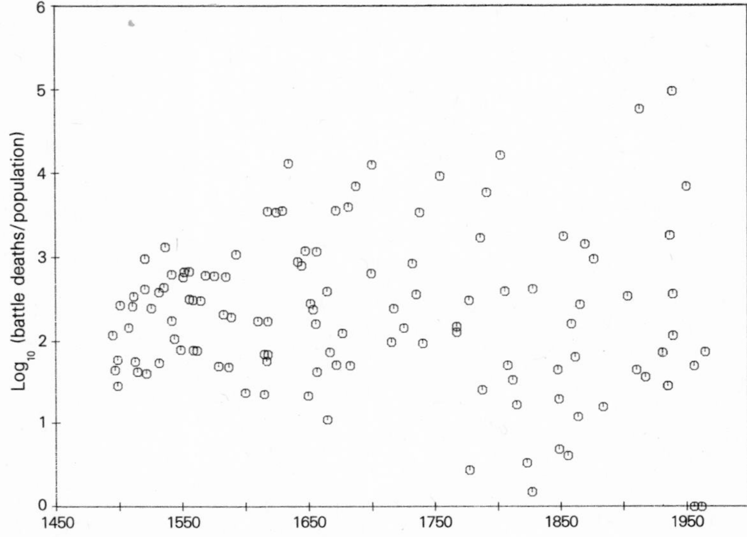

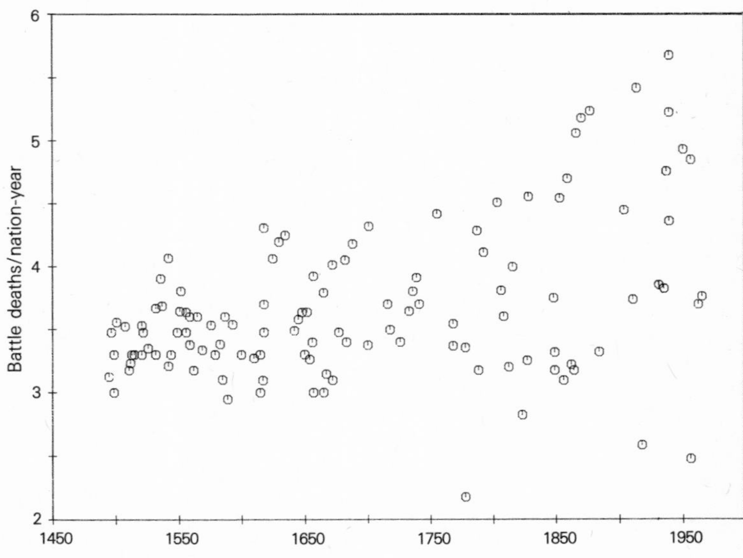

None of the linear trends in war appears particularly dramatic. Perhaps the most noticeable is that interstate wars involving the Powers are getting shorter in duration. Figure 6.2a reveals that only one war of the post-Vienna period has lasted longer than seven years, whereas in the pre-Vienna period there were nearly twenty wars of this duration. This downward trend in the duration of war is confirmed by the statistics presented in Table 6.1.

The downward trend, as indicated by the negative tau-*b* and *b*, is fairly strong. The *b* of –.0064 indicates that individual wars are diminishing in duration by about .0064 years (2.3 days) each year (regardless of whether a war actually occurs). This is equivalent to a decline of about three years per war since the beginning of the system in 1495, which is dramatic considering that the average war during this period was only four and a half years long.

The scattergram of the extent indicator demonstrates an interesting pattern, but no long-term trends. The low *b* and tau-*b* in Table 6.1 (small enough that they have opposite signs) indicate that the number of Powers participating in these wars has changed very little over time.

The magnitude of war also follows an interesting pattern. Other than the two world wars the only time wars have exceeded twenty in magnitude was from the late sixteenth century to the early nineteenth century, followed by a particularly low magnitude in the nineteenth century. The slightly downward trend overall is confirmed by Table 6.1. The magnitude of war has declined by .0073 nation-years of war per year, or 3.5 nation-years over the entire span of the system. This decline is fairly strong (the mean is ten nation-years) but not as strong as the decline in the duration of war, as demonstrated by the standardized betas. The downward trend in both indicators can be explained in part by the occurrence in the first two centuries of the system of several protracted Turkish wars.

The scattergram shows that the severity of war has become increasingly variable over time and that the number of battle deaths has been increasing, but that this trend is not as great as we might have expected. This positive but relatively small increase is confirmed by

Table 6.1. Historical Trends in War: Tau-*b* and Regression Coefficients for the Individual Wars

Dimension	Tau-*b*	*b*	*b**	Significance Level of *b*
	Interstate Wars Involving the Powers			
Duration	−.17	−.0064	−.20	.03
Extent	−.06	.0005	.05	.6
Magnitude	−.16	−.0073	−.08	.4
Severity	.04	.00015	.02	.8
Intensity	−.05	−.00069	−.10	.3
Concentration	.25	.0018	.42	.000
	Great Power Wars			
Duration	.02	−.0022	−.06	.6
Extent	.32	.0058	.48	.000
Magnitude	.14	.022	.18	.16
Severity	.27	.0027	.40	.001
Intensity	.20	.0020	.31	.01
Concentration	.36	.0029	.57	.000

Note: The regression coefficients (*b* and *b**) and significance levels for the severity, intensity, and concentration indicators are from the regressions of the logged values of the indicators against time.

tau-*b* (0.4), *b* (.00015), and *b** (0.2). Beta indicates that the number of battle deaths per war has been increasing at the average rate of .015 percent per year, but this is not statistically significant.

Before rejecting the common view that casualties from war have been increasing dramatically, we must recognize that these conclusions may reflect the particular methodological procedures used. A logarithmic transformation result in a slight downward bias on observed trends. If battle deaths (rather than their logarithm) are regressed against time, a fairly strong positive trend emerges ($b = 2200$, $b^* = .22$, significant at $p = .013$), indicating that the average battle deaths per war have increased by a million (or four times the mean) over the span of five centuries. This result demonstrates the sensitivity of the analysis to the methods used. Yet some methods are more appropriate than others for certain questions and certain data. When there are a limited number of outlying cases, it is neither appropriate nor conventional to use a least-squares method on untransformed data. The use of logarithms is entirely consistent with existing practice for data of this sort,[12] and the fact that another acceptable method (tau-*b*) gives similar results tends to provide additional support for this analysis. It is true that the most severe wars of any age are becoming increasingly destructive in loss of life.[13] With respect to the general question of historical trends in war, however, we must conclude that the severity of interstate wars involving the Great Powers is increasing but at an extremely slow rate.[14]

It is not surprising to find similar trends in the intensity of war, given the high correlation between severity and intensity. The intensity of war may actually be decreasing slightly over time, as indicated by tau-*b* and *b* (not statistically significant). The intensity of wars has been declining by about .07 percent per year, suggesting that the destructiveness of war has not quite kept up with the increase in population.[15] The historical increase in the concentration of war is less ambiguous (see Figure 6.1f). Fatalities per nation-year of war have been increasing by .18 percent per year, faster than any other indicator and about ten times as fast as the severity of war. This finding confirms the view of Wright and others that war is becoming much more concentrated in space and time.

Thus except for their duration and concentration dimensions, interstate wars involving the Great Powers have changed little over time. The nature of Great Power wars has changed, however, as is evident from the scattergrams for the Great Power war indicators, which are presented in Figure 6.3a–d. The intensity and concentration indicators are excluded because of the similarity of their distributions to that of the severity of Great Power war and to the intensity and concentration indicators for interstate wars involving the Great Powers.

The scattergrams suggest an increase in most of the indicators except perhaps duration. These impressions are confirmed by the beta

Figure 6.3. Scattergrams: Characteristics of Great Power Wars

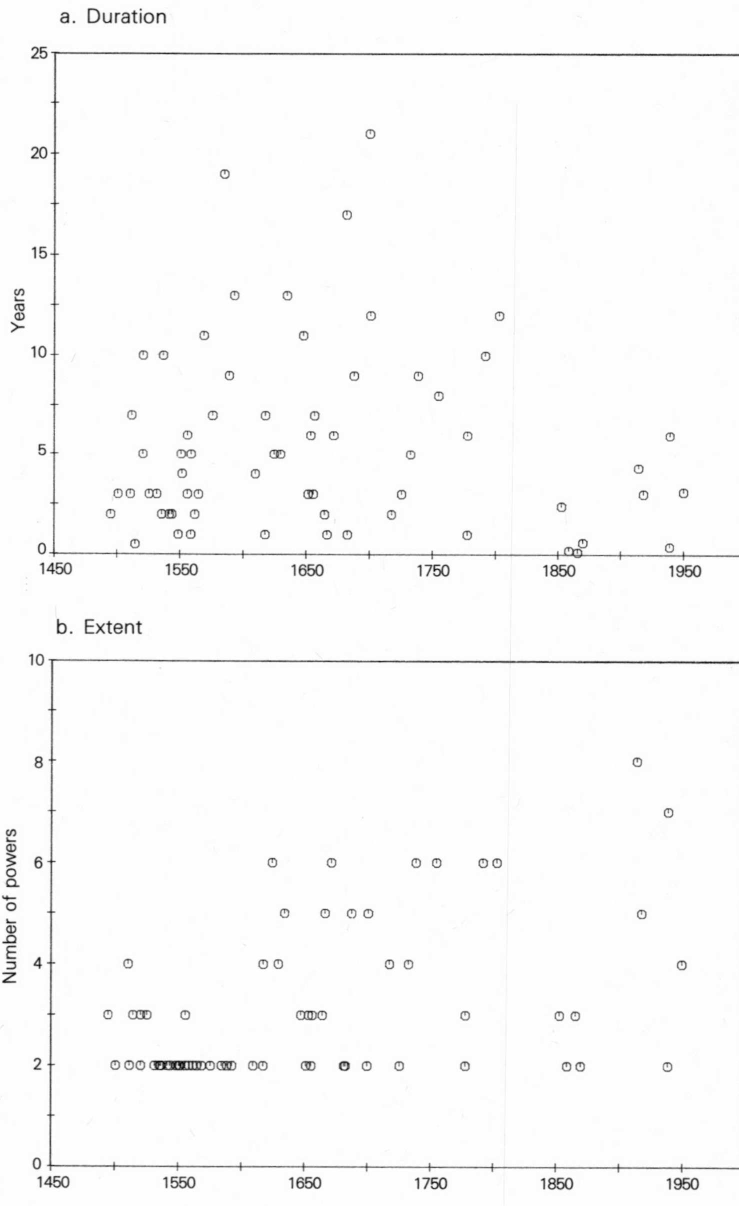

Figure 6.3, continued

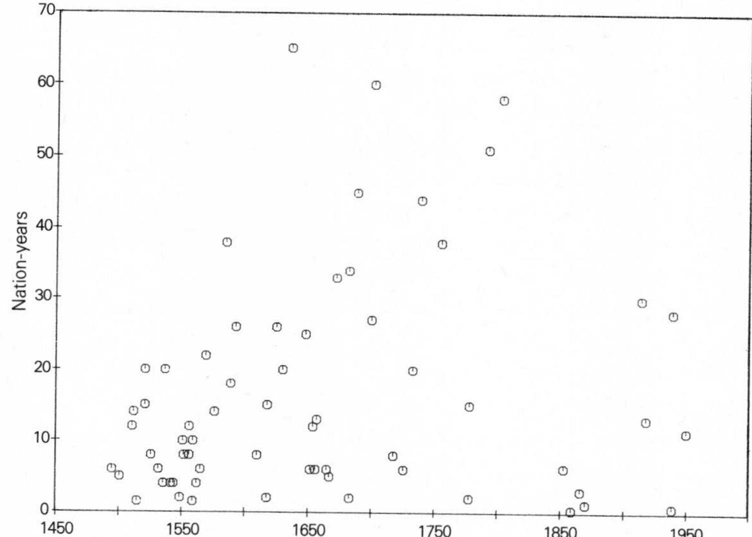

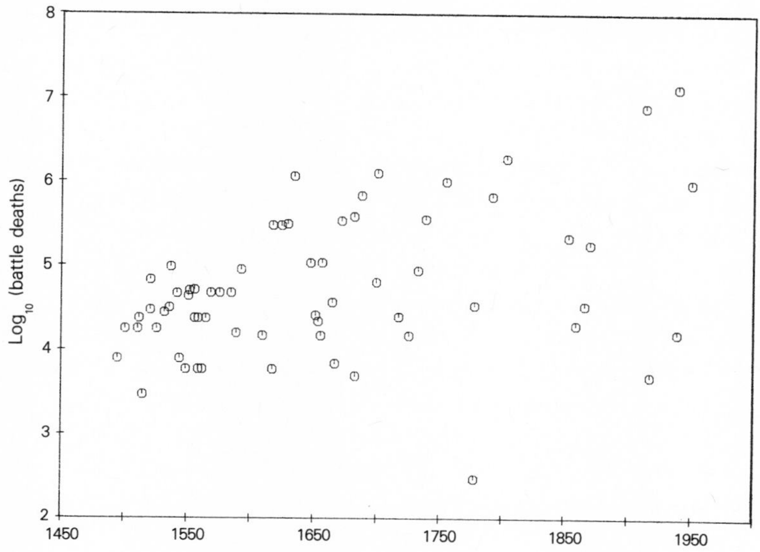

coefficients and rank-order correlation coefficients presented at the bottom of Table 6.1. The duration of Great Power wars has remained basically constant since the late fifteenth century, but their extent has increased sharply. The *b* of .0058 indicates that the number of Powers participating in Great Power war has been increasing by approximately .006 per year, or by over one Power every two centuries. (Recall that the average number of Powers participating in a single Great Power war is only 3.2 and the median only 2.5). The scattergram in Figure 6.3b reveals additional information. Before the Thirty Years' War, no conflict involved more than four Powers and most wars involved two Powers. From the early seventeenth century to the early nineteenth century, the number of warring Powers varied from two to six, the median being four. No war in the nineteenth century involved more than three Powers, but the two world wars in the twentieth century involved seven and eight Powers, respectively. Furthermore, the proportion of Great Power wars involving a large number of Powers is much higher in recent times than previously. Since Vienna, for example, two-thirds of these wars have involved three or more Powers, whereas previously this ratio was less than half. Thus the proportion of conflicts that expanded into larger wars involving several Powers has been increasing over time.[16]

The magnitude of Great Power war has also been increasing but less than half as fast as its extent (as indicated by the b^* of .18 compared to .48 for extent). The *b* of .022 suggests that the magnitude of war has been increasing by over two nation-years each century (compared to a mean of 16, median of 11). This is not statistically significant, however ($p = .16$), given the large variance in magnitude.

All of the fatality-based indicators show that Great Power wars have also become increasingly destructive, as demonstrated by the tau-*b* and regression coefficients. The severity of Great Power war has been increasing at an average rate of .62 percent each year. At this rate, the average number of battle deaths in a Great Power war has doubled every 110 years or so. The intensity of war has increased nearly as rapidly (.46 percent per year), doubling every 150 years. The most pronounced trend in Great Power war, as indicated by the b^*

of .57, is its increasing concentration over time. The number of battle deaths has increased at a rate of .67 percent per year, doubling every 100 years. An examination of the scattergrams of the data clearly reveals that these upward trends are not simply the product of the enormous destructiveness of two world wars but would hold true without them.

The Aggregate Amount of War

It is clear that the frequency of interstate war involving the Powers has been declining while the individual wars themselves have become more serious in some respects and less serious in others. Great Power wars have declined markedly in frequency but have become more serious in every respect but duration. The question here is the impact of these divergent trends on the aggregate amount of interstate war involving the Great Powers. Are the yearly fatalities from war or the total magnitude of war increasing or decreasing? An answer to these questions requires that we examine the yearly amount of war under way and the amount of war beginning in a given period.

The relevant indicators for the annual amount of war and Great Power war under way are the number of wars and Great Power wars under way, the number of Powers at war, and the annual magnitude, severity, and concentration of war under way. The scattergrams of these indicators are very revealing in many respects and will provide the basis for some of the analysis that follows. Each consists of 481 annual data points, however, and therefore does not provide a clear and uncluttered plot of manageable size. For this reason these scattergrams are not presented here.

The scattergrams would show a noticeable decline in the yearly number of wars under way. There have been a disproportionately large number of years without war in the post-Vienna period (about 60 percent of the years are without war) compared to the continuity of war in earlier times (when only 10 percent of the years were without war). Moreover, rarely in the last three centuries have more than two wars been under way in any given year, a phenomenon that was common in earlier historical periods. The decline of Great Power war is even more pronounced. There has been a relative absence of Great Power war in the nineteenth and twentieth centuries, when it has been under way only about one-sixth of the time. In the sixteenth, seventeenth, and eighteenth centuries, by contrast, Great Power war was under way about 80 percent of the time. During the first 250 years of the system there were only eighteen years in which all of the Powers were at peace and only twenty-five years in which two or more Great Powers were not at war. The simultaneous existence of more than one (and up to four) Great Power war was common before the eighteenth century but extremely rare since then.

A related fact is that the phenomenon of precisely two Powers at war, common before the nineteenth century, has practically ceased to exist, occurring only three times since the early nineteenth century. In the last two centuries only three Great Power wars have been limited to two Powers (whereas eight have involved three or more Powers). In the previous three centuries about half of the wars were limited in this manner. Thus in earlier times dyadic wars between two Powers did not always escalate through the intervention of third Powers. Such restraint by a third Power is much less common in more recent times. One possible explanation is that the capabilities and resources available to the Great Powers makes it more feasible than in the past to intervene quickly in an ongoing war, particularly in remote areas. Another explanation, based on incentives rather than capabilities, is that more often in recent times than in the past the Great Powers have perceived their vital security interests to be seriously threatened by dyadic wars between other Powers. This classic balance-of-power behavior is as evident in the nineteenth and twentieth centuries as it was in the Golden Age of the balance of power in the eighteenth century and before. It would be interesting to hypothesize that this strong tendency for two-Power wars to escalate may be an added deterrent to war and may help explain the relative infrequency of war since 1815. The correlation between the extent of the average war and the frequency of Great Power war is negative (particularly at twenty-five-year intervals), which tends to support this view.

The patterns in the magnitude of war under way generally follow those for the number of Great Powers at war and need not be discussed any further here. The scattergrams of the (logged) severity and concentration indicators are more difficult to interpret because of the gap between the values of the indicators for war and no-war years (which derives from the war/no-war dichotomy and the use of the 1,000 battle-death threshold to define war). If we look only at years in which war was under way, we find a slight upward trend in severity and concentration. The relative infrequency of war in recent times results, however, in an overall, though very slight, decrease in these indicators over time.

The observed downward trends in all of the war indicators are confirmed by a statistical analysis based on a regression of the indicators against time and a rank-order correlation analysis. The correlation and regression coefficients are presented in Table 6.2.

All of these coefficents are statistically significant[17] and all are negative, indicating that the annual amount of war under way has been declining over time for all dimensions, including severity and concentration. The amount of this decline can be evaluated in comparison with the average values of the indicators (refer back to Table 5.3 for five-year averages).[18] The average number of wars under way has dropped by 1.9 over the 480-year span of the system, which exceeds the average number of wars under way (1.3). The decline in the number of Great Power wars under way is even more dramatic —1.6 wars over the span of the system, twice the size of the mean (.8). The declines in the number of Powers at war and in the magnitude of war under way are not as large as those in the number of wars, but the total decline of each still equals its average annual value (2.7 fewer Powers at war compared to an annual average of 2.7, and 3.4 fewer nation-years of war, compared to an annual average of 3.2). The yearly severity and concentration of war have declined by .5 percent and .4 percent, respectively. Again, this is contrary to the common impression that losses of life from war have been increasing rapidly over time.

These historical trends in the aggregate amount of interstate war

Table 6.2. Historical Trends in the Amount of War Under Way: Tau-*b* and Regression Coefficients

Indicator	tau-*b*	*b*	*b**
Number wars under way	–.39	–.0039	–.47
Number GP wars under way	–.47	–.0033	–.55
Number powers at war	–.24	–.0056	–.34
Magnitude	–.26	–.0071	–.35
Severity	–.10	–.005	–.35
Concentration	–.05	–.0039	–.32

Note: The regression coefficients (*b* and *b**) for the severity and concentration indicators are from the regressions of the logged values of the indicators against time. All beta coefficients are significant at the .001 level.

involving the Great Powers are generally confirmed further if we examine the amount of war beginning for various periods of aggregation as well as the annual amount of war under way. Graphs of the amount of interstate wars involving the Powers per twenty-five-year period are presented in Figure 6.4a–f. The patterns for intensity are nearly identical to those for severity, so the former is excluded. The rank-order correlations (tau-*b*) and regression coefficients for five-, ten-, and twenty-five-year intervals and for both interstate war involving the Great Powers and Great Power war are presented in Table 6.3. The results show a consistent pattern of decline in war over time. Both tau-*b* and *b* are negative (and most are statistically significant) for all periods of aggregation and for Great Power wars as well as all wars, for the frequency, duration, extent, and magnitude indicators. This is unambiguous evidence of the decline in the amount of war over time along these dimensions. The statistics for the severity and concentration indicators are more ambiguous, however, for their direction and strength vary somewhat with the length of the period of aggregation. If five- and ten-year periods are used, the severity and concentration of both war and Great Power war appear to be declining slightly, whereas the use of a twenty-five-year period points more in the direction of a slight increase in the severity and concentration of wars and

Figure 6.4. Graphs: Amount of War, Twenty-five-Year Periods

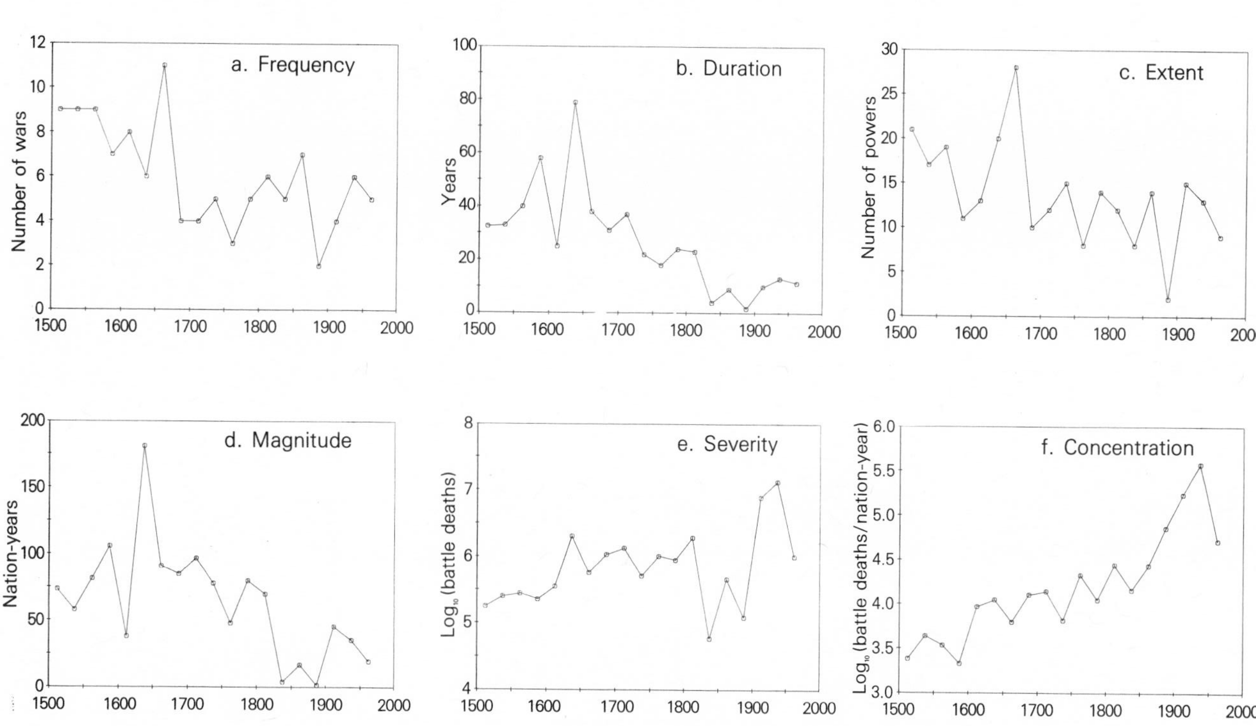

Table 6.3. Historical Trends in the Amount of War Beginning: Tau-*b* and Regression Coefficients

Indicator	All Wars			Great Power Wars		
	Unit of Aggregation					
	5-year	10-year	25-year	5-year	10-year	25-year
	*Regression Coefficients (*b*)*					
Frequency	–.0024	–.0041	–.01	–.0027	–.0054	–.013
Duration	–.019	–.038	–.095	–.016	–.033	–.081
Extent	–.0048	–.0086	–.022	–.0052	–.010	–.025
Magnitude	–.034	–.069	–.17	–.031	–.065	–.16
Severity	–.0036	*–.0029*	*.0017*	–.0065	–.0069	*–.0017*
Concentration	*–.0015*	–.00063	.0037	–.0047	–.0042	*.00069*
	*Rank-Order Correlations (tau-*b*)*					
Frequency	–.23	–.26	–.42	–.36	–.44	–.61
Duration	–.27	–.37	–.59	–.32	–.40	–.63
Extent	–.21	–.26	–.36	–.25	–.31	–.39
Magnitude	–.23	–.31	–.45	–.26	–.30	–.45
Severity	–.12	*–.05*	.31	–.20	*–.11*	.30
Concentration	*.04*	.18	.77	–.17	*–.03*	.46

Note: All statistics except those in italics are significant at the .05 level. The regression coefficients for the severity and concentration indicators are from the regressions of the logged values of the indicators against time.

of Great Power wars. This difference in results shows the importance of aggregation in the analysis of time-series data. The explanation for the differences observed here lies in the fact that all but two of the ten five-year periods from 1900 to 1950 were characterized by a relatively small number of battle deaths from wars beginning in those periods. In seven of the ten periods there were no fatalities from Great Power war. These wars naturally shift the regression lines downward if five- or ten-year periods are used, since these eight periods dominate over the two with the world wars. Similarly, the analysis of the amount of war under way on a yearly basis showed downward trends in severity and concentration. A twenty-five-year period of aggregation, however, collapses these ten periods into two, each encompassing one of the world wars. Thus the periods without fatalities are absorbed into the periods dominated by the world wars. Similarly, the many other periods in the last century and a half that are characterized by the absence of war are absorbed into adjacent periods of war, thus reducing their impact on the trend lines and rank orders.

In this sense, these results may be partially an artifact of the particular statistical methods used. It must be concluded, however, that the data are sufficiently ambiguous to point against the argument that the aggregate severity and concentration of war have been increasing rapidly over time. It can be concluded that the most violent periods (measured by fatalities from war) have become even more violent and the most severe Great Power wars have become more severe, but in general there has been no significant increase in the total losses of life from wars involving the Great Powers or from Great Power wars.

Summary of Linear Trends

In the previous section a variety of indicators, representing different levels, dimensions, and units of analysis of war, were used to determine the nature of historical trends over time. The results are not perfectly congruent across all of these indicators, but some overall patterns emerge. In general, interstate war involving the Great Powers has been diminishing over time. There has been a strong decline in the frequency of war and particularly in the frequency of Great Power war. The amount of war under way in any given year has also been declining, for all dimensions. The yearly amount of war has been decreasing in nearly every respect, increasing only in that the bloodiest years are getting bloodier—absolutely, as a proportion of the population, and for each Great Power. The patterns for the characteristics of the individual wars are somewhat different. Interstate wars involving the Powers have become considerably shorter, slightly lower in magnitude, much greater in concentration, and unchanged in the number of Powers involved and in severity and intensity. The most severe wars, however, are becoming more severe. In contrast to the general decline of war in most respects, Great Power wars are becoming much less frequent, but those that do occur are much greater in extent, severity, intensity, and concentration, somewhat greater in magnitude, and unchanged in duration.[19]

Cyclical Trends

To this point the concern has been with increasing or decreasing trends in war over time. It is possible that superimposed upon these secular trends may be cyclical fluctuations. The possibility of periodicity in war is an interesting descriptive question in its own right. It is also of some relevance for substantive theoretical considerations. Many hypotheses regarding the causes or consequences of war or systemic transformation involve cyclical variables and imply cyclical trends in war, so that the existence or nonexistence of cyclical trends has an important bearing on the validity of these hypotheses. Some of these hypotheses are related to the phenomenon of war contagion and will be discussed in the following chapter. The concern here is with the question of the actual existence of cyclical trends and with empirical research dealing with it.

There have been a number of attempts to determine empirically the existence or absence of any cyclical trends in war. It is consistently found that the outbreak of war is random rather than contagious, regardless of whether we look at short-term contagion or long-term periodicity. Sorokin finds "no regular periodicity, no uniform rhythm, no universal uniformity" in war during the ancient Greek system or in the European system. He finds little more than a "trendless shifting in the rhythm and in the number of recurring internecine wars." Wright's data are somewhat ambiguous. He claims to see fluctuations of war and peace every fifty years of modern civilization. Denton and Warren Phillips, using Wright's data, find that before 1680 there was a peak in the amount of war (per five-year period) every twenty years.

Since 1680 the period of each cycle has been about thirty years. Richardson, however, finds no periodicity in Wright's data over the last five centuries. Singer and Small find no evidence of periodicity (of forty years or less) in either the frequency or magnitude of international war since 1815. Singer and Cusack confirm this finding: "Clearly, the evidence does not support the cyclical view; the intervals are too irregular, and the occurrence of war entries have been indifferent to the passage of time since the prior war. Moreover, when we control for the outcome of the prior war or its duration or its fatality level, we still find that the probability of the next war entry is basically unrelated to the passage of time." Similarly, Sorokin concludes: "History seems to be neither as monotonous and uninventive as the partisans of the strict periodicities and 'iron laws' and 'universal uniformities' think; nor so dull and mechanical as an engine, making the same number of revolutions in a unit of time. It repeats its 'themes' but almost always with new variations. In this sense it is ever new, and ever old, so far as the ups and downs are repeated. So much for periodicity, rhythms, and uniformity."[20]

The absence of empirical support in the literature for hypotheses of cyclical trends in war is confirmed by a visual inspection of the scattergrams presented earlier in this chapter. There are no hints of any cyclical patterns in either the occurrence of war or in any of its other dimensions. For each of the war indicators, the highest peaks in war as well as the periods of no war appear to be scattered at random.

It would be possible, of course, to test for cyclical trends statistically. The statistical tests required for this purpose, however, are very complex. Singer and Small, for example, apply spectral analysis, which is based on a Fourier transform of the autocovariance function.[21] In the absence of any hints of the existence of cyclical trends either in the scattergrams or in earlier studies, however, it is very unlikely that sophisticated statistical techniques could uncover any patterns that are sufficiently strong to have any substantive significance. For this reason these tests are not applied here. This tentative finding of the absence of cyclical trends in war will draw further support in the following chapter, for the analysis of short-term contagion in war has direct implications for the existence of short-term cyclical trends.

Comparison of Historical Periods

An examination of the relative amounts of war in various historical eras is useful for several reasons. It will permit an assessment of the historical validity of many of the conventional wisdoms concerning this question. It will also provide empirical evidence bearing on some macrohistorical theories of conflict or systemic transformation. Finally, this analysis is relevant to our earlier discussion of linear trends in war and can be interpreted as an alternative means of identifying those trends.

The basis for comparison of these different historical periods is simply the average amount of war for each period, as measured by the following indicators: (1) percentage of years of war under way; (2) average yearly amount of war, measured in frequency, duration, extent, magnitude, severity, and concentration; and (3) the characteristics of the average war, measured in median duration, extent, magnitude, severity, and concentration. Measures of the average amount of Great Power war will also be considered. The significance of the differences between centuries will be evaluated with respect to the estimated measurement error in each indicator. The measurement error ranges from 5-10 percent for the frequency and extent of war to 10-15 percent for the duration and magnitude of war and 25-30 percent for the fatality-based indicators. Differences less than this measurement error will not be treated as substantively significant.

First, the relative amount of war in each of the last five centuries is compared. The percentage of years of war, average yearly amounts of war, and characteristics of the typical (median) war for each of the centuries are given in Table 6.4. The rankings of the centuries along each war indicator can be computed, and the average rank of each century over all indicators is given at the bottom of Table 6.4 (with

Table 6.4. Comparison of the Centuries by Amount of War

Indicator	Century 16th	17th	18th	19th	20th
Years war under way	95%	94%	78%	40%	53%
	Average Yearly Amount of War				
Frequency	.34	.29	.17	.20	.20
Duration	1.60	1.7	1.0	.38	.45
Extent	.68	.71	.49	.36	.49
Magnitude	3.20	4.0	3.0	.93	1.3
Severity	9400	40000	38000	26000	290000
Concentration	2900	10000	13000	28000	220000
	Average War (Median)				
Duration	3.1	4.0	4.8	.95	1.4
Extent	2.0	1.9	2.2	1.4	1.3
Magnitude	7.2	6.0	8.0	1.0	1.4
Severity	18000	15000	34000	5600	16000
Concentration	3000	3000	4400	4000	23000
Average rank[a]	2.71	2.42	2.46	4.29	3.12

[a] Based on the mean rank order of each century across all indicators, 1.0 being the most warlike.

1.0 being the most warlike).[22] These average rankings provide a rough indicator of the relative amount of war in each century. They should be interpreted with caution, however, for they are based on the simplifying but not fully acceptable assumption that each of the twelve indicators is equally important as a measure of war.

As expected on the basis of the earlier analysis of the relationships among the various dimensions of war, the rankings of the centuries according to the amount of war vary with the particular war indicator used as the basis for comparison. Some generalizations can be made, however. First, the nineteenth century is without question the most peaceful; for only one of the twelve indicators—the average yearly concentration of war—was this century more warlike than the average. Second, the twentieth century is particularly warlike only in the fatality-based indices. The average yearly severity and concentration of war in the twentieth century are dramatically higher than in earlier times (although the severity of the typical war in the twentieth century is just about average). In all other respects, however, the twentieth century ranks below average. War has been under way about half the time, compared to 95 percent of the time in the sixteenth and seventeenth centuries and nearly 80 percent of the time in the eighteenth century; only the nineteenth century ranks lower, with war under way 40 percent of the time.

The eighteenth century was the least war-prone with regard to frequency, yet the wars that did occur were generally more serious than the typical wars of other centuries. This finding is precisely the opposite of the hypothesis that eighteenth-century wars were frequent but limited in nature. In addition, the number of years of war under way and the average yearly amount of war in the eighteenth century were just about average.

The greatest continuity in war is to be found in the sixteenth and seventeenth centuries, which are similar in nearly all of the war indicators, yet different from later periods. Of all the centuries, these two were the most warlike in terms of the proportion of years of war under way (95 percent), the frequency of war (nearly one every three years), and the average yearly duration, extent, and magnitude of war. The average yearly severity and concentration were relatively low, however (particularly in the sixteenth century), and the typical war during these periods was about average in most respects (though very low in concentration). To the extent that the average overall rankings reflect (though imperfectly) some measure of the relative amount of war, the sixteenth, seventeenth, and eighteenth centuries were considerably more warlike than the twentieth and particularly the nineteenth centuries, with the sixteenth century being slightly more belligerent than the two centuries that followed. These patterns confirm the general trend discovered earlier toward the diminishing level of war in the system over time.

These conclusions refer to interstate war involving the Great Pow-

Table 6.5. Comparison of the Centuries by Amount of Great Power War

	Century				
Indicator	16th	17th	18th	19th	20th
Years GP war under way	89%	88%	64%	24%	25%
	Average Yearly Amount of War				
Frequency	.26	.17	.10	.05	.07
Duration	1.4	1.0	.77	.15	.22
Extent	.58	.59	.40	.16	.35
Magnitude	2.9	3.2	2.7	.69	1.1
Severity	8800	38000	35000	23000	290000
Concentration	3000	12000	13000	33000	260000
	Average War (Median)				
Duration	3.2	5.2	6.5	.6	3.1
Extent	2.1	3.1	4.0	2.8	5.0
Magnitude	8.2	13	21	3.0	13
Severity	24000	110000	68000	180000	960000
Concentration	3000	6200	3200	50000	85000
Average rank[a]	3.25	2.42	2.75	3.96	2.62

[a] Based on the mean rank order of each century across all indicators, 1.0 being the most warlike.

ers. The patterns for Great Power wars are somewhat different, as seen in Table 6.5. The nineteenth century was still the most peaceful, and, except for the twentieth century, there has been a general decline in the average yearly frequency, duration, extent, and magnitude of Great Power war and proportion of years with war under way. The precipitous drop in the number of years with war under way in the nineteenth and twentieth centuries (as well as the mild decline in the eighteenth century) is particularly noticeable. Overall, however, the twentieth century appears relatively more warlike than it did in the earlier analysis of interstate war involving the Powers, in the sense that the relatively few Great Power wars that did occur were typically more serious than those in earlier centuries. The sixteenth century, on the other hand, appears more peaceful relative to other centuries than in the earlier analysis. It ranks first in frequency of Great Power wars, but these wars were typically rather limited. This finding may not be very meaningful, however, in the context of hypotheses relating to limited war. The concept of limited war suggests that the empirical domain not be restricted to Great Power wars, as is done here. For this reason, interstate war involving the Great Powers (Table 6.4) is generally a better approximation of the total amount of war in the system.

Some will object to the preceding analysis, however, and argue that a periodization of the centuries based strictly on time is artificial and that a more substantively based periodization would be more meaningful. Such a periodization, following the conventions of historians, would exclude the Napoleonic Wars from the nineteenth century and the French Revolutionary Wars, Spanish Succession, and Second Northern Wars from the eighteenth century.[23] The latter two are generally included in an "extended" seventeenth century, while the French Revolutionary and Napoleonic Wars are often excluded altogether. This exclusion raises serious questions regarding the validity of such a periodization, but because it is conventional the results are presented in Table 6.6.

It is clear that of the modified centuries the nineteenth was still by far the most peaceful, ranking above fourth on only one war indicator (yearly concentration). The seventeenth century was the most warlike, ranking lower than average only on the concentration indicator. The sixteenth century is characterized by below-average severity and concentration of war, but it ranks high on most of the other indicators. Generally less warlike than the sixteenth century are the twentieth and (attenuated) eighteenth centuries. War in the modified eighteenth century was relatively infrequent (tied for last with the nineteenth century) and only average in both the characteristics of the typical war and the average yearly amount of war. The common argument that eighteenth-century wars were frequent but limited is still contradicted.

These findings have bearing on some common assumptions and

Table 6.6. Comparison of Modified Centuries by Amount or War

Indicator	Period 1500–1599	1600–1713	1714–1789	1816–1899	1900–1975
Years war under way	95%	95%	71%	29%	53%
	Average Yearly Amount of War				
Frequency	.34	.27	.18	.18	.20
Duration	1.6	1.8	.76	.18	.45
Extent	.68	.69	.47	.30	.49
Magnitude	3.2	4.3	2.2	.28	1.3
Severity	9400	47000	24000	7600	290000
Concentration	2900	11000	11000	27000	220000
	Average War (Median)				
Duration	3.1	4.2	3.5	.7	1.4
Extent	2.0	2.0	2.0	1.4	1.3
Magnitude	7.2	6.3	6.3	1.0	1.4
Severity	18000	22000	16000	5600	16000
Concentration	3000	3000	3500	2100	23000
Average rank[a]	2.3	1.9	3.0	4.6	3.0

[a] Based on the mean rank order of each century across all indicators, 1.0 being the most warlike.

practices in the theoretical and empirical literature on international conflict. First, the patterns of warfare involving the Great Powers in the sixteenth, seventeenth, and eighteenth centuries were fundamentally similar. No significant turning point in the history of warfare occurred at the mid-seventeenth century, as some have suggested. This conclusion supports my earlier argument that the Treaty of Westphalia was merely a formal ratification of a system that had been operating for over a century, that the diplomacy and war behavior of the Powers did not change after Westphalia, and that there is no compelling reason to exclude the pre-Westphalia period from a study of international war involving the Great Powers.

These findings also have certain implications for the common practice in contemporary empirical research to distinguish between the nineteenth and twentieth centuries. Most of the studies associated with the Correlates of War Project conduct separate analyses for these centuries and often find significant differences in substantive relationships involving war. It has repeatedly been demonstrated, for example, that the alliance-war relationship was negative in the nineteenth century but positive in the twentieth century.[24] Singer argues more generally that the findings of the Correlates of War project "suggest rather strongly that (a) today's world *is* different from that of the nineteenth century; but (b) the most discernible changes occurred around the turn of the century and not with World War I or II or [the nuclear era]."[25]

Although the differences between the nineteenth and twentieth centuries cannot be denied, it would be wrong to infer that the beginning of the twentieth century marks a new era in warfare. Rather, the nineteenth century should be viewed as an anomaly in an otherwise continuous pattern of warfare over the last five centuries. By almost any indicator the nineteenth century was unquestionably the most peaceful of the modern period. The twentieth century, though characterized by a high severity and concentration of war and low frequency of Great Power war, is generally comparable to the earlier centuries in most other respects. According to the key indicators used here, the similarities between twentieth-century war involving the Great Powers and sixteenth-to-eighteenth-century warfare are more profound than their differences. It does not necessarily follow that the causes (or consequences) of twentieth-century war are similar to those of earlier centuries, but that possibility cannot be excluded. These findings suggest that the assumed irrelevance of pre-nineteenth-century warfare for an understanding of present and future war involving the Great Powers may be seriously exaggerated.

Interpretation of Historical Trends

The description of historical trends is of course easier than their explanation. To attempt to explain the observed trends in all of the indicators of different levels and dimensions of war would be impractical. The focus here is on what are undeniably among the most important—the trends in Great Power war. It has been found that during the last five hundred years Great Power wars have been rapidly diminishing in frequency but increasing in extent, severity, intensity, concentration, and (to a certain degree) magnitude. How can these trends be explained?

Before it could be fully accepted any explanation would have to be tested against the historical evidence, which would require the operationalization and measurement of the explanatory variables (and plausible control variables as well) in as systematic a manner as has been done with the dependent variable. This is an enormous task lying far beyond the scope of this study. Having rigorously and systematically described longitudinal trends in Great Power wars, here I can only hypothesize about their theoretical explanations by identifying the important variables and suggesting plausible theoretical linkages.

Of all the trends, perhaps most puzzling is the relatively unchanging duration of Great Power war. We might have expected that improvements in communications and logistics would have increased the speed of military operations on the battlefield and that innovations in military technology and the increasing destructiveness of military conflict would have increased the costs of war. Both would presumably force an earlier termination of the hostilities. Obviously, there are other variables that have counteracted this tendency.[26] While the costs of war have become much greater, the gradual industrialization of basically agricultural societies has increased their economic capacity to sustain a war and accept the costs. We might also hypothesize that, in spite of the enormous changes in military technology, the defense has managed to keep up with the offense, so that it takes equally long to obtain a decisive advantage on the battlefield.[27] Finally, the increasing organizational momentum and incrementalism generated by a larger and more firmly entrenched bureaucracy, and the increasing political insecurity of elites (deriving from the decline of dynastic legitimacy) in conjunction with increasing nationalist pressures, both make it ever more difficult to withdraw from a costly but inconclusive war.[28]

An ever-increasing number (and proportion) of Great Powers have been participating in these wars. We might hypothesize that this derives in part from the increasing interdependence of the modern Great Power security system. As the Great Powers evolved from dynastic to nation-states their interests, as well as their capabilities to project power in defense of these interests, tended to expand, and their commercial relationships became closer. The Great Powers came increasingly to perceive their own strategic and economic interests as dependent on power relationships in the system as a whole and were increasingly likely to intervene in external wars to maintain a balance of power or their own influence and prestige. Hence the extent (and also the magnitude) of Great Power war has increased over time.[29]

Let us now consider the increasing destructiveness of war as measured by severity, intensity, and concentration. The most obvious explanation, of course, is technological: the major changes not only in the destructive power of weapons but also in their range, accuracy, volume of fire, mobility, and penetrability, and the speed and efficiency of military transport and communications systems. In addition, there has been an increasing economic capacity to produce a larger quantity of weapons and support systems. Much of the increased capacity for violence over the past centuries can be traced to the changes in production and transport generated by the industrial revolution; the mechanization of war at the beginning of the twentieth century;[30] the development of airpower a few decades later; and (in potential for future destruction) the development of nuclear weapons and global delivery systems by the second half of this century.

Technological innovation alone, however, cannot fully explain the increasing destructiveness of Great Power wars in the last five centuries. Several interrelated political, socioeconomic, and cultural factors have also contributed to the gradual emergence of total war. Let us briefly consider these in approximate chronological sequence.[31] First was the increasing rationalization of military power under the state, beginning in the late fifteenth century and intensifying after the legal codification of the existing sovereign state system at Westphalia.[32] The wars for the personal honor, vengeance, and enrichment of kings and nobles in the Middle Ages (which may have contributed to their frequent but limited nature) were increasingly replaced by the "rational" use of force as an efficient instrument of policy for the achievement of political objectives, first by dynastic/territorial political systems and ultimately by nation-states. The seriousness of the wars grew proportionally with the expansion of these political objectives, from personal gain, to the territorial aggrandizement of the state, to the national ambitions of an entire people.

Reinforcing the rational use of force was the increasing centralization of political power within the state. Feudal interests were gradually subordinated to centralized state authority in the early sixteenth century, and the centralization of power intensified in the late seventeenth century with the development of an administrative and financial system capable of supporting a military establishment and providing the logistical basis for an expanded military effort.[33]

Contributing further to the power of states and their ability to make war was the commercialization of war beginning in the early seventeenth century. The relationship between the state and the commercial classes became increasingly symbiotic. Commerce generated the wealth necessary to sustain war,[34] and war in turn became a means of expanding commerce. In the mercantilist conception, commerce was a continuation of war (with an admixture of other means) and war was a continuation of commerce.[35] The merchants' enthusiasm for war diminished somewhat as the mercantilist system was replaced by free trade in the late eighteenth century, but the link was not broken, and subsequent economic progress contributed further to the state's capacity for war.

This period also marked the emerging popularization of war: the rise of nationalism and popular ideology, the institution of conscripted manpower, and the creation of the "nation in arms."[36] Each of these phenomena contributed to the enhancement of the military power of the state.

The state's ability to use these expanding resources was furthered by the professionalization of military power in the late nineteenth century—the development of a peacetime military establishment directed by a new professional military elite that was independent of the aristocracy, headed by a general staff system, run according to new principles of scientific management, and supported by a system of military academies.[37] These developments not only increased the efficiency of the conduct of war. They also enhanced the legitimacy of the military profession and contributed to the trends toward militarism, defined by the acceptance of the values of the military subculture as the dominant values of society.[38] At the same time, the earlier moral and cultural restraints on war associated with the Christian and humanist traditions were gradually eroded by the materialism and individualism of industrial society.[39]

These trends culminated in World War II with what Millis calls the scientific revolution in war: the harnessing, for the first time, of the entire scientific, engineering, and technological capacities of the nation directly for the conduct of the war.[40] Mobilization of the intellectual as well as material and social resources of the nation for the purposes of enhancing military power continues now in peacetime. These political, social, and cultural developments, in conjunction with technological innovation, have been largely responsible for the increasing destructiveness of war.

Let us consider some plausible explanations for the declining frequency of Great Power war. It can generally be argued that the potential benefits of Great Power war have not kept up with their rising human and economic costs. Warfare has resulted in enormous increases in casualties and human suffering, the physical destruction of industrial infrastructure, and opportunity costs for society deriving from increasing costs of weapons systems, manpower, and logistics. The greater tendency toward external intervention in Great Power war (described above) further raises the costs or reduces the potential benefits from war, whether by adding the military burden of an additional enemy or by necessitating the sharing of the gains with an ally. The declining legitimacy of Great Power war has increased its diplomatic and domestic political costs. Finally, the changing bases of national power and the declining value of territorial conquest have reduced the potential benefits of Great Power war,[41] as has the increasing congruence between state and ethnic boundaries (at least for the Great Powers). These increasing costs of Great Power war relative to its perceived benefits have reduced its utility as a rational instrument of state policy and largely account for its declining frequency.[42]

These statements should be interpreted as hypotheses to be tested rather than empirically confirmed theoretical generalizations. The existing literature on the evolution of war, much of which has been cited earlier in this study, provides an ample reservoir of information from which data can be extracted to test these hypotheses. Such a task, however, would involve very difficult analytical and methodological problems.

7

War Contagion

The last two chapters have provided a quantitative description of the nature of international war involving the Great Powers and an analysis of historical trends in war over the past five centuries. The theoretical question to be examined in this chapter is whether the occurrence of one war has any impact on subsequent war. Is international war involving the Great Powers characterized by diffusion over time and space, much like the epidemiological phenomenon of the spread of contagious disease? Does war beget war, inhibit war, or have no impact on subsequent war? This question has attracted considerable attention in the literature on international conflict.

Conceptualization of War Contagion

Several theoretical arguments have been advanced in support of the view that war begets war. (1) The victorious state may be stimulated by its success and its newly acquired power and seek to further its gains (revolutionary France). (2) The defeated state may move to recover its losses from an earlier war (Austria after the Silesian Wars) or overturn a punitive peace settlement (Germany after Versailles). (3) A dispute over the division of the spoils of war may turn the victorious states against one another (the Second Balkan War). (4) The expansion of an ongoing war by the use of military force against nonbelligerents may be perceived as necessary for victory or the achievement of other national objectives (the Japanese attack against Pearl Harbor as an expansion of the Sino-Japanese War). Wars also frequently expand because of the (5) intervention of third states to defend an ally, protect their own interests, maintain the existing balance of power, or perhaps demonstrate their own credibility (World War I). Similarly, (6) these nonbelligerents may perceive that their rivals have been militarily weakened or diplomatically isolated by war and decide to exploit this opportunity and intervene militarily (the Italian intervention in the Austro-Prussian War). (7) Seeing that third states are engaged in a war that precludes their intervention elsewhere, a state may take that opportunity to advance its interests by force in another country (the French invasion of Mexico in 1862).

There are also a number of theoretical arguments why war, rather than begetting war, should reduce the likelihood of subsequent war. (8) War may deplete a nation's resources and leave it incapable of fighting another war. (9) War, particularly if unsuccessful, may generate the belief that another war should not be undertaken unless the likelihood of victory is nearly certain. (10) War, particularly if unsuccessful, may induce a change in the political elite and bring to power those committed to a more peaceful policy. Or, (11) war, especially if it is long and destructive, may generate a general revulsion against violence and an immunity against subsequent war until the memory of war gradually fades—the well-known war-weariness hypothesis. Richardson, for example, argues that "a long and severe bout of fighting confers immunity on most of those who have experienced it."[1] It is more difficult to imagine how (12) war-weariness might inhibit subsequent war by others, though there may be some historical cases (the systemic effects of U.S. use of the atomic bomb). A more likely form of negative contagion is (13) a war between states A and B rendering the subsequent use of force by state C unnecessary against the weakened loser and too risky against the strengthened winner.

Toynbee also speaks of war-weariness and the resulting cycles of war and peace. He suggests, however, that these cycles can be better explained as manifestations of the underlying dynamics of the international system. A bid for world domination evokes a defensive coalition of all other Great Powers and a "General War" to maintain the balance of power. The result is the defeat of the "arch-aggressor" and a "breathing-space" of peace. Such a peace is uneasy, transient, and improvised, for the unsettled issues over which the general war was fought are not yet capable of resolution. The result is a burst of short and relatively mild wars ("Supplemental Wars"), which resolve the outstanding issues and generate a tranquil and lasting "General Peace." Ultimately the gradual building of new forces explodes into a new episode of general war as a new Power seeks domination, and the cycle begins anew, approximately once every century.[2]

There are other cyclical theories of war. Closely related to Toynbee's theory is Modelski's "long cycle" of global politics and wars, driven by the struggle for world leadership based on military power of global reach. Doran and Parsons speak of a cycle of national power and wars governed by internal capability changes and political dynamics rather than international interactions.[3] Other cyclical theories are based on business cycles, American isolationism and interventionism, and even astrological phenomena.[4] Not all of these cyclical theories should be conceptualized as war contagion, however, a point to which I will return.

It is clear that the occurrence of war may affect the likelihood of subsequent war in a variety of ways that involve different causal linkages operating at different levels of analysis and over different periods of time. First, a state's participation in war may lead to subsequent war behavior by that same actor, as suggested in arguments 1-4 above. This is what William W. Davis, George T. Duncan, and Randolph M. Siverson call "addiction" and Benjamin A. Most and Harvey Starr call "positive reinforcement." Alternatively, war behavior by one dyad may increase the likelihood of war involvement by other actors (arguments 5-7 above). This contagion process involves new actors and is analytically distinct from addiction. It is referred to as "infection" or "positive spatial diffusion."[5] A further analytic distinction between two kinds of infectious contagion which is not emphasized in the literature is the intervention by external actors in an ongoing war and their initiation of a new war. This involves the systemic level of analysis and the difficult question of how a single war is to be defined, a point to which I will return. Contagion can also be negative. War participation by one actor may reduce the likelihood of subsequent war behavior by the same actor (arguments

8-11), which Most and Starr call "negative reinforcement." Or, war behavior by some may reduce the likelihood of subsequent war behavior of others (arguments 12-13), referred to as "negative spatial diffusion."[6]

The cyclical theories mentioned above are more difficult to fit into neat analytical categories. The phenomenon of long-term periodicity or cyclical fluctuations in war is generally thought of as distinct from contagion and involving different causal linkages, but this distinction has not been adequately conceptualized.[7] Davis, Duncan, and Siverson differentiate between contagion and heterogeneity and appear to classify most cyclical theories of war as involving time-heterogeneous processes. They see the probability of war as a function of time: "The evolution of the process may be governed by different rules at different times." This analytical distinction is valid if the cyclical fluctuations in war are driven by factors themselves generated independently of war (such as climatological or seasonal changes). Yet many of the factors generating fluctuations in war behavior are affected by previous war, and in this case the distinction between contagion and heterogeneity begins to blur. Davis, Duncan, and Siverson recognize that "warfare changes the factors which determine the future incidence of warfare" and that these other sources of time heterogeneity are "not so easily handled."[8] Thus contagion and heterogeneity are very difficult to distinguish empirically.[9] It appears that the implicit criterion most often used to distinguish between war contagion and cyclical theories of war is time. Contagion refers to relatively short-term causal effects (less than five or ten years at the most), while most cyclical theories posit wavelengths of at least twenty years. This study is restricted to the analysis of short-term war contagion rather than long-term periodicity, which was examined in the previous chapter.

It was noted in the previous chapter that most empirical studies of short-term war contagion as well as long-term periodicity have concluded that the outbreak of war is random rather than contagious.[10] Evidence has been accumulating, however, that the expansion of war is characterized by contagion. That is, a war already under way may expand by drawing in external actors through an infectious process.

Davis, Duncan, and Siverson focus on the dyad rather than the nation as the unit of analysis and conclude that the outbreak of dyadic war over the 1815–1965 period follows an infectious contagion model. Infection is enhanced by geographical contiguity, as Richardson and Starr and Most have demonstrated.[11] Alliances also play a key role in the infection process, as Siverson and Joel King find. Certain characteristics of alliances are particularly conducive to contagion.[12]

The weakest aspect of the empirical literature on war contagion is the analysis of short-term contagion in the outbreak (as opposed to expansion) of war. These analyses are usually the by-products of longer-term periodicity studies and lack the intensive focus on the short term that is necessary to uncover important but subtle relationships. These studies have also failed to answer other questions. First, are the findings for the 1815-1965 period based on the Singer-Small data also valid for earlier historical eras? The few studies for earlier periods are of questionable validity because of the limitations of existing data. Second, is the absence of contagion or periodicity also valid for the wars of the Great Powers? Many contagion studies fail to distinguish between wars involving secondary states and those involving the Great Powers. Given the central role of the Powers in international politics, it is important to know whether their wars are contagious. Finally, are some kinds of wars more contagious than others and does the seriousness of a war or series of wars have any impact on its contagious effects? Most of the contagion and periodicity studies focus on the question of whether the outbreak of one war leads to another and fail to examine the possible effects of other dimensions.

For these reasons the focus here is on the question of short-term contagion in the outbreak of war involving the Great Powers over an extended historical period, with particular attention to the question of whether war might be affected by the nature or seriousness as well as the occurrence of previous wars. Hypotheses suggesting that civil, imperial, or small power wars may affect the likelihood of wars involving the Great Powers (or vice versa), while not unimportant, cannot be tested here with the available data.

This study is conducted at the systemic level. Some contagion hypotheses, such as social-psychological addiction hypotheses, are most appropriate at the national or dyadic level, whereas others are appropriate at the systemic level. Given the interdependence of the Great Powers with respect to security issues, it is reasonable to ask whether the likelihood of interstate war anywhere in the Great Power system is affected by previous war in the system (as statesmen continuously claim), regardless of which Powers participate. To answer the question of whether war is contagious at the systemic level it is not necessary to make the distinction between addictive and infectious contagion. Furthermore, given the equal plausibility of the various arguments for positive and negative contagion presented earlier, this study is exploratory in purpose, in an attempt to determine the net contagion effects of these diverse causal linkages. The descriptive question of whether or not contagion exists is important in itself.

My inquiry is guided by the following theoretical questions, derived from the contagion literature and representing a series of refinements of the more general question of whether war begets war. First, is the outbreak of war generally followed by the outbreak of subsequent wars, either while the first is still in progress or soon after its termination? Do the various dimensions of the first war have any impact on the subsequent outbreak of war? Are particularly severe wars more likely to be followed by relatively infrequent wars or by a prolonged period of peace, as the war-weariness hypothesis might suggest? Do history's most destructive wars have a unique impact on subsequent war? Second, is there any relationship between the frequency of war in one period and the frequency of war in the following period? Third, are any of the key measures of the amount of war in one period related to the incidence of subsequent war? Which dimensions of war, if any, have the greatest contagion effects? Is the outbreak of war affected more by the number of earlier wars or by their destructiveness? Does the total amount of war in one period, measured by a combination of war indicators, have any impact on war in the subsequent period?

The Contagion of Individual Wars

The first question concerns the possible contagion of individual wars. One hypothesis is that the occurrence of war increases the probability of the outbreak of another war while the first is still in progress. The empirical testing of this hypothesis is more difficult than would first appear. The most serious problem concerns the aggregation or disaggregation of simultaneous wars, treated in Chapter 3. If the second war is defined as an extension of the first rather than as a separate war, the possibility of contagion is defined away. This problem can be avoided by focusing on the dyad rather than the war as the unit of analysis (as Davis, Duncan, and Siverson and Siverson and King have done), but the systemic-level orientation followed here requires focusing on the war as the unit of analysis. In Chapter 2 considerable attention was given to the problems involving the aggregation of war —and to the lack of serious attention to these problems in the literature. The coding rules used in this compilation of war data involve the aggregation of wars unless there are compelling reasons to do otherwise. This tendency not to identify "new" conflicts as separate wars generates a bias in favor of the null hypothesis of no contagion. Since the most difficult cases involve the aggregation of simultaneous wars rather than the temporal aggregation of sequential wars, the bias noted above is strongest with respect to the infectious contagion of an ongoing war (spatial diffusion) and weakest for the contagion of a war that has already ended.

A second problem involves the questions of causality and spuriousness. If wars are frequently followed by other wars, is this empirical correlation the result of the causal effect of the first war or are both wars caused independently by the same antecedent variables? Especially if the systemic causes of war dominate, two temporally proximate wars may have the same set of causes without the first war having any causal impact on the second. This problem is related to the earlier discussion of the contagion/heterogeneity distinction. It is particularly serious because it involves the possibility of a systematic bias that cannot be assumed to be mitigated by the randomization of extraneous variables over the lengthy temporal domain of the study. No answer is provided here, for the empirical resolution of the problem would require a fully operational theory of the causes of war and the measurement of all relevant variables over the five-century span of the modern system.

The hypothesis is tested by comparing the average frequency of war when war is under way with the average frequency of war over the entire span of the system, regardless of whether war is under way. The yearly average number of wars occurring while another is under way is .37, compared to .25 wars per year over the period as a whole. This difference indicates a slight tendency for wars to occur while another is under way, but it is not statistically significant at the conventional .05 level (t-test, $p = .10$).[13] Similarly, wars are somewhat more likely to occur while Great Power wars are under way (.34 wars per year) than at other times (.25 wars per year), but this is not statistically significant ($p = .15$). The average frequency of Great Power war is .13 wars per year, but increases to .17 wars per year while another war is under way ($p = .15$) and .21 wars per year while a Great Power war is under way ($p = .07$). There may be a slight tendency, therefore, for the likelihood of war to increase while another war is under way, particularly for Great Power wars. The p-values fall slightly outside the critical range for statistical significance, but this is outweighed by the strong bias toward the null hypothesis noted earlier.[14] This conclusion is consistent with the finding by Davis, Duncan, and Siverson of positive contagion in the expansion of war.

Does this possible contagious effect also hold true after the first war has ended, as many hypotheses suggest? Because my concern is short-term contagion, the three years following the termination of war are examined. The average yearly number of wars occurring in the three-year period following war is .25 (or .26 following Great Power war), compared to .25 wars per year overall. The incidence of Great Power wars during these periods is .16 per year, only slightly greater than their overall average of .13. Neither of these differences is statistically significant.[15] We can conclude that the likelihood of war does not increase during the period immediately following the termination of a previous war.

The next question that arises is whether the incidence of war is affected by the characteristics of the war that is under way. This set of relationships is best measured by a simple correlation analysis involving each of the war indicators and various measures of the incidence of subsequent war: the number of wars occurring within three years after the termination of war, the number of Great Power wars during and immediately after war, the time elapsed until the outbreak of the next war and the next Great Power war, and similar measures of the number of wars following a Great Power war. The resulting product-moment correlations are presented in Table 7.1.[16]

The results in Table 7.1 demonstrate the absence of any meaningful relationship between the seriousness of a given war and the outbreak of subsequent war. None of the correlations exceeds .3, indicating that no indicator of war can account for 10 percent of the variance in any measure of the incidence of subsequent war. Most of the correlations involving the number of wars are negative, indicating that the more serious wars are followed by a slightly lower incidence of war, but these correlations are too small to be meaningful. A few are statistically signficant but the absence of any consistent pattern lessens their substantive significance. Although correlations are weak their general direction runs contrary to the popular war-weariness hypothesis that the most destructive wars are followed by the longest periods of peace. First, the elapsed time indicator is inversely related to most of the war indicators, suggesting that more serious wars are followed by a shorter period of time until the next war. Second, the severity of war, which is generally regarded as the best measure of its destructiveness, has the weakest associations with subsequent war. All of these findings also hold for the contagion of Great Power wars. We can conclude that none of the attributes of war has any significant impact on the number of wars occurring during or immediately after that war or on the length of the period until the next war.

Table 7.1. Correlation (r) between War Indicators and Measures of Subsequent War

Indicators of Subsequent War ($W_{t+1,i}$)	War Indicators ($W_{t,j}$) Dur	Ext	Mag	Sev	Con
Yearly number of new wars during a war	−.10	−.10	−.11	−.04	.04
Yearly number of wars within 3 years	.04	−.13	−.04	−.11	−.17*
Yearly number GP wars during a war	−.04	−.09	−.11	−.06	−.08
Yearly number GP wars within 3 years	.04	−.16*	−.07	−.10	−.17*
Elapsed time to next war	−.29*	−.10	−.22*	−.08	.10
Time to next GP war	−.20*	−.03	−.10	.00	.18*

*Denotes statistical significance at the .05 level.

Some would argue, however, that the war-weariness hypothesis does not imply a linear relationship between the seriousness of a war and the peacefulness of the following period but rather a threshold effect—once the seriousness of a war reaches a certain level, war-weariness and therefore a period of relative peace are induced. Such effects should be reflected in the linear correlation method applied earlier, but a more direct and perhaps better test of this hypothesis can be performed by examining the consequences of general wars involving nearly all the Great Powers and high casualties (as defined in Chapter 3). For each of these general wars, the number of wars and number of Great Power wars occurring within ten years after its termination and the length of time to the next war and the next Great Power war are determined. The averages of these summary measures can then be compared with those for the typical ten-year period over the entire span of the system and with the mean duration of peace following the average war in the system to determine the relative peacefulness of the periods following general wars.[17]

The results of this analysis are as follows. The average number of wars in the ten-year period immediately following the end of a general war is 2.0 wars and 1.3 Great Power wars, compared to the 2.5 wars and 1.3 Great Power wars during the average ten-year period over the last five centuries. These differences are not statistically significant, suggesting that, contrary to the hypothesis, war is no more or less likely to occur in periods following general wars than in any other period.

This finding is confirmed by the use of another method based on a Poisson probability model. A Poisson process describes the number of events per unit of time generated from a random, independent, stationary, stochastic process. If the distribution of wars deviates from a Poisson distribution, it can be concluded that wars are not distributed randomly and that they are not independent (that is, the occurrence of one war in some way alters the likelihood of subsequent wars). If, on the other hand, the distribution of wars does fit a Poisson, then we cannot reject the null hypotheses that the wars are distributed randomly and that they are independent.

More technically, if events are generated randomly, the number of periods in which x events occur is given by

$$Ne^{-\lambda} \lambda^k / k!$$

where N is the total number of observations (for example, 96 five-year periods) and λ is the average number of events per period (119 wars/96 periods = 1.24). The actual number of periods characterized by k wars (where $k = 0, 1, 2, \ldots$) can be computed from the data. The observed and theoretical distributions can then be compared by a chi-square goodness-of-fit test.[18]

If wars occur randomly (independently of general wars), the number of ten-year periods containing zero wars, one war, and so on can be determined by a Poisson probability model and compared with the observed distribution by a chi-square test. It is found that the periods following general wars are no different with regard to the frequency of interstate war or Great Power war than would be expected from a purely random distribution of wars ($p = .32$ and .67, respectively). Also, the median elapsed time between the end of a general war and the incidence of another war (or Great Power war) is five years, compared to an average of 1.8 years between the end of one war and the beginning of the next and 6.1 years until the next Great Power war. Thus after general wars there are on average a few extra years of peace until the outbreak of a new war but a slightly shorter period until the outbreak of the next Great Power war, as compared with the average periods following interstate wars involving the Powers. The war-weariness hypothesis would have predicted, if anything, the opposite—a longer delay before a Great Power war, with perhaps a few minor wars in the interim. The thrust of this evidence, then, is contrary to the war-weariness hypothesis. There is no empirical evidence that periods following wars are more peaceful than other periods, nor is there any evidence that periods following the more serious wars are any more peaceful than those following less serious wars. This does not mean that no war ever induces an inhibition against war, but only that this is not a general tendency that repeatedly occurs.

In this section it has been found that the incidence of war (or Great Power war) may increase slightly after the outbreak of an earlier war but only while the first war is under way and independently of the attributes of that war. The incidence of war is unaffected by the outbreak of an earlier war once that war has been concluded. It is conceivable, however, that the incidence of war is affected not by the existence or seriousness of a single preceding war but rather by the number of wars occurring within a given period of time.

Frequencies of War in Successive Periods

The question here is whether the frequency of war in one period is related to the frequency of war in the period immediately following. Because of the focus on relatively short-term contagion effects, a five-year period of temporal aggregation is used.[19] Longer time lags would be more relevant to questions of cyclical trends or periodicity than contagion.

Several statistical techniques can be used to test the hypothesis of empirical association. The most direct is a simple correlation analysis. The product-moment correlation between the frequencies of wars in successive periods is –.07 for wars involving the Powers and .17 for Great Power wars. Both are relatively low, and neither is statistically significant at the .10 level, suggesting the absence of any relationship. This finding is confirmed by a Durbin-Watson test for autocorrelation. The Durbin-Watson *d*-statistic is defined as a function of the residuals e_t:

$$d = \frac{\sum_t (e_t - e_{t-1})^2}{\sum_t e_t^2}$$

By comparing the *d* calculated from the actual residuals with the *d* predicted by the theoretical sampling distribution (derived from a population characterized by no serial correlation), the existence of serial correlation in the data can be determined.[20]

The resulting Durbin-Watson coefficients of 2.24 for all wars and 2.09 for Great Power wars are well within the limits denoting the absence of autocorrelation. This result provides additional support for the argument that the number of wars in one period has no effect on the frequency of war in the years that follow.

Still more evidence for the sequential independence of war initiations is provided by a Poisson test for randomness. The actual distribution of wars can be compared with a theoretical Poisson distribution for randomly generated wars. The results are presented in Table 7.2.

The distribution of the frequency of war appears to fit the theoretical Poisson distribution, but a more formal statistical test is necessary

Table 7.2. The Distribution of Wars: Theoretical Poisson vs. Observed

	Number of Wars per Five-Year Period (k)						
	0	1	2	3	4	5	6
Number periods with k wars	28	36	20	8	2	1	1
Theoretical Poisson ($Ne^{-\lambda}\lambda^k/k!$)	27.8	34.4	21.4	8.8	2.7	0.7	0.1

for confirmation. The appropriate method here is a chi-square goodness-of-fit test. The chi-square statistic is defined as

$$\chi^2 = \sum_k \frac{(f_o - f_e)^2}{f_e}$$

where f_o is the observed frequency and f_e is the expected frequency based on the theoretical distribution (in this case the Poisson) for each category or period k. The chi-square value computed from the data can then be compared to the theoretical sampling distribution for chi-square, and the level of statistical significance can be determined. When the chi-square test is run on the war data, collapsing the last two categories, the result is $\chi^2 = 2.4$. This is a rather low chi-square value, representing a minimal deviation between the observed and theoretical distributions. Its level of statistical significance is about .5, indicating that a truly random process would generate a chi-square this large about half the time. We must conclude, therefore, that the occurrence of war does fit a Poisson distribution and that the null hypothesis of sequentially independent wars cannot be rejected. A similar analysis for Great Power wars yields a p-value of .35 for the goodness-of-fit test, suggesting the independence of sequential Great Power wars. Analyses based on other units of temporal aggregation generally yield similar results.

The convergence in the results from the three different methods of analysis increases our confidence in their validity. It must be concluded that there is no relationship between the frequency of war in one period and the frequency in the following period, either for wars involving the Great Powers or for Great Power wars.

Contagion of the Total Amount of War

It has been found that the likelihood of war is not affected by the occurrence of a previous war, the seriousness of such a war, or the frequency of these wars. It is conceivable, though, that the likelihood of war may be affected by the total amount of war in the period immediately preceding, in terms of battle-deaths, nation-years of war, or any of the other indicators or combinations of them. The questions here are whether any measure of the aggregate amount of war in one period affects the frequency of war in the period that follows and which dimensions of war have the greatest impact on subsequent war or peace.

The most direct way of determining whether the incidence of war is related to any of the temporally aggregated dimensions of war in the previous period is a simple correlation analysis. The correlations between the frequency of war in one period and each of the war indicators for the previous period, using a five-year period of aggregation, are presented in Table 7.3. The results for wars involving the Powers and for Great Power wars are included. The relatively low correlations and their lack of statistical significance demonstrate the absence of relationships between the frequency of war in one period and any other dimension of war in the previous five-year period.[21]

These are only simple correlations. To compare the impacts of the various indicators and determine the total impact of all of the indicators a multiple regression analysis must be used. It would be redundant to include all of the war indicators in the analysis because of the intercorrelations among them. Instead, the analytically independent dimensions of frequency, duration, extent, and severity are used as

Table 7.3. Correlations (*r*) between Frequency of War and Lagged War Indicators

Lagged War Indicator	Interstate War	Great Power Wars
Frequency	–.07	.17
Duration	–.05	.02
Extent	–.10	.02
Magnitude	–.12	–.09
Severity[a]	–.02	.08
Concentration[a]	.03	.09

Notes: Five-year period of aggregation. None of the *r*'s is significant at the .10 level.

[a]The logarithms are used because of the highly skewed nature of these distributions.

lagged variables predicting to the frequency of war in the following period. The standardized beta coefficients and total amounts of variance explained are presented in Table 7.4.

The incidence of interstate war among the Great Powers is basically unaffected by the total amount of war in the five-year period immediately preceding. Only 3 percent of their variance can be accounted for by the lagged war indicators. This result is consistent with the earlier findings of the absence of war contagion.

The results for Great Power wars are more ambiguous. The frequency of Great Power war is affected to a certain degree by the total amount of Great Power war in the period immediately preceding, in that 11 percent of its variance can be accounted for by the lagged indicators. Although this is statistically significant, the low R^2 suggests a relatively weak relationship. It indicates that the contagious effects of Great Power war are limited and far less important than the causal effects of other substantive variables in the processes leading up to war. Note that the frequency of previous war and the total number of Powers involved have the greatest impact on subsequent outbreaks of war, while severity has the least impact but in a positive direction. Although these relationships are relatively weak, these

Table 7.4. Regression of Frequency of War on Lagged War Indicators: Standardized Betas and Variance Explained

Lagged Indicator	Interstate War	Great Power War
Frequency	.02	.71*
Duration	–.04	–.20
Extent	–.28	–.62*
Severity	.24	.18
R^2	.03	.11
Significance	.55	.03

*Statistically significant at .05.

findings contradict the implications of the war-weariness hypothesis that the bloodiest wars should have the strongest negative contagion effects.[22]

Summary and Interpretation

This chapter has been concerned with short-term war contagion rather than long-term periodicity in war and with the outbreak of new war rather than the expansion of ongoing war. It has considered the impact of various attributes of war and of the frequency of these wars. The analysis has been guided by a number of more specific hypotheses representing different operational perspectives on the general theoretical question of war contagion and has used a multiplicity of statistical techniques. Regardless of how the question is defined or operationalized the results are remarkably consistent. There may be a slight tendency for the occurrence of war to increase the likelihood of the outbreak of a second war, but only while the first is under way and independently of its characteristics. Once a war (or a series of wars) is over, neither its incidence nor its seriousness has any impact on the likelihood of war in the period immediately following, regardless of its characteristics or frequency of occurrence and regardless of the total amount of war in a given period. These findings are valid for Great Power wars as well as for interstate wars involving the Powers over the last five centuries of the modern Great Power system.

These findings are generally consistent with recent empirical research on war contagion, though they are generated by a different conceptual orientation and operational procedures. These findings appear to be consistent with those of Davis, Duncan, and Siverson regarding the infectious contagion of dyadic wars. Although my focus on wars as the unit of analysis differs from their focus on dyads, it is clear that there is considerable empirical overlap between the concurrent outbreak of new war and the contagion of dyadic war.[23] In spite of the differences between these studies,[24] or perhaps because of them, my finding of positive contagion of ongoing wars reinforces their finding of the positive infection of dyadic war, for I have demonstrated that this phenomenon operates at the systemic as well as dyadic level of analysis and over the sixteenth to eighteenth as well as the nineteenth to twentieth centuries.

More generally, our findings are consistent with a long line of empirical research going back to Sorokin. These earlier studies have repeatedly demonstrated the absence of contagion or periodicity in the outbreak of war. The similarity of the empirical generalizations in conjunction with the distinctiveness of the approach I have used makes this an important contribution to the contagion literature. The demonstration of the absence of contagion in the outbreak of war over this spatial/temporal domain establishes the generality and comprehensiveness of earlier findings and greatly enhances confidence in their validity.

Particularly interesting are the implications of these findings for the popular war-weariness hypothesis. Not only are most of the relevant test statistics relatively weak and statistically insignificant, but they tend to run in a direction contrary to that implied by the hypothesis. Neither war nor a series of wars retards subsequent war (or Great Power war). The severity of war has the smallest (rather than the largest) impact, and periods of most destructive war (as measured by severity) tend to be followed by more (not fewer) Great Power wars.

If anything, the duration of war appears to have the greatest impact, but the longer wars tend to be followed by the shortest elapsed time until the next war or Great Power war. Finally, Great Power wars follow even more quickly after the very destructive general wars than after other wars. These tendencies run counter to the implications of the war-weariness hypothesis, but they are too weak to provide support for hypotheses of positive war contagion.

These findings of the absence of contagion do not necessarily mean, however, that none of the separate contagion hypotheses summarized earlier is valid. They mean only that there are no net systemic contagion effects of all of these separate processes operating simultaneously. Even if there are no individual contagion effects, there are several other possibilities: (1) some or all of these distinct contagion linkages may operate but simply cancel out; (2) under some conditions war begets war but under other conditions war retards war; (3) war is positively contagious for some states but negatively contagious for others. Each of these possibilities, or some combination of them, could generate the observed results of no net contagion at the systemic level. The contagion process, in other words, may be considerably more complex than indicated by present theory and empirical research. The discovery of the absence of any net contagion effects has been important in itself. Now that this question has been resolved, subsequent research ought to be directed toward the construction and testing of more complex causal models of the contagion process, with attention given to the question of spuriousness and antecedent variables.

8

Conclusion: A Base for Further Investigation

This concludes the first part of a multiphase study of war in the modern Great Power system. The primary objectives have been to define and identify the Great Powers, to generate a data base for all international wars involving the Powers over the last five centuries, and to analyze the characteristics of the wars, their changes over time, and the impact of war on subsequent war. Given the nature of these tasks, their completion does not easily lead to an extensive summary or grand conclusion at this point. This study has made several important contributions to the literature on international conflict, however, and these should be put in perspective.

First, this is one of the few attempts to define the concept of a Great Power, identify the primary behavioral characteristics of the Powers, and use these operational criteria to determine the historical identity of the Powers over the last five centuries of the modern system. Second, the data base generated in this study provides the foundation for the systematic empirical analysis over an extended time span of some important theoretical questions regarding the causes and consequences of international war involving the Great Powers. A third major contribution of this study is the descriptive empirical analysis of the nature of the wars, their interrelationships, and their changes over time.

First, consider the nature of the wars themselves. Over the 480-year span of the system, there have been 119 interstate wars involving the

Great Powers, or about one every four years. Slightly over half have been Great Power wars, and nine have been general wars involving most of the Powers and resulting in very high casualties. The typical war lasts about three years and involves about two Powers, five nation-years of war, and 17,000 fatalities (about 180 per million European population and about 3,400 per year for each participating Power). Many wars are considerably more serious than this average. Ten involve more than thirty nation-years of war and five result in more than a million casualties. War is present three times more frequently than it is absent, and in the typical year there are about 6,500 fatalities from war. There is a moderate empirical association between most of the war indicators, but there is no relationship between the number of Powers in the system and the frequency or destructiveness of the wars that occur. Interstate wars involving the Powers tend to be slightly more destructive during those quarter centuries in which they are least frequent. This relationship is sensitive to the time span under consideration, however, and is not valid for shorter periods. Therefore there is mixed evidence for the hypothesis that the frequency and seriousness of war are inversely related.

With respect to historical trends in war, it has been found that interstate war involving the Great Powers has generally been diminishing over time. The frequency of war has been declining. Every dimension of the yearly amount of war has been decreasing except that the bloodiest years are getting bloodier. The wars that do occur have become considerably shorter, slightly lower in magnitude, and much greater in concentration. They are no greater in the number of Powers involved or in severity, although the most severe wars are becoming worse. Although Great Power wars have become much less frequent, when they do occur they are much more serious than in earlier times in every respect but duration. The nineteenth century was by far the most peaceful, and the twentieth century has been about average (or slightly below) in every respect except severity and concentration. The sixteenth and seventeenth centuries were generally the most warlike, although they involved relatively few casualties. Wars occurred relatively infrequently in the eighteenth century but those that did occur were serious, a finding that contradicts the popular conception of that century as one characterized by frequent but limited wars. There is no evidence of any cyclical patterns in war over time.

Finally, there is little empirical support for most war contagion hypotheses. War appears to be contagious only in the sense that the likelihood of war breaking out is greatest while another war is under way. This contagion effect is independent of the attributes of the first war and ceases once the first war is concluded. The length of the peace is unaffected by the seriousness of the previous war. Neither the frequency of war nor the aggregate amount of war (along several dimensions) in one period has any impact on the frequency or aggregate amount of war in the following period. Moreover, the severity of war has the least impact on subsequent war. These results are directly contrary to the war-weariness hypothesis.

This study has been restricted to the univariate analysis of international war involving the Great Powers and has been primarily descriptive-empirical in orientation. The next phase of this ongoing research project is to use the war data generated here to test some important theoretical propositions regarding the causes of war. Of particular interest are balance-of-power theory and related *realpolitik* hypotheses that have long dominated the study of international conflict. The systematic testing of these hypotheses requires, however, the prior definition, operationalization, and measurement of all key causal variables (and also of all extraneous variables whose impact is to be controlled) over the five-century span of the modern system. This is an enormous task, which must be reserved for subsequent studies. A central aim of the first phase of this project has been to generate the data base that make further studies possible. In this way, I hope, the present study will ultimately help to expand our knowledge of the causes of war.

Appendix: Estimation of Missing Battle Death Data

As noted in Chapter 3, battle fatality data are incomplete for several wars. In this Appendix general principles are suggested for the estimation of the missing battle death data, and these principles are applied to particular cases.

Wars of the Ottoman Empire

A simple way to estimate these data would be to assume that Turkish casualties were similar to those of the enemy, whose battle deaths are known in most cases. Various historical accounts suggest, however, that the Turks often suffered much greater casualties than their opponents. Consequently, I shall attempt to estimate an average ratio of the battle deaths for Turkey as compared to her opponents. My source was Harbottle's *Dictionary of Battles.* For purposes of comparison, all battles involving Turkey and for which casualty estimates are given for both sides were selected. The ratio of Turkish fatalities to enemy fatalities for each of the resulting nine battles is computed. This ratio ranges from 1.4 (Battle of Villach in 1492) to 58 (Battle of Zenta in 1679), with a median ratio of 6. This result is as expected, given superior European technology and the prolonged and costly sieges embarked upon by the Turks. Yet large battles cannot be taken as fully representative of the wars as a whole, and an average ratio computed from the data probably would be excessive. I have decided, therefore, to make a more conservative estimate and assume that in wars with another Great Power Turkish casualties were twice those of the enemy. When additional states (Great Powers or otherwise) allied against Turkey, creating more than one front so that Turkish forces were spread out and consequently weakened, it is assumed that Turkish casualties were three times those listed for the enemy Great Powers. To estimate the casualties for the Ottoman Empire in bivariate wars against lesser European states, a different approach is needed, because casualty data are not available for the latter. Here, the average Turkish casualty rate in bivariate wars with the Great Powers is estimated. For eleven wars, the average rate was 3,800 battle deaths per year. Assuming that the Turkish casualty rate was the same in wars with lesser powers, the total number of battle deaths for the entire war can be estimated. One exception here is the Polish-Turkish War of 1583–90. Sorokin gives Polish casualty figures of 1,200 for a 1582 war (which is excluded here). If we assume the same rate (based on 30,000 troops and a 4 percent casualty rate), and again assume twice this many for Turkey, we get 16,800 battle fatalities for Turkey.

Wars Involving Other Powers

For other wars, a variety of estimation procedures are used. In bivariate wars between Powers of roughly equal strength, equal casualties are assumed. If another comparable war between the given Powers is identified easily, figures from that war are used as a basis of comparison. If data on army size are available, the Sorokin estimation procedures are used. Other quantitative sources mentioned previously (Bodart and Vedel-Peterson) are also referred to.

Here I list the war in question, the Powers for which casualty data are not available, known battle-death data for key states, and other relevant information. On the basis of this information, approximate estimates of the missing battle death data are induced.

1536-38 Third War of Charles V

Missing data for France. Sorokin estimates losses of 26,000 for the United Hapsburgs. This war was concurrent with the Ottoman war against the Hapsburgs. The French effort was directed largely against Venice and consisted primarily of a naval war. French casualties are estimated at 5,000.

1589-98 War of the Three Henries

Missing data for Spain. French casualties were 8,000, and assuming equal losses, Spanish battle deaths are estimated at 8,000.

1618-48 Thirty Years' War

Missing data for Sweden. Mowat estimates 36,000 Swedish troops in Germany. Sorokin estimates 20,000 French troops and 100,000 Hapsburg (Austrian) troops in Germany. In the second phase of the war, Sweden fought against Prussia and Poland (9,000 casualties). Army strength for Sweden is estimated as follows: Phase II—20,000; Phases III and IV—35,000. The casualty rates for the Thirty Years' War ranged from one-fourth to one-third, so the Swedish casualty rate is estimated at 30 percent (per year). The Swedish casualties can then be estimated:

Phase II (3 years)	20,000 troops	18,000 battle deaths
Phase III (5 years)	35,000 troops	52,000 battle deaths
Phase IV (13 years)	35,000 troops	136,000 battle deaths

1650–51 Scottish War

Missing data for England. Previous wars between England and Scotland, excluding those with French intervention, resulted in 4,500 (2 years), 3,000 (1 year), and 7,500 (4 years) battle deaths, or an average of 2,100 per year. English fatalities are estimated at 2,000.

1654-60 Great Northern War

Missing data for Sweden. Russia (10,000 battle deaths), Poland (9,-600), Prussia (1,800), and Denmark formed a coalition against Sweden. Swedish battle deaths are estimated at 15,000.

1665-66 Sweden-Bremen War

Missing data for both. Given the limited nature of this short war, Swedish casualties are estimated at 1,000.

1672-78 Dutch War of Louis XIV

Missing data for Sweden, which invaded Brandenburg (1675-78) as an ally of France. The Germans suffered 1,600 casualties in one year, while Sweden suffered "disastrous" defeats at Fehrbellin and Kioge (naval war). I estimate 10,000 battle deaths for Sweden in three years.

1700-21 Second Northern War

Missing data for Sweden. A coalition against Sweden consisted of England (average 580 battle deaths per year), Russia (16,700), Prussia (600), and Poland (2,000). A conservative estimate is 3,000 battle deaths per year for Sweden, or approximately 60,000 battle fatalities for the entire war.

1726-29 British-Spanish War

Missing data for both. This was a naval war and a land siege of Gibraltar. A comparison was made with the three-year war of 1656-59 between the two, resulting in 7,500 casualties each. The same number of casualties is assumed here.

1739-48 War of the Austrian Succession

Missing data for Russia. The main Russian fighting lasted one year with 10,000 troops. The French and English casualty rate was 11 percent each, so the same is assumed for Russia. The estimate is 1,000 battle deaths.

1806-12 Russo-Turkish War

Missing data for Britain. A British squadron forced passage of the Dardannelles, losing two ships, and occupied Alexandria against vigorous opposition. A conservative estimate is 500 British fatalities.

Notes

Chapter 1. Introduction: The Empirical Study Of War

1. A good summary and critical appraisal of the recent "scientific study" of international politics, including many conflict studies, can be found in Dina A. Zinnes, *Contemporary Research in International Relations.* For a summary and critique of four of the leading research projects on international conflict, including a bibliography for each, see Francis W. Hoole and Dina A. Zinnes, eds., *Quantitative International Politics.*

2. Quincy Wright, *A Study of War;* Lewis F. Richardson, *Statistics of Deadly Quarrels;* and J. David Singer and Melvin Small, *The Wages of War, 1816-1965.* The Singer-Small data have been updated in Small and Singer, *Resort to Arms.* Other empirically based works have used case study or comparative case study methodologies.

3. A recent bibliography of studies associated with the Correlates of War Project can be found in Small and Singer, *Resort to Arms.* Some of the more useful of these can be found in J. David Singer, ed., *The Correlates of War I and II;* and Singer et al., *Explaining War.*

4. Exceptions include J. David Singer, Stuart A. Bremer, and John Stuckey, "Capability Distribution, Uncertainty, and Major Power War, 1820-1965"; and Charles Gochman, "Status, Capabilities, and Major Power War."

5. Harold Nicolson, *The Congress of Vienna;* Sir Charles Webster, *The Congress of Vienna,* pp. 80-84.

6. Leopold von Ranke, "The Great Powers," pp. 65-101; A. J. P. Taylor, *The Struggle for Mastery in Europe, 1848-1918,* p. xix. Taylor's history of seventy years of European diplomacy is explicitly a history of Great Power relations.

7. Walter L. Dorn writes that eighteenth-century international affairs were "controlled by a small group of great powers which applied the doctrine of the balance of power only to themselves, not to their relations with smaller and weaker states" (*Competition for Empire, 1740-1763,* p. 3).

8. Kenneth N. Waltz, *Theory of International Politics,* pp. 72-73.

9. Wright, *Study of War,* pp. 220-21.

10. For over half the states in this study (excluding those that have always or have never been Great Powers), the average frequency of war participation during the time the state enjoyed Great Power status was more than twice that during its period(s) of non-Great Power status. These calculations are based on my definition of the Great Powers and Wright's listing of wars for the 1495-1964 period.

11. Frederick Adams Woods and Alexander Baltzly, *Is War Diminishing?*

12. Singer and Small, *Wages of War,* pp. 70-71. These figures are based on the Singer-Small definitions of wars and major powers.

13. George Modelski, "Wars and the Great Power System," pp. 43-44.

14. Immanuel Wallerstein, "The Rise and Future Demise of the World Capitalist System," pp. 387-415; Wallerstein, *The Modern World System;* Christopher Chase-Dunn, "Interstate System and Capitalist World-Economy," pp. 19-42; George Modelski, "The Long Cycle of Global Politics and the Nation-State," pp. 214-35; Modelski and William R. Thompson, "Testing Cobweb Models of the Long Cycle of World Leadership." For a related conceptualization of the global political economy see Robert Gilpin, *War and Change in World Politics.* For a brief analysis of the differing assumptions and propositions of the realist and world system paradigms see my "World System Analysis."

15. Wright, *Study of War;* Pitirim A. Sorokin, *Social and Cultural Dynamics,* vol. 3: *Fluctuation of Social Relationships, War, and Revolution;* Woods and Baltzly, *Is War Diminishing?*

16. Ranke, "Great Powers"; George Modelski, *Principles of World Politics,* chap. 8; Robert L. Rothstein, *Alliances and Small Powers,* chap. 1; Hedley Bull, *The Anarchical Society,* chap. 9; Taylor, *Struggle for Mastery,* pp. xix-xxxvi. Historical treatments include George Modelski, *World Power Concentrations;* Michael Haas, *International Subsystems Data, Codebook;* Singer and Small, *Wages of War,* p. 23; Wright, *Study of War,* pp. 647-49.

Chapter 2. The Modern Great Power System

1. Leading alternative frameworks include the complex interdependence paradigm of Keohane and Nye, the issue-based paradigm of Mansbach and Vasquez, the capitalist world-economy of Wallerstein and Chase-Dunn, and the global political economy of Modelski and Thompson and of Gilpin. See Robert O. Keohane and Joseph S. Nye, *Power and Interdependence;* Richard W. Mansbach and John A. Vasquez, *In Search of Theory;* Wallerstein, "Rise and Demise" and *Modern World System;* Chase-Dunn, "Interstate System";

Modelski, "Long Cycle"; Modelski and Thompson, "Testing Cobweb Models"; and Gilpin, *War and Change.*

2. Most realist theories recognize the leading role of the Great Powers. Many realists, however, would argue that the same general principles guide the behavior of all states and that only the power configurations are different. The Great Power framework attempts to identify a distinct set of testable hypotheses applicable to the actions and interactions of the Great Powers.

3. Waltz makes the more general claim that in any self-help system, including economic systems of oligopolistic competition as well as anarchic political systems, the structure and processes of the system are determined by the interactions of the strongest units (*Theory of International Politics,* p. 72).

4. Leading proponents of political realism include Thucydides, *The Peloponnesian War;* Hans J. Morgenthau, *Politics among Nations;* Raymond Aron, *Peace and War;* Arnold Wolfers, *Discord and Collaboration;* Martin Wight, *Power Politics;* Edward Hallett Carr, *The Twenty Years' Crisis, 1919-1939;* and Henry Kissinger, *A World Restored.* Although these scholars share basic realist assumptions, their specific theoretical orientations differ in significant respects.

5. Conceptualizations of the impact of international anarchy can be found in Jean Jacques Rousseau, *The State of War* and *Discourse on the Origin and Foundation of Inequality among Men;* Kenneth N. Waltz, *Man, the State and War,* chaps. 6-7; Waltz, *Theory of International Politics;* Wolfers, *Discord and Collaboration;* Robert Jervis, "Cooperation under the Security Dilemma"; and Bull, *Anarchical Society.*

Some realists trace this high-threat environment to an aggressive human nature, whether it be based on the theological perspective of a St. Augustine, the secular philosophy of a Spinoza, the instinct theory of a Lorenz, or the psychoanalytical orientation of a Freud. See the summary in Waltz, *Man, the State and War,* chap. 2. The importance of human nature as the source of international conflict should not be exaggerated, however. If the human nature concept is conceived broadly, the hypothesis is nonfalsifiable and the concept devoid of explanatory power. If conceived narrowly, human nature has a limited causal impact and its utility to a theory of conflict is at least open to question.

6. K. J. Holsti defines international system as "any collection of independent political entities—tribes, city-states, nations, or empires—that interact with considerable frequency and according to regularized processes" (*International Politics,* p. 27). Here the Great Power system has been defined in terms of security issues. For a general discussion of the importance of the concept of issue-area in any conception of an international system, see Donald E. Lampert, Lawrence S. Falkowski, and Richard W. Mansbach, "Is There an International System?"

7. Modelski, *Principles of World Politics* and *World Power Concentrations;* Bull, *Anarchical Society;* Charles F. Doran, *The Politics of Assimilation.*

8. Conceptualizations of the realist paradigm generally include the assumption that states are not only the dominant actors but also are unitary actors pursuing the national interest in the absence of internal controversy or constraints (see Morgenthau, *Politics among Nations;* Keohane and Nye, *Power and Independence;* and Mansbach and Vasquez, *In Search of Theory*). That is, state decision makers define a consistent set of foreign policy goals and agree on the means by which these goals are to be achieved. This standard assumption is unnecessarily strong. The Great Power framework can incorporate overlap between foreign and domestic policy and the impact of internal constraints on the selection, pursuit, and accomplishment of foreign policy objectives (see Stephen D. Krasner, *Defending the National Interest*). The Great Power framework therefore allows some role for bureaucratic politics, misperceptions, public opinion, private interests, and other internal variables but asserts that they may modify but do not dominate the pursuit of the national interest defined as security. To the extent that internal variables affect the foreign policies of the Great Powers, they help shape the international system.

9. For an excellent analysis of several distinct international systems see Adda Bozeman, *Politics and Culture in International History.*

10. Singer and Small, *Wages of War,* p. 23.

11. Rothstein, *Alliances and Small Powers,* p. 14.

12. Taylor, *Struggle for Mastery,* p. xxiv; Modelski, *Principles of World Politics,* p. 149; J. David Singer and Thomas Cusack, "Periodicity, Inexorability, and Steermanship in International War"; Ranke, "Great Powers," p. 86.

13. This class of Superpowers might include the United States and the Soviet Union from 1945 on, Britain from 1815 to 1871 or so, France from 1659 to 1713 and from 1789 to 1814, the United Hapsburgs from 1519 to 1556, and Spain from 1556 to 1588.

14. Michael Haas, "International Subsystems," p. 122.

15. Wight, *Power Politics,* p. 18; Taylor, *Struggle for Mastery,* p. xxiv; Rothstein, *Alliances and Small Powers,* pp. 24-29; Stanley Hoffmann, *The State of War,* p. 138.

16. Hedley Bull, "Society and Anarchy in International Relations," p. 27.

17. Hoffmann goes further and argues that "the main object of a larger power is to maximize gains (defined in a variety of ways) rather than to minimize risks" (*State of War,* p. 135).

18. Michael Howard, *Studies in War and Peace,* p. 254; Michael Haas, *International Conflict,* pp. 330-31.

19. Rothstein, *Alliances and Small Powers,* p. 14; Modelski, *World Power Concentrations,* p. 2; Modelski and Thompson, "Testing Cobweb Models"; William R. Thompson, "Seapower in Global Politics, 1500-1945."

20. One of the better discussions of the elements of military power and potential is Klaus Knorr, *Military Power and Potential.*

21. John Stuckey and J. David Singer, "The Powerful and the Warprone."

22. A.F.K. Organski and Jacek Kugler correctly predict the outcome of the Arab-Israeli wars by constructing an alternative index of military power that incorporates an indication of tax effort to measure the ability and willingness of the government to extract resources from society (*The War Ledger,* chap. 2).

23. For the construction of the power index and resulting rank ordering of nations based on this index see Stuckey and Singer, "The Powerful and the Warprone." The Singer-Small system of major powers can be found in their *Wages of War,* p. 23. Subsequent references to their power rankings and their major power system refer to these sources and pages.

24. For further discussion of this point see Modelski, *Principles of World Politics,* chap. 8, and *World Power Concentrations;* Bull, *Anarchical Society,* chap. 9. This concern for order maintenance may include a desire to order the system under its own hegemony, the consequences of which may be very destabilizing.

25. The question of the origins of a state system is distinct from that of the origins of states themselves, for the latter does not necessarily involve a system of interactive behavior. F. H. Hinsley appears to define a state system as one in which no state holds a hegemonial position or seeks to dominate. Not only is this definition conceptually unsatisfactory, but his analysis is historically questionable, for he ignores Napoleon and Hitler (*Power and the Pursuit of Peace,* pp. 153-57).

26. Frederick L. Schuman, *International Politics,* pp. 37, 41.

27. Garrett Mattingly, *Renaissance Diplomacy,* chaps. 15 and 22.

28. Richard A. Preston and Sydney F. Wise, *Men in Arms,* p. 102; Lynn Montross, *War through the Ages,* p. 205; Oman quoted in Theodore Ropp, *War in the Modern World,* pp. 25-26.

29. See R. B. Mowat, *A History of European Diplomacy, 1451-1789,* p. 7; Denys Hay, Introduction, pp. 5-8; Preston and Wise, *Men in Arms,* p. 99.

30. Sir Charles Petrie, *Earlier Diplomatic History,* pp. 1-2, 11; Charles Oman, *The Sixteenth Century,* p. 16; René Albrecht-Carrié, "European Diplomacy and Wars (c. 1500-1914)," pp. 1081-82.

31. Ludwig Dehio, *The Precarious Balance,* p. 23; David Jayne Hill, *A History of Diplomacy in the International Development of Europe,* 2:209;

Arnold J. Toynbee, *A Study of History,* 9:227; Mattingly, *Renaissance Diplomacy,* pp. 124-25.

32. Preston and Wise, *Men in Arms,* p. 98; Ropp, *War,* pp. 19, 24; Michael Howard, *War in European History,* pp. 19-20. See also Bernard Brodie and Fawn M. Brodie, *From Crossbow to H-Bomb,* p. 51.

33. Niccolo Machiavelli, *The Prince;* see also Frederick Meinecke, *Machiavellism.*

34. H. C. Darby, "The Face of Europe on the Eve of the Great Discoveries," pp. 40-41.

35. Wallerstein, *Modern World System,* vol. 1; Modelski, "Long-Cycle"; Thompson, "Seapower."

36. Preston and Wise, *Men in Arms,* chap. 7; Nef, chap. 2; Ropp, *War,* pp. 19, 24; Brodie and Brodie, *From Crossbow to H-Bomb,* chap. 3; Jon M. Bridgman, "Gunpowder and Governmental Power"; Trevor N. Dupuy, *The Evolution of Weapons and Warfare,* p. 107; Montross, *War,* pp. 205-11; J. R. Hale, "International Relations in the West," pp. 281-88.

37. For a discussion of the mercenary system see Howard, *War in European History,* chap. 2; J. R. Hale, "Armies, Navies, and the Art of War," pp. 481-509; Andre Corvisier, *Armies and Societies in Europe, 1494-1789,* chap. 3.

38. Ropp, *War,* p. 19. For an opposing view see Howard, *War in European History,* chap. 2. Robert E. Osgood dates this "rationalization" of force nearly two centuries later ("The Expansion of Force," pp. 42-45).

39. I have defined a single Great Power system over time, in which the identity of the particular Powers is continuously changing. A common alternative is to posit a series of distinct historical systems over time, defined by certain structural characteristics or the identity of the Great Powers. Thus Haas defines ten major European subsystems since 1649; Rosecrance defines nine historical systems since 1740; and Kaplan identifies several analytically distinct systems on the basis of certain power distribution parameters. The utility of defining an international system transformation on the basis of a change in one or two variables is open to question. I prefer to define one system, characterized by several distinct variables (such as power distributions, alliances, technology), and to study the changes in and interrelationships among these variables within the system. The effects of all but the most cataclysmic changes in international politics can be studied with equal if not greater efficiency within the theoretical construct of a single system. See Haas, "International Subsystems," p. 103; Richard N. Rosecrance, *Action and Reaction in World Politics;* and Morton A. Kaplan, *System and Process in International Politics.*

40. Wright, *Study of War,* p. 649; Haas, "International Subsystems," p. 102.

41. Modelski makes a similar argument (*Principles of World Politics,* p. 150).

42. It might be argued that the actual temporal sequence is reversed: the decline of power and hence the loss of Great Power status induces aggression by others. Even if this were true, the resulting bias would be minimal. In the vast majority of cases when a Power's departure from the system is marked by the end of a war, that war is a general one involving nearly all the Powers (examples are the Netherlands, Sweden, Italy, and Japan). A different coding rule would not affect the existence of a Great Power war (the one case to the contrary would be the Ottoman Empire), and the contribution of the one Power in question to the other dimensions of the war would be marginal. The hypothesis that the decline of power precipitates war is fully testable, for neither the declining states nor their wars have been excluded from the system.

43. This decision is consistent with Steven Spiegel's conceptualization, which defines both primary powers (the United States and the Soviet Union) and secondary powers (Britain, France, West Germany, Japan, and China) as Great Powers (*Dominance and Diversity,* p. 98). Singer and Small (*Wages of War,* p. 23) include—in addition to the United States and the Soviet Union —Britain, France, and China. Haas adds only Britain (*International Subsystems Data,* p. 28); Bull (*Anarchical Society,* pp. 203-4) adds only China.

44. The rankings for 1960 were as follows: United States, Soviet Union, China, Britain, West Germany, France, India, and Japan.

45. Singer and Small include France in their contemporary major power system but Haas does not.

46. Petrie, *Earlier Diplomatic History,* pp. 5-8. Wolf and Palmer and Colton take more extreme views. Wolf argues that England played a "secondary role in European high politics" until after the Glorious Revolution in 1688. Palmer marks 1713 as the date of England's appearance as a Great Power. See John B. Wolf, *Toward a European Balance of Power, 1620-1715,* p. 143; R. R. Palmer and Joel Colton, *A History of the Modern World,* p. 171.

47. Cited in Mowat, *History of European Diplomacy,* p. 42.

48. Hill, *History of Diplomacy,* 2:294; Mattingly, *Renaissance Diplomacy,* p. 108; Dehio, *Precarious Balance,* p. 28.

49. This decision is consistent with both Singer and Small and Haas.

50. The Great Power rank of the Austrian Hapsburgs at the end of the fifteenth century is explicitly recognized by Hill (*History of Diplomacy,*

2:238), Mattingly (*Renaissance Diplomacy,* p. 108), Dehio (*Precarious Balance,* p. 28), Albrecht-Carrié ("European Diplomacy," pp. 1081-82), and others. See also Robert A. Kann, *A History of the Hapsburg Empire, 1526-1918,* chap. 1.

51. See Karl Brandi, *The Emperor Charles V,* p. 14; H. G. Koenigsberger, *The Hapsburgs and Europe, 1516-1660,* pp. 14-19; Hill, *History of Diplomacy,* 2:358.

52. For example, Fernand Braudel, *The Mediterranean and the Mediterranean World in the Age of Philip II,* 2:673-74; Hill, *History of Diplomacy,* 2: chaps. 5-6; Brandi, *Emperor Charles V,* p. 14; Dehio, *Precarious Balance,* p. 35.

53. Braudel, *The Mediterranean,* 2: pt. 3.

54. Hill (*History of Diplomacy,* 2:294); Mattingly (*Renaissance Diplomacy,* p. 108); and Dehio (*Precarious Balance,* p. 28) all consider Spain under Ferdinand and Isabella one of the four Great Powers of Europe. Albrecht-Carrié also attributes Great Power rank to Spain. See also J. H. Elliott, *Imperial Spain, 1469-1716.*

55. See Wolf, *Toward a European Balance of Power,* chap. 5.

56. M. S. Anderson, *Eighteenth Century Europe, 1713-1789,* pp. 6, 23-24; Hill, *History of Diplomacy,* 3:400, 438, 468, 505; Mowat, *History of European Diplomacy,* chaps. 26-27.

57. Stanford J. Shaw, *History of the Ottoman Empire and Modern Turkey,* 1: chap. 4; Lord Kinross, *The Ottoman Centuries,* chap. 3; V. J. Parry, "The Ottoman Empire (1481-1520)," pp. 395-419.

58. Hale, "Armies," pp. 485-86.

59. Paolo Giovio, *Turcicarum Rerum Commentarius,* p. 83, quoted in ibid., p. 485.

60. Petrie, *Earlier Diplomatic History,* pp. 49-50; Dehio, *Precarious Balance,* chap. 1.

61. J. F. C. Fuller, *A Military History of the Western World,* 1:555-56; Braudel, *The Mediterranean,* 2:905, and pt. 3, chap. 2; Petrie, *Earlier Diplomatic History,* p. 54; Oman, *Sixteenth Century,* p. 82; Mattingly, *Renaissance Diplomacy,* p. 154.

62. Braudel, *The Mediterranean,* 2:1088, 1141.

63. For various aspects of the decline of the Ottoman Empire, see Shaw, *History of the Ottoman Empire,* chap. 6; Kinross, *Ottoman Centuries,* p. 4; Wolf, *Toward a European Balance of Power,* pp. 76-78; A. N. Kurat, "The Retreat of the Turks, 1683-1730," chap. 19.

64. Shaw, *History of the Ottoman Empire,* pp. 223-25; Kurat, "Retreat of the Turks," pp. 626-29; Hill, *History of Diplomacy,* 3:266; Petrie, *Earlier Diplomatic History,* p. 209.

65. It is puzzling that Haas identifies the Ottoman Empire as a major power only during the years 1815-47, long after its political, economic, and military decay (*International Subsystems Data,* pp. 22-23).

66. For the importance of Dutch naval power see Alfred Thayer Mahan, *The Influence of Seapower upon History, 1660-1783,* pp. 58-60; J. P. Cooper, "Sea Power."

67. Immanuel Wallerstein, "The Three Instances of Hegemony in the History of the Capitalist World-Economy"; Modelski, "Long Cycle," pp. 220-25. See also Carl J. Friederich, *The Age of the Baroque, 1610-1660,* chap. 5.

68. Mahan, *Influence of Seapower,* p. 60.

69. This argument is generally accepted in the literature. See Petrie, *Earlier Diplomatic History,* p. 89; Anderson, *Eighteenth Century Europe,* pp. 7-8; Hill, *History of Diplomacy,* 3: chap. 5. Admittedly, an argument can be made for extending the Great Power status of the Dutch through the end of the War of the Quadrangle Alliance and the London Treaty in 1720. Haas does not consider the Netherlands a Great Power during any period.

70. See M. Roberts, "Sweden and the Baltic, 1611-54."

71. C. V. Wedgwood, *The Thirty Years War.*

72. This argument is explicitly supported by Mowat, *History of European Diplomacy,* p. 199; Dehio, *Precarious Balance,* p. 105; Hill, *History of Diplomacy,* 3:343; Anderson, *Eighteenth Century Europe, pp. 9, 14;* and Ragnhild Hatton, *"Charles XIII and the Great Northern War,"* p. 679. An argument could be made for marking Sweden's exit from the system twelve years earlier, after Poltava. Haas is on very weak ground in including Sweden as a major power from 1714 to 1789 *(International Subsystems Data,* p. 20).

73. M. S. Anderson, *Europe in the Eighteenth Century, 1713-1783,* pp. 2, 217-18; Albrecht-Carrié, "European Diplomacy," p. 1092.

74. Robert K. Massie, *Peter the Great,* pt. 2.

75. W. Bruce Lincoln, *The Romanovs,* chap. 7; Massie, *Peter the Great,* chaps. 58-59; M. S. Anderson, "Russia under Peter the Great and the Changed Relations of East and West"; B. H. Sumner, *Peter the Great and the Emergence of Russia.*

76. The date 1721 is supported by Petrie, *Earlier Diplomatic History,* p. 217. Haas (*International Subsystems Data,* p. 20) begins a few years earlier. Anderson (*Europe,* pp. 2, 225-26) is vague on this point. J. O. Lindsay implies that Russia's status as a Great Power did not begin until the War of the Polish Succession ("International Relations," p. 204).

77. I have argued previously that the Soviet Union should not be excluded from the Great Power system for the brief period of the Russian civil war, 1918-21.

78. Anderson, *Eighteenth Century Europe,* p. 15.

79. Gerhard Ritter, *The Sword and the Scepter,* vol. I.

80. Osgood, "Expansion of Force," p. 49. For the development of the Prussian army, see Gordon A. Craig, *The Politics of the Prussian Army, 1640-1645,* pt. 1; also Dorn, *Competition for Empire,* pp. 90-99.

81. This date is supported by B. H. Liddell Hart, *Strategy,* p. 106; Lindsay, "International Relations," p. 206; Dorn, *Competition for Empire,* p. 134. Hass prefers 1714.

82. Neither Singer and Small nor Haas includes West Germany during this period.

83. See R. Harrison Wagner, "The Decision to Divide Germany and the Origins of the Cold War"; Klaus Epstein, "The German Problem, 1945-1950."

84. For the Soviet concern with Germany, see Thomas W. Wolfe, *Soviet Power and Europe, 1945-70,* pp. 27-31. Adam Ulam argues that the issue of Berlin was used by the Soviets primarily as an instrument to gain a guarantee against West Germany obtaining nuclear weapons. (*Expansion and Coexistence,* p. 663).

85. I have argued earlier why Germany should not be excluded from the system during the few years following its defeat in the two world wars.

86. René Albrecht-Carrié, *A Diplomatic History of Europe since the Congress of Vienna,* p. 235; Taylor, *Struggle for Mastery,* pp. xxii-xxx.

87. This determination is consistent with Taylor, *Struggle for Mastery,* p. xxiii. Singer and Small begin a year earlier, which is premature; Haas uses 1872.

88. See Ernest R. May, *Imperial Democracy;* Foster Rhea Dulles, *America's Rise to World Power, 1898-1954;* Howard K. Beale, *Theodore Roosevelt and the Rise of America to World Power.* This date is also used by Singer and Small, *Wages of War,* p. 23.

89. This view is consistent with that of Albrecht-Carrié, *Diplomatic History,* p. 245, and Modelski, *Principles of World Politics,* p. 150. The Anglo-Japanese Treaty of 1902 is not enough to advance Japan's rise to Great Power status.

90. Singer and Small, as well as Haas and Modelski (*Principles of World Politics,* p. 150), exclude Japan during this period.

91. One of the best examples is the testimony of Secretary of State Dean Rusk before the Senate Foreign Relations Committee in 1966 (*The Vietnam Hearings,* pp. 3-58). See also the November 1964 memo from Assistant Secretary of Defense John T. McNaughton to Robert McNamara, noted in *The Pentagon Papers,* p. 255.

92. China is included as a Great Power by Singer and Small, Modelski (*Principles of World Politics,* p. 150), and Bull (*Anarchical Society,* pp. 203-5).

93. A good discussion of the decline of Venice can be found in G. V. Scammell, *The World Encompassed,* pp. 132-54.

94. Venice is often mentioned as a maritime power, but rarely as a Great Power, in most historical studies of the period. See Petrie, *Earlier Diplomatic History,* chap. 2; Dehio, *Precarious Balance,* p. 26.

95. Albrecht-Carrié, "European Diplomacy," p. 1082.

96. Montross, *War,* p. 204.

97. Modelski, "Long Cycle," pp. 218-19.

98. Mattingly (*Renaissance Diplomacy,* pp. 156-57) refers to Portugal as "almost a major power" and the "greatest of the lesser powers" in the sixteenth century on the basis of the wealth from her empire.

99. A contrary view is that of Barbara Jelavich, who includes Poland as a Great Power for a time (*A Century of Russian Foreign Policy, 1814-1914,* p. 4).

100. As noted earlier, the decision to treat the union of the Hapsburgs under Charles V as a single Great Power might also be challenged.

Chapter 3. Definition and Identification of the Wars

1. Bronislaw Malinowski, "An Anthropological Analysis of War," p. 247. This definition is similar to the one suggested by L. L. Bernard in *War and Its Causes,* p. 28.

2. Wright defines war as "the legal condition which equally permits two or more hostile groups to carry on a conflict by armed force" (*Study of War,* p. 8). This legalistic focus is not relevant to the military conflicts in the pre-Westphalia period before the codification of international law or to the contemporary period of undeclared and unconventional wars. Wright modifies this definition later when he provides operational criteria for the identification of wars. He includes "all hostilities . . . which were recognized as states of war in the legal sense or which involved over 50,000 troops . . . [or which] led to important legal results such as the creation or extinction of states, territorial transfers, or changes of government" (p. 636). The troop requirement is not consistent with Wright's definition and will be discussed later. The criterion of "important legal results" is not very useful because it is subjective and raises additional problems by defining a phenomenon in terms of its consequences. Moreover, many important legal results are achieved without war.

3. For alternative definitions of war, see Karl von Clausewitz, *On War,* chap. 1; Julian Lider, *On the Nature of War;* Wright, *Study of War,* chap. 17; Bernard, *War,* chap. 2.

4. Richardson, *Deadly Quarrels,* pp. 6-7. Gaston Bodart; *Losses of Life in Modern Wars,* p. 79; Singer and Small, *Wages of War,* p. 35. This criterion applies only to formal members of the international system, defined by their population and diplomatic recognition (pp. 19-22).

5. Singer and Small, *Wages of War,* p. 35-37.

6. For a more favorable evaluation of these apsects of Richardson's work, see David Wilkinson, *Deadly Quarrels.* There is no doubt about the originality of Richardson's pioneering effort or his ingenious application of mathematical models in testing hypotheses about war. The Singer-Small data have been used far more widely, however.

7. Sorokin, *Social and Cultural Dynamics,* 3:283.

8. Wright, *Study of War,* Appendix XX.

9. To evaluate the seriousness of this problem, I consulted several diplomatic histories. Few of the wars identified in only one of the data sets are even mentioned in the histories, and none was particularly significant.

10. This procedure represents improvement upon a different one used in an earlier version of this study: William L. Langer's *Encyclopedia of World History* was used in place of Woods and Baltzly's *Is War Diminishing?* to arbitrate any discrepancies between Wright and Sorokin. See my "Military Power, Alliances and Technology."

11. Thomas Harbottle, *Dictionary of Battles.*

12. The approximate level of casualties can often be inferred from a historical reference. For example, the first war of the Falkland Islands between Britain and Spain in 1770, identified by both Wright and Woods and Baltzly, is excluded because the latter describes it as "friction" and because it is elsewhere described as a seizure of land and fleet action which was "nearly the cause of war."

13. Wright, *Study of War,* p. 638.

14. Singer and Small, *Wages of War,* pp. 19-22.

15. This procedure follows the conventions established by Singer and Small, *Wages of War,* pp. 33-34. A bias is introduced, because this procedure tends to reduce the frequency of war for Great Powers that have attempted to maintain the status quo by means of external military intervention. In addition, some groups that are not states are excluded on the basis of legalistic criteria in spite of their undeniable political importance (for example, the PLO or the early Viet Minh). Interstate war is important in itself, however, and problems such as these cannot be avoided.

16. Ibid., p. 34.

17. Small and Singer, *Resort to Arms,* p. 227. The Western allies attempted to seize the Russian war stocks at Murmansk, Archangel, and Vladivostok to keep them out of German hands. This action brought them into direct

conflict with the Bolshevik army. Japan sought to control the northern end of the Manchurian railroad in China and to win concessions from the Russians in Kamchatka, Siberia, and Sakhalin. The conflicts were exacerbated by ideological differences between the Bolshevik regime and the other Powers. For an analysis of the allied interventions, see Robert D. Warth, *The Allies and the Russian Revolution;* George F. Kennan, *Russia and the West under Lenin and Stalin,* chaps. 5-8; Ulam, *Expansion and Coexistence,* chap. 3.

18. Another general issue raised by the Russian Civil War is what casualty figures to include for internationalized civil wars. The measurement of battle deaths will be discussed in the following chapter, but a few comments are necessary here. When the regime against which the rebellion is being conducted is a Great Power, should—and can—the casualties from the interstate dimension of the war be determined separately from those from the internal dimension of the war? This question is important because many civil wars involve enormous casualties. In the Russian Civil War, for example, there were roughly a half million fatalities, but less than three thousand of these belonged to the Western allies (presumably the number was comparable for the Soviet Union in her war against the allies). Lumping all casualties together would greatly exaggerate the seriousness of the international dimension of the war. For this reason, casualties from the internal civil war should be excluded from the estimates for the interstate war. The Sorokin data are presented in a way that generally makes separation possible. When no breakdown is given, estimates can be made based on the data for the other Powers in conjunction with the general criteria for estimating missing data presented in the Appendix.

19. Singer and Small, *Wages,* p. 34; Richardson, *Deadly Quarrels,* p. 179.

20. See John Gallagher and Ronald Robinson, "The Imperialism of Free Trade."

21. One minor difficulty arises because a particular military conflict is often given different names. Singer and Small ignore the war labels altogether in comparing the Wright, Sorokin, and Richardson compilations with their own. Yet some description is useful for the purposes of identification, and in cases for which Wright, Sorokin, and Woods and Baltzly differ, I consult other historical authorities.

22. Wright, *Study of War,* p. 636.

23. Ibid.

24. Richardson, *Deadly Quarrels,* pp. 15-16.

25. Singer and Small, *Wages of War,* p. 45.

26. R. Ernest Dupuy and Trevor N. Dupuy, *The Encyclopedia of Military History.*

27. Wright, *Study of War,* p. 636.

28. Singer and Small, *Wages of War,* pp. 79-80.

29. Wright, *Study of War,* Table 33. Wright also identifies ten distinct peace treaties settling different aspects of the conflict: Nikolsburg, Ulm, Münster, Lübeck, Strohm, Cherasco, Osnabruck, Prague, Münster, and Bromsbro.

30. Langer, *Encyclopedia of World History,* p. 431. Mowat and Wright identify identical periods, with only negligible differences. Wright ends the Bohemian period in 1623 and Mowat in 1624; Mowat begins the last period in 1636 and calls it the Franco-Swedish period (Mowat, *History of European Diplomacy,* p. 93; Wright, *Study of War,* Table 33).

31. Wright, *Study of War,* Tables 36-37; Sorokin, *Social and Cultural Dynamics* 3:551-52.

32. See Singer and Small, *Wages of War,* chap. 5.

33. This definition of general war as one involving nearly all the Powers is consistent with the definitions of "general war," "hegemonic war," or "world war" by Blainey, *Causes of War,* p. 196; Toynbee, *Study of History,* 9:251; Osgood, "Expansion of Force," p. 52; Gilpin, *War and Change,* p. 200; Mandlebaum, *Nuclear Revolution,* p. 71; Wallerstein, "Three Instances of Hegemony," p. 6. Wright's definition (*Study of War,* p. 649) is considerably broader.

34. Here involvement is defined to require at least 1,000 battle fatalities, as measured in the following chapter. Wars in which many Powers participate but only in a nominal way (the Korean War, for example) are excluded.

35. This list is similar to Gilpin's (*War and Change,* p. 200); the primary difference is the inclusion here of the two great wars of the mid-eighteenth century, the War of the Austrian Succession and the Seven Years' War. The most noticeable exclusion from this list, the Crimean War (involving three out of five of the Great Powers), is often noted for its failure to escalate into a general European war. (Richard Smoke, for example, in *War,* includes the Crimean War in his comparative case studies for this reason.) The Crimean War was both less severe and less intense than any of the nine general wars identified here. Wars satisfying the extent but not the intensity criterion are the Russian Civil War (1918-20), War of the Polish Succession (1733-38), the First and Second Wars of Charles V (1521-26, 1526-29), and the War of the Holy League (1511-14). None of these is usually regarded as being as important as any of the general wars listed in Table 4.

Chapter 4. Measurement of the Wars

1. For a good summary of various conceptualizations of internal war, see Small and Singer, *Resort to Arms,* chap. 12.

2. Singer and Small, *Wages of War,* chap. 3. They also make some use of the duration and frequency dimensions.

3. Blainey, *Causes of War,* p. 196; Osgood, "Expansion of Force," p. 52; Toynbee, *Study of History,* 9:251; Michael Mandelbaum, *The Nuclear Revolution,* p. 71.

4. For some purposes, the total number of states participating in war might also be useful. This dimension might be called the *scope* of war but is not included in this study. The number of participating Great Powers is generally more important than the number of participating states.

5. This usage follows that of Singer and Small rather than Richardson, who defines magnitude as the logarithmic transformation of the number of battle deaths.

6. The magnitude of war is not fully dependent mathematically upon the extent and duration measures, for it is the length of the war for each Power (and not the duration of the war as a whole) that determines the magnitude.

7. Singer and Small (*Wages of War,* p. 130) state that "the single most valid and sensitive indicator of the 'amount of war' experienced by the system is that of battle deaths, or severity." The number of battle deaths is also the central concern of Bodart *(Losses of Life),* Samuel Dumas and K. O. Vedel-Peterson *(Losses of Life Caused by War),* and Richardson *(Deadly Quarrels).*

8. Singer and Small, *Wages of War,* chap. 3.

9. In this study the intensity indicator is based on the total population of Europe rather than that of individual states.

10. Singer and Small, *Wages of War,* pp. 147-49.

11. Ibid., p. 45.

12. This concept of the magnitude of war assumes that the contribution of one year is equivalent to that of one Great Power. For example, a war involving two Powers and lasting four years is equal in magnitude to one involving four Powers and lasting two years. The indicator also assumes that all Powers are somehow equal and that all years are equal. It is true, of course, that for some years and some Powers the conflict is more "intense" than for others, but the magnitude indicator is to tap only the spatial and temporal aspects of war and not the intensity.

13. Richardson, *Deadly Quarrels,* pp. 8-9.

14. Singer and Small, *Wages of War,* p. 48.

15. Ibid.

16. Richardson, *Deadly Quarrels,* p. 7.

17. Singer and Small, *Wages of War,* p. 50.

18. Sorokin, *Social and Cultural Dynamics,* 3:285.

19. Ibid., p. 382

20. Ibid., chap. 10.

21. With the geographical expansion of the Great Power system in the twentieth century, the population rates for some of the non-European Powers may deviate from the population rates for Europe.

22. Walter F. Wilcox, ed., *International Migrations,* p. 78; Alexander M. Carr-Saunders, *World Population;* R. R. Kuczynski, "Population," p. 241 (Kuczynski's original source was Wilcox, and the same data are reprinted in Wright, *Study of War,* p. 612); John V. Grauman, "Population." Grauman's estimates for the year 1910 are his own. For the years before 1900 Grauman's estimates are identical to those of Kuczynski, so these two data sets can be merged.

23. See William Wu-Shyong Wei, "The Effect of Temporal Aggregation on Discrete Dynamic Time Series Models"; Arnold Zellner and Claude Montmarquette, "A Study of Some Aspects of Temporal Aggregation Problems in Econometric Analysis"; R. F. Engle and T. C. Liu, "Effects of Aggregation over Time on Dynamic Characteristics of an Econometric Model."

24. A good example of a questionable choice of the unit of aggregation is the study of nineteenth-century alliance formation by Patrick J. McGowan and Robert M. Rood, "Alliance Behavior in Balance of Power Systems." A one-year period of aggregation is used, and the conclusion is that alliance formation is independent of past alliance formation. Since the test for independence of events (alliance formation) is based on the Poisson distribution the crucial factor is the number of events in each period, from which the number of periods having x alliances is determined. If two alliances are not in the same period, they might as well be separated by fifty years as far as the model is concerned. Consider the numerous alliances of the Bismarckian period, 1872-90. Using a one-year period of aggregation, few of these alliances would fall into the same period, whereas a five-year period would reflect the temporal concentration of alliances in this era. Since one year is too short to reveal any sequential dependence in alliance formation, a different conclusion might result if a five-year period were used.

Chapter 5. Characteristics of the Wars

1. The values of these indicators are plotted on a logarithmic scale in Figure 5.1 d-f, which collapses the scale and partially conceals the skewness. The skewness is enhanced by the fact that most conflicts involving under 1,000 battle deaths have been excluded by the operational criteria used to define the wars.

2. A war is defined as under way in a given year if any fighting takes place in that year, regardless of how long that fighting lasts. The number of wars in which a Power participates is incorporated into the magnitude of war under

way but not into the number of Powers at war (so that the latter is not equivalent to the extent indicator defined in Chapter 3). The severity and concentration of war under way present a problem, however, for battle death data are not available on a yearly basis. As noted previously, yearly fatalities can be approximated by assuming that the number of battle fatalities in any war is distributed evenly over the course of the war. The intensity indicator is excluded because it so closely resembles severity (see Figure 5.1e). Histograms of the magnitude and concentration indicators have been excluded; the first resembles that for the number of Powers at war and the second resembles that for severity.

3. The twelve years in which casualties exceeded one million are those of the two world wars in this century. Of the years exceeding 100,000 casualties only 40 percent were in this century, indicating that earlier historical periods also suffered from huge losses of life in war.

4. Although I can be fairly confident that my data correctly establish which of two wars involve more fatalities or more nation-years of war, I am much less confident regarding the actual differences in fatalities (or other characteristics) between two wars. An interval-level statistic such as Pearson's product-moment coefficient *(r)* implies exact knowledge of differences as well as rank. Another ordinal measure of association that might be used is Spearman's rho, but that statistic is excessively sensitive to a large number of ties and is therefore inappropriate for this data. (In general, the correlations between the war indicators tend to be about 20 percent higher for Spearman's rho than for Kendall's tau-b.)

5. For an argument for the applicability of significance tests for statistical populations, see Margaret Jarman Hagood, "The Notion of a Hypothetical Universe."

6. These criteria are technically more appropriate for the Pearson's r, where $r = .7$ indicates that about 50 percent of the variance in one variable is accounted for by the other, which is fairly high. An r of .3, on the other hand, indicates that less than 10 percent of the variance is accounted for, which is fairly low. In the analysis of the war data I have found that the magnitude of Kendall's tau-b differs little from that of Pearson's r, except for the fatality-based indicators. These cutoff points can be applied, therefore, to the tau-b statistic.

7. This is consistent with the findings of Charles W. Ostrom, Jr., and John H. Aldrich, "The Relationship between Size and Stability in the Major Power International System."

8. Preston and Wise, *Men in Arms,* chap. 9; Inis L. Claude, Jr., *Power and International Relations,* p. 71.

9. The characteristics of the average war in the kth period are defined by each of the i indicators $\overline{W}_{ki} = W_{ki}/\text{freq}_k$, where freq_k is the frequency of wars

in period k and W_{ki} is the sum of the values of indicator i over all wars in period k. Periods in which there are no wars are excluded from the analysis, for in these cases the average is undefined. The alternative of defining the averages as zero in the absence of war would introduce a serious bias into the analysis.

10. In a different study, I have conducted a similar analysis including the imperial wars of the Great Powers and their other wars involving fewer than 1,000 fatalities. It was found that the frequency and seriousness of war are inversely related but that the relationship is not particularly strong (Jack S. Levy and T. Clifton Morgan, "Are Wars Either Frequent But Limited or Infrequent But Serious?").

Chapter 6. Historical Trends in War

1. Singer and Small, *Wages of War,* chap. 8; their analysis controls for the size of the international system.
2. Richardson, *Deadly Quarrels,* chap. 4.
3. Frank H. Denton, "Some Regularities in International Conflict."
4. Richardson, *Deadly Quarrels,* p. 167.
5. Woods and Baltzly, *Is War Diminishing?* chap. 2.
6. Sorokin, *Social and Cultural Dynamics,* 3:336-37, 347, 360-62.
7. Wright, *Study of War,* pp. 121, 237, 242, 248, 638.
8. Sorokin excludes Turkey, Sweden, the United States, and Japan from his analysis but includes Poland (*Social and Cultural Dimensions,* chap. 11). Wright includes Savoy, Denmark, and Poland as well as the Great Powers defined here (*Study of War;* Appendix XX). In addition to the Austrian Hapsburgs, England, France, Holland, Prussia, Russia, Spain, Sweden, and Turkey, Woods and Baltzly include Denmark and Poland.
9. Ronald J. Wonnacott and Thomas H. Wonnacott, *Regression,* pp. 120-24; Edward R. Tufte, *Data Analysis for Politics and Policy,* pp. 124-28.
10. Since I am using common logarithms, the percentage change in the war indicator, or growth rate, is given by r = beta*log10(e), or 2.3 beta. The doubling time is then .69/r.
11. Problems of autocorrelation or heteroscedasticity can arise in regression analysis. An examination of the scattergrams shows that several of the indicators, and particularly the severity-based ones, are heteroscedastic, generally with increasing variances over time. Also, a Durbin-Watson test for serial correlation reveals autocorrelation in the duration and possibly the magnitude indicators but in none of the others. These problems of heteroscedasticity and autocorrelation would not result in biased estimators of the population regression coefficent (which is the main concern here), but they would result in underestimation of the variance of and reduction in the

efficiency of the estimator. However, I am using the least square method only to describe a trend in an existing set of data. I am dealing with the universe rather than a sample so there is no need to estimate population parameters. Problems of heteroscedasticity and autocorrelation therefore do not affect this analysis. Furthermore, they have no impact on the rank-order correlations used to supplement the regression analysis. See J. Johnston, *Econometric Methods,* pp. 214-21; Arthur S. Goldberger, *Econometric Theory,* pp. 238-41; Taro Yamane, *Statistics,* p. 1000.

12. The use of logarithmic transformations in an analysis of historical trends in the severity of war has ample precedent. Richardson defines his indicator as the log of the fatalities (*Deadly Quarrels,* p. 6), and Singer and Small use logarithms in analyzing historical trends (*Wages of War,* p. 200).

13. At the same time, it appears (Figure 6.2d) that the least severe wars are becoming less destructive. Unfortunately, this latter trend is in part a manifestation of my selection procedures and demonstrates the sensitivity of the analysis to the particular operational indicator used to represent a general theoretical concept. In operationally defining wars, I have followed Singer and Small and included wars in which there were fewer than 1,000 fatalities if more than 1,000 active troops were involved. This method tends to include more low-severity wars in recent times because the Singer-Small data are good enough to identify these wars. If all wars under 1,000 in severity are excluded, we find that in a logged regression analysis of severity against time, tau – b = .13, b = .0013, and b^* = .22, with a statistical significance of .02. This finding suggests a somewhat stronger trend toward an increasing severity of war.

14. It should be recalled from Chapter 3 that the severity indicator has been defined as battle-connected deaths of military personnel. Most common hypotheses regarding casualties from war are ambiguous, so that it is generally unclear whether they refer only to fatalities of military personnel or to all possible battle-related casualties, including civilians. If the concern is with the latter, however, there may be a slight downward bias in the trends uncovered in this analysis. As noted in Chapter 3, in more recent times battle-related civilian casualties have become substantial in interstate wars. (A study of civil war would be more seriously affected by the exclusion of civilian casualties.)

15. If the untransformed intensity indicator is used, we find a moderate increase in the intensity of war over time. Or, if all wars with fewer than 1,000 fatalities are eliminated we get a tau–b = .03 and b = .0005, both positive but neither strong nor statistically significant.

16. Earlier it was demonstrated that neither the extent indicator nor any of the others are even moderately correlated with the size of the system. This

suggests that the upward trend in these war indicators is not simply a function of the slight increase in the size of the system.

17. The very low p-values (.000) are deceiving, for they derive as much from the large n (481) as from the strength of the relationships.

18. The mean is used for all but the severity and concentration indicators; the medians are smaller and would make these declines in war appear even greater.

19. These results are fairly stable in that they are not particularly sensitive to small changes in the data generated by changes in coding rules. In an earlier study I conducted a similar analysis using a slightly different data base, with 108 wars rather than 119 (and 58 Great Power wars rather than 64) and some other small changes ("Military Power," chap. 5). The resulting changes in the beta coefficients in the regression analyses are practically insignificant. For example, in the regression analysis of the individual war indicators against time, the changes in beta are about .003 for duration, .00025 for extent, and .007 for magnitude. The standardized beta for the frequency of Great Power war changes from .19 to .20. As noted earlier, the statistical significance of the coefficients is another indicator of their stability. The changes in the other statistics are equally small.

20. Sorokin, *Social and Cultural Dynamics,* 3:352-60; Wright, *Study of War,* p. 378; Frank H. Denton and Warren Phillips, "Some Patterns in the History of Violence"; Richardson, *Deadly Quarrels,* pp. 128-31; Singer and Small, *Wages of War,* pp. 205-7; Singer and Cusack, "Periodicity." When Singer and Small examine the magnitude of international war under way rather than beginning in a given period, however, "a rather strong periodicity emerges, with the dominant peaks about 20 years apart." Furthermore, this trend is more pronounced for central system (European) wars. They admit, though, that "the evidence is far from conclusive" (*Wages of War,* pp. 215-16). Sorokin, *Social and Cultural Dynamics,* 3:359-60.

21. Singer and Small, *Wages of War,* pp. 206-7. See also George E. P. Box and Gwilym M. Jenkins, *Time Series Analysis,* chap. 2.

22. When the difference between centuries is less than the estimated measurement error, tied ranks are used.

23. M. S. Anderson, for example, entitles his books *Europe in the Eighteenth Century, 1713-1783* and *18th Century Europe, 1713-1789.*

24. J. David Singer and Melvin Small, "Alliance Aggregation and the Onset of War, 1815-1945."

25. Singer, Bremer, and Stuckey, "Capability Distribution," p. 296. For other examples of distinct findings for the nineteenth and twentieth centuries, Bruce Bueno de Mesquita, "Systemic Polarization and the Occurrence

and Duration of War"; Gochman, "Status"; Yoshinobu Yamamoto and Stuart Bremer, "Wider Wars and Restless Nights."

26. If the duration of a war were inversely related to its costs, a strong negative correlation between duration and concentration would be expected. The tau-*b* of .07 suggests the absence of any significant relationship.

27. Wright (*Study of War,* pp. 1519-20) argues that military invention has in the long run tended to benefit defense more than offense, generating a stalemate that would result in wars of increasing duration. Wright is not always consistent on this point, however (see p. 292).

28. Fred Charles Iklé, *Every War Must End.*

29. This argument would appear to contradict the classic liberal notion that economic interdependence is the best guarantee of peace (see Edmund Silberner, *The Problem of War in Nineteenth Century Economic Thought*.) The emphasis in my study, however, is on the interdependence of the security system rather than the economic system.

30. Walter Millis, *Arms and Men,* chaps. 2 and 4; J. F. C. Fuller, *The Conduct of War, 1789-1961,* chap. 5; Osgood, "Expansion of Force."

31. This conceptualization generally follows and attempts to build upon that of Osgood, "Expansion of Force."

32. Osgood (ibid., pp. 42-45) suggests that the rationalization of force did not begin until the eighteenth century. This argument minimizes the importance of the use of force as a political instrument by territorial states. See the discussion in Chapter 1, above.

33. Osgood, "Expansion of Force," pp. 44-45.

34. Blainey, *Causes of War,* chap. 6.

35. Howard, *War in European History,* p. 47.

36. Osgood, "Expansion of Force," pp. 51-52; Millis, *Arms and Men,* chap. 1; Preston and Wise, *Men in Arms,* chap. 12.

37. Osgood, "Expansion of Force," pp. 53-56; Millis, *Arms and Men,* chap. 3; Samuel P. Huntington, *The Soldier and the State,* pt. 1.

38. Howard, *War in European History,* pp. 109-10; Alfred Vagts, *A History of Militarism.*

39. Nef, *War,* chaps. 6, 17, 19.

40. Millis, *Arms and Men,* chap. 5.

41. Klaus Knorr, *On the Uses of Military Power in the Nuclear Age,* chaps. 2-3.

42. Since the frequency of Great Power war has declined but its extent has increased, I have hypothesized that the initiation of Great Power war has become less rational (in perceived benefits relative to costs) and that intervention in an ongoing war between Great Powers has become more rational (at least in the prenuclear age). These hypotheses are consistent if the structure

of threats and opportunities is sufficiently asymmetric to ensure that the incentive to maintain the status quo is far greater than the incentive to change it in one's favor.

Chapter 7. War Contagion

1. Richardson, quoted in Blainey, *Causes of War,* p. 6.
2. Toynbee, *Study of History,* 3:251-54, 322-23. Toynbee applies his theory to the post-Alexandrine Hellenic and post-Confucian Sinic international systems as well as the modern Western system (1494 on).
3. Modelski, "Long Cycle"; Charles F. Doran and Wes Parsons, "War and the Cycle of Relative Power."
4. A. L. Macfie, "The Outbreak of War and the Trade Cycle"; Frank Klingberg, "The Historical Alternation of Moods in American Foreign Policy"; Sorokin, *Social and Cultural Dynamics,* 3:353.
5. William W. Davis, George T. Duncan, and Randolph M. Siverson, "The Dynamics of Warfare, 1816-1965," pp. 777-78; Benjamin A. Most and Harvey Starr, "Diffusion, Reinforcement, Geopolitics, and the Spread of War," p. 933.
6. Most and Starr, "Diffusion," p. 933.
7. Nor is this distinction always explicit in the empirical literature on contagion. Much of this literature is descriptive rather than explanatory, focusing on whether contagion exists rather than its possible causes. Although the explanations for these phenomena may be different, many of the mathematical models are the same (with different parameters, of course), and the same statistical methods are used to analyze both phenomena.
8. Davis, Duncan, and Siverson, "Dynamics of Warfare," p. 776.
9. Given the interrelationships among many social phenomena, the main question is not simply the existence or absence of a causal connection with earlier war, but rather the relative strength or weakness of the causal effect and its proximity or remoteness along the causal chain. This is hardly conducive to a neat analytical distinction or a practical operational criterion for differentiating between heterogeneity and contagion.
10. Singer and Small find, however, some tendency for victorious states to be more inclined to embark on another war ("Foreign Policy Indicators").
11. Richardson, *Deadly Quarrels,* pp. 273-87; Harvey Starr and Benjamin A. Most, "The Substance and Study of Borders in International Relations Research," pp. 608-10; Most and Starr, "Diffusion."
12. Randolph M. Siverson and Joel King, "Alliances and the Expansion of War, 1815-1965"; Siverson and King, "Attributes of National Alliance Membership and War Participation, 1815-1965."

13. More weight is given to significance levels in this chapter than previously. Whereas the focus in the earlier discussion was on the population of wars as a whole, here different samples within that population are compared. Significance tests are clearly appropriate to determine whether these samples deviate from those that might be randomly generated.

14. Since the relationships under consideration are very sensitive to minor changes in operational procedures for the aggregation of wars, these results should be taken as tentative until aggregation procedures are further refined and fully operationalized.

15. It was noted earlier that the definitional bias toward the null hypothesis is less for cases of sequential wars than for simultaneous wars.

16. There is no significant difference if tau-*b* is used instead of *r*.

17. A ten-year period (instead of three years) is used because it is often suggested that general wars have more prolonged (as well as more intense) effects than most wars. A ten-year period allows this hypothesis to be tested. If we look at the three years immediately after general wars we find that the incidence of war (.55 wars per three years) is slightly lower than average (.74 wars per three years). Similarly, there are an average of .33 Great Power wars (compared to .40 normally). These differences are not statistically significant, however. In addition, the small number of wars (five) following within three years of the nine general wars makes generalization very difficult.

18. James S. Coleman, *Introduction to Mathematical Sociology,* chap. 10; Yamane, *Statistics,* chap. 20.

19. The use of ten-year periods yields similar results for each of the statistical techniques applied here.

20. For a discussion of the Durbin-Watson *d*-statistic, see Charles W. Ostrom, Jr., *Time Series Analysis,* pp. 31-35; Johnston, *Econometric Methods,* pp. 250-52; Yamane, *Statistics,* pp. 1000-1006.

21. The finding that all but one of the correlations for interstate wars involving the Powers are negative and all but one of the correlations for Great Power wars are positive is precisely the opposite that a war-weariness hypothesis would predict, for the more serious Great Power wars should be more likely to retard other wars. The observed relationships are very weak, however. These results are nearly identical for a ten-year period of aggregation.

22. The positive frequency coefficient in conjunction with the negative extent coefficient suggest that numerous "small" (and short) Great Power wars are more likely to be followed by subsequent Great Power wars than one larger war. These results must be interpreted with caution, however, for some bias may be generated by the procedures for the aggregation of wars. A single, lengthy war involving many Powers and extending into the following period may increase the chances that any new conflict initiation in that period will

be classified as a continuation of an ongoing war rather than a new war (because of the aggregation procedures). The observed relationship between small wars and subsequent war is consequently weaker than the statistics imply.

23. Some of their dyadic infections would not be considered new war initiations in my analysis, but all of my concurrent war initiations would be classified as separate dyadic wars.

24. The main difference, and perhaps a significant one, is the longer temporal span of their infectious process.

Selected Bibliography

Albrecht-Carrié, René. *A Diplomatic History of Europe since the Congress of Vienna.* New York: Harper & Brothers, 1958.

———. "European Diplomacy and Wars (c. 1500-1914)." In *Encyclopedia Britannica.* 15th ed. 6:1081–1115.

Anderson, M. S. *Eighteenth Century Europe, 1713-1789.* London: Oxford University Press, 1966.

———. *Europe in the Eighteenth Century, 1713-1783.* 2d ed. London: Longman, 1961.

———. "Russia under Peter the Great and the Changed Relations of East and West." In *The New Cambridge Modern History,* vol. 6: *The Rise of Great Britain and Russia, 1688-1725,* chap. 21. Cambridge: Cambridge University Press, 1970.

Aron, Raymond. *Peace and War.* London: Weidenfeld and Nicolson, 1966.

Beale, Howard K. *Theodore Roosevelt and the Rise of America to World Power.* New York: Collier, 1962.

Beer, Francis A. "How Much War in History: Definitions, Estimates, Extrapolations, and Trends." Sage Professional Papers in International Studies, vol. 3, #02-030. Beverly Hills: Sage, 1974.

———. *Peace Against War.* San Francisco: Freeman, 1981.

Bernard, L. L. *War and Its Causes.* New York: Henry Holt, 1944.

Blainey, Geoffrey. *The Causes of War.* New York: Free Press, 1973.

Bodart, Gaston. *Losses of Life in Modern Wars.* Oxford: Clarendon, 1916.

Box, George E. P., and Gwilym M. Jenkins. *Time Series Analysis.* Rev. ed. San Francisco: Holden-Day, 1976.

Bozeman, Adda B. *Politics and Culture in International History.* Princeton: Princeton University Press, 1960.

Brandi, Karl. *The Emperor Charles V.* Translated by C. V. Wedgwood. New York: Knopf, 1939.

Braudel, Fernand. *The Mediterranean and the Mediterranean World in the Age of Philip II.* Translated by Sian Reynolds. 2 vols. New York: Harper & Row, 1972.

Bremer, Stuart. "National Capabilities and War Proneness." In *Correlates of War II,* edited by J. David Singer, pp. 57-82. New York: Free Press, 1980.

Bridgman, Jon M. "Gunpowder and Governmental Power: War in Early Modern Europe (1494-1825)." In *War: A Historical, Political, and Social Study,* edited by L. L. Farrar, pp. 105-11. Santa Barbara: ABC-Clio, 1978.

Brodie, Bernard, and Fawn M. Brodie. *From Crossbow to H-Bomb.* Bloomington: Indiana University Press, 1973.

Bueno de Mesquita, Bruce. "Systemic Polarization and the Occurrence and Duration of War." *Journal of Conflict Resolution* 22 (June 1978):241-67.

———. *The War Trap.* New Haven: Yale University Press, 1981.

Bull, Hedley. *The Anarchical Society.* New York: Columbia University Press, 1973.

———. "Society and Anarchy in International Relations." In *International Politics,* edited by Robert J. Art and Robert Jervis, pp. 21-28. Boston: Little, Brown, 1973.

Carr, Edward Hallett. *The Twenty Years' Crisis, 1919-1939.* New York: Harper & Row, 1964.

Carr-Saunders, Alexander M. *World Population: Past Growth and Present Trends.* Oxford: Clarendon, 1936.

Carter, Charles. *The Western European Powers, 1500-1700.* Ithaca: Cornell University Press, 1971.

Chase-Dunn, Christopher. "Interstate System and Capitalist World-Economy: One Logic or Two?" *International Studies Quarterly* 25 (March 1981):19-42.

Claude, Inis L., Jr. *Power and International Relations.* New York: Random House, 1962.

Clausewitz, Carl von. *On War.* Edited by Anatol Rapoport. Baltimore: Penguin, 1968.

Coleman, James S. *Introduction to Mathematical Sociology.* New York: Free Press, 1964.

Cooper, J. P. "Sea Power." In *The New Cambridge Modern History,* vol. 4. *The Decline of Spain and the Thirty Years War,* chap. 7. Cambridge: Cambridge University Press, 1971.

Corvisier, Andre. *Armies and Societies in Europe, 1494-1789.* Translated by Abigail T. Siddall. Bloomington: University of Indiana Press, 1979.

Craig, Gordon A. *The Politics of the Prussian Army, 1640-1945.* Oxford: Oxford University Press, 1955.

Cusack, Thomas. "The Major Powers and the Pursuit of Security in the Nineteenth and Twentieth Centuries." Ph.D. dissertation, University of Michigan, 1978.

Darby, H. C. "The Face of Europe on the Eve of the Great Discoveries." In *The New Cambridge Modern History,* vol. 1: *The Renaissance, 1493-1520,* chap. 2. Cambridge: Cambridge University Press, 1957.

Davis, William W., George T. Duncan, and Randolph M. Siverson. "The Dynamics of Warfare, 1816-1965." *American Journal of Political Science* 22 (November 1978):772-92.

Dehio, Ludwig. *The Precarious Balance.* New York: Vintage Books, 1962.

Denton, Frank H. "Some Regularities in International Conflict." *Background* 9 (February 1966):283-96.

Denton, Frank H., and Warren Phillips. "Some Patterns in the History of Violence." *Journal of Conflict Resolution* 12 (June 1968):182-95.

Doran, Charles F. *The Politics of Assimilation.* Baltimore: Johns Hopkins University Press, 1971.

Doran, Charles F., and Wes Parsons. "War and the Cycle of Relative Power." *American Political Science Review* 74 (December 1980):947-65.

Dorn, Walter L. *Competition for Empire, 1740-1763.* New York: Harper & Row, 1963.

Dulles, Foster Rhea. *America's Rise to World Power 1898-1954.* New York: Harper Torchbooks, 1954.

Dumas, Samuel, and K. O. Vedel-Peterson. *Losses of Life Caused by War.* Oxford: Clarendon, 1923.

Dupuy, Trevor N. *The Evolution of Weapons and Warfare.* Indianapolis: Bobbs-Merrill, 1980.

Dupuy, R. Ernest, and Trevor N. Dupuy. *The Encyclopedia of Military History.* Rev. ed. New York: Harper & Row, 1970.

Elliot, J. H. *Imperial Spain, 1469-1716.* New York: New American Library, Meridian Books, 1963.

Engle, R. F., and T. C. Liu. "Effects of Aggregation over Time on Dynamic Characteristics of an Econometric Model." In *Econometric Models of Cyclical Behaviors,* vol. 2, edited by B. G. Hickman, pp. 673-737. New York: Columbia University Press, 1972.

Epstein, Klaus. "The German Problem, 1945-1950." *World Politics* 20 (January 1968):279-300.

Friedrich, Carl J. *The Age of the Baroque, 1610-1660.* New York: Harper & Row, 1953.

Fuller, J. F. C. *The Conduct of War, 1789-1961.* London: Eyre & Spottiswoode, 1961.

———. *A Military History of the Western World.* 3 vols. New York: Funk and Wagnalls, 1954.

Gallagher, John, and Ronald Robinson. "The Imperialism of Free Trade." *Economic History Review* 6, no. 2 (1963):1-15.

Gilpin, Robert. *War and Change in World Politics.* Cambridge: Cambridge University Press, 1981.

Giovio, Paolo. *Turcicarum Rerum Commentarius.* Paris, 1539.

Gochman, Charles. "Status, Capabilities, and Major Power War." In *Correlates of World War II: Testing Some Realpolitik Models,* edited by J. David Singer, pp. 83-123. New York: Free Press, 1979.

Goldberger, Arthur S. *Econometric Theory.* New York: Wiley, 1964.

Grauman, John V. "Population: Population Growth." In *International Encyclopedia of the Social Sciences.* New York: Macmillan, 1968, 12:376-81.

Haas, Michael. *International Conflict.* Indianapolis: Bobbs-Merrill, 1974.

———. *International Subsystems Data, Codebook.* Ann Arbor: Inter-university Consortium for Political Research, International Relations Archive, 1968.

———. "International Subsystems: Stability and Polarity." *American Political Science Review* 64 (March 1970):98-123.

Hagood, Margaret Jarman. "The Notion of a Hypothetical Universe." In *The Significance Test Controversy,* edited by Denton E. Morrison and Ramon E. Henkel, chap. 4. Chicago: Aldine, 1970.

Hale, J. R. "Armies, Navies, and the Art of War." In *The New Cambridge Modern History,* vol. 2: *The Reformation, 1520-59,* chap 16. Cambridge: Cambridge University Press, 1958.

———. "International Relations in the West: Diplomacy and War." In *The New Cambridge Modern History,* vol. 1: *The Renaissance, 1493-1520,* chap. 9. Cambridge: Cambridge University Press, 1957.

Harbottle, Thomas. *Dictionary of Battles.* New York: Thomas Y. Crowell, 1967.

Hart, B. H. Liddell. *Strategy.* Rev. ed. New York: Praeger, 1954.

Hatton, Ragnhild. "Charles XII and the Great Northern War." In *The New Cambridge Modern History,* vol. 6: *The Rise of Great Britain and Russia, 1688-1725,* chap. 20, pt. 1. Cambridge: Cambridge University Press, 1970.

Hay, Denys. Introduction. *The New Cambridge Modern History,* vol. 1: *The Renaissance.* Cambridge: Cambridge University Press, 1957.

Hill, David Jayne. *A History of Diplomacy in the International Development of Europe.* 3 vols. London: Longmans, Green, & Co., 1914.

Hinsley, F. H. *Power and the Pursuit of Peace.* Cambridge: Cambridge University Press, 1967.

Hoffman, Stanley. *The State of War.* New York: Praeger, 1968.

Holsti, K. J. *International Politics.* Englewood Cliffs, N.J.: Prentice-Hall, 1967.

Hoole, Francis W., and Dina A. Zinnes, eds. *Quantitative International Politics.* New York: Praeger, 1976.

Howard, Michael. *Studies in War and Peace.* New York: Viking, 1971.

———. *War in European History.* Oxford: Oxford University Press, 1976.

Huntington, Samuel P. *The Soldier and the State.* New York: Vintage, 1957.

Iklé, Fred C. *Every War Must End.* New York: Columbia University Press, 1971.

Jelavich, Barbara. *A Century of Russian Foreign Policy, 1814-1914.* Philadelphia: J. B. Lippincott, 1964.

Jervis, Robert. "Cooperation under the Security Dilemma." *World Politics* 30 (January 1978):167-214.

Johnston, J. *Econometric Methods.* Second ed. New York: McGraw-Hill, 1972.

Kann, Robert A. *A History of the Hapsburg Empire, 1526-1918.* Berkeley and Los Angeles: University of California Press, 1974.

Kaplan, Morton A. *System and Process in International Politics.* New York: Wiley, 1957.

Kennan, George F. *Russia and the West under Lenin and Stalin.* New York: Mentor Books, 1960.

Keohane, Robert O., and Joseph S. Nye. *Power and Interdependence.* New York: Little, Brown, 1977.

Kinross, Lord. *The Ottoman Centuries: The Rise and Fall of the Turkish Empire.* New York: Morrow Quill, 1977.

Kissinger, Henry A. *A World Restored.* New York: Grosset & Dunlap, 1964.

Klingberg, Frank L. "The Historical Alternation of Moods in American Foreign Policy." *World Politics* 4 (January 1952):239-73.

Knorr, Klaus. *Military Power and Potential.* Lexington, Mass.: D. C. Heath, 1970.

———. *On the Uses of Military Power in the Nuclear Age.* Princeton: Princeton University Press, 1966.

Koenigsberger, H. G. *The Hapsburgs and Europe, 1516-1660.* Ithaca: Cornell University Press, 1971.

Krasner, Stephen D. *Defending the National Interest.* Princeton: Princeton University Press, 1978.

Kuczynski, R. R. "Population." In *Encyclopedia of the Social Sciences.* 15 vols. New York: Macmillan, 1930-1935. vol. 12, pp. 240-48.

Kurat, A. N. "The Retreat of the Turks, 1683-1730." In *The New Cambridge Modern History,* vol. 6: *The Rise of Great Britain and Russia, 1688-1725,* chap. 19. Cambridge: Cambridge University Press, 1970.

Lampert, Donald E., Lawrence S. Falkowski, and Richard W. Mansbach. "Is There an International System?" *International Studies Quarterly* 22 (March 1978):143-66.

Langer, William L., ed. *An Encyclopedia of World History.* 4th ed. Boston: Houghton-Mifflin, 1948.

Levy, Jack S. "Alliance Formation and War Behavior: An Analysis of the Great Powers, 1495-1975," *Journal of Conflict Resolution* 25 (December 1981):581-614.

———. "The Contagion of Great Power War Behavior," *American Journal of Political Science* 26 (August 1982):

———. "Historical Trends in Great Power War," *International Studies Quarterly* 26 (June 1982):278-301.

———. "Military Power, Alliances, and Technology: An Analysis of Some Structural Determinants of International War among the Great Powers, 1495-1975." Ph.D. dissertation, University of Wisconsin-Madison, 1976.

———. "World System Analysis: A Great Power Perspective." In *World System Analysis: Competing Perspectives,* edited by William R. Thompson. Beverly Hills: Sage, 1983.

Levy, Jack S., and T. Clifton Morgan. "Are Wars Either Frequent But Limited or Infrequent But Serious?" Mimeograph. Austin: University of Texas, 1982.

Lider, Julian. *On the Nature of War.* Westmead, England: Saxon House, 1977.

Lincoln, W. Bruce. *The Romanovs.* New York: Dial Press, 1981.

Lindsay, J. O. "International Relations." In *The New Cambridge Modern History,* vol. 7: *The Old Regime, 1713-63,* chap. 9. Cambridge: Cambridge University Press, 1970.

Macfie, A. L. "The Outbreak of War and the Trade Cycle." *Economic History* 4 (February 1938):89-97.

McGowan, Patrick J., and Robert M. Rood. "Alliance Behavior in Balance of Power Systems: Applying a Poisson Model to Nineteenth Century Europe." *American Political Science Review* 69 (September 1975):859-70.

Machiavelli, Niccolo. *The Prince.* Translated and edited by Thomas G. Bergin. New York: Appleton-Century-Crofts, 1947.

McNeill, William H. *The Pursuit of Power.* Chicago: University of Chicago Press, 1982.

Mahan, Alfred Thayer. *The Influence of Seapower upon History, 1660-1783.* New York: Hill and Wang, 1957.

Malinowski, Bronislaw. "An Anthropological Analysis of War." In *War,* rev. ed., edited by Leon Bramson and George W. Goethals, pp. 245-268. New York: Basic Books, 1968.

Mandlebaum, Michael. *The Nuclear Revolution.* Cambridge: Cambridge University Press, 1981.

Mansbach, Richard W., and John A. Vasquez. *In Search of Theory: A New Paradigm for Global Politics.* New York: Columbia University Press, 1981.

Massie, Robert K. *Peter the Great.* New York: Ballantine, 1980.

Mattingly, Garrett. *Renaissance Diplomacy.* Baltimore: Penguin, 1955.

May, Ernest R. *Imperial Democracy: The Emergence of America as a Great Power.* New York: Harper & Row, 1961.

Meinecke, Frederick. *Machiavellism: The Doctrine of Raison d'Etat and Its Place in Modern History.* New York: Praeger, 1965.

Millis, Walter. *Arms and Men.* New York: Mentor Books, 1956.

Modelski, George. "The Long Cycle of Global Politics and the Nation-State." *Comparative Studies in Society and History* 20 (April 1978):214-35.

———. *Principles of World Politics.* New York: Free Press, 1972.

———. "Wars and the Great Power System." In *War: A Historical, Political and Social Study,* edited by L. L. Farrar, Jr., pp. 43-56. Santa Barbara: ABC-Clio, 1978.

———. *World Power Concentrations: Typology, Data, Explanatory Framework.* Morristown, N.J.: General Learning Press, 1974.

Modelski, George, and William R. Thompson. "Testing Cobweb Models of the Long Cycle of World Leadership." Paper presented at the 1980 annual meeting of the American Political Science Association, Washington, D.C.

Montross, Lynn. *War through the Ages.* Rev. ed. New York: Harper & Row, 1960.

Morgenthau, Hans J. *Politics among Nations.* 4th ed. New York: Knopf, 1967.

Most, Benjamin A., and Harvey Starr. "Diffusion, Reinforcement, Geopolitics, and the Spread of War." *American Political Science Review* 74 (December 1980):932-46.

Mowat, R. B. *A History of European Diplomacy, 1451-1789.* London: Edward Arnold, 1928.

Nef, John V. *War and Human Progress.* New York: Norton, 1950.

Nicolson, Harold. *The Congress of Vienna.* New York: Viking Press, 1946.

Oman, Charles. *A History of the Art of War in the Middle Ages.* London: Methuen, 1968.

———. *The Sixteenth Century.* New York: Dutton, 1936.

Organski, A. F. K., and Jacek Kugler. *The War Ledger.* Chicago: University of Chicago Press, 1980.

Osgood, Robert E. "The Expansion of Force." In *Force, Order, and Justice,* edited by Robert E. Osgood and Robert W. Tucker, pp. 41-120. Baltimore: Johns Hopkins Press, 1967.

Ostrom, Charles W., Jr. *Time Series Analysis.* Beverly Hills: Sage, 1978.

Ostrom, Charles W., Jr., and John H. Aldrich. "The Relationship between Size and Stability in the Major Power International System." *American Journal of Political Science* 22 (November 1978):743-71.

Padfield, Peter, *Tide of Empires: Decisive Naval Campaigns in the Rise of the West.* 4 vols. London: Routledge & Kegan Paul, 1982.

Palmer, R. R., and Colton, Joel. *A History of the Modern World.* 3d ed. New York: Knopf, 1965.

Parry, V. J. "The Ottoman Empire (1481-1520)." In *The New Cambridge Modern History,* vol. 1: *The Renaissance, 1493-1520,* chap. 14. Cambridge: Cambridge University Press, 1957.

The Pentagon Papers. New York Times edition. New York: Bantam Books, 1971.

Petrie, Sir Charles. *Earlier Diplomatic History.* London: Hollis and Carter, 1947.

Preston, Richard A., and Sydney F. Wise. *Men in Arms: A History of Warfare and Its Interrelationships with Western Society.* 4th ed. New York: Holt, Rinehart, and Winston, 1979.

Ranke, Leopold von. "The Great Powers" (1833). In Leopold von Ranke, *The Theory and Practice of History,* edited by George G. Iggers and Konrad von Moltke, pp. 65-101. Indianapolis: Bobbs-Merrill, 1973.

Richardson, Lewis F. *Statistics of Deadly Quarrels.* Chicago: Quadrangle, 1960.

Ritter, Gerhard. *The Sword and the Scepter: The Problem of Militarism in Germany,* vol. 1: *The Prussian Tradition, 1740-1890.* Translated by Heinz Norden. Coral Gables, Fla.: University of Miami Press, 1969.

Roberts, M. "Sweden and the Baltic, 1611-54." In *The New Cambridge Modern History,* vol. 4: *The Decline of Spain and the Thirty Years War, 1609-48/59,* chap. 13. Cambridge: Cambridge University Press, 1971.

Ropp, Theodore. *War in the Modern World.* Rev. ed. New York: Macmillan/Collier, 1962.

Rosecrance, Richard N. *Action and Reaction in World Politics.* Boston: Little, Brown, 1963.

Rothstein, Robert L. *Alliances and Small Powers.* New York: Columbia University Press, 1968.

Rousseau, Jean Jacques. *The State of War* and *Discourse on the Origin and Foundation of Inequality among Men.* Translated by C. E. Vaughan. London: Constable & Co., 1917.

Rummel, Rudolph J. "Dimensions of Dyadic War, 1920-1952." *Journal of Conflict Resolution* 11 (June 1967):176-83.

———. *The Dimensions of Nations.* Beverly Hills: Sage, 1972.

Russett, Bruce M. *Trends in World Politics.* New York: Macmillan, 1965.

Russett, Bruce M., and Harvey Starr. *World Politics.* San Francisco: Freeman, 1981.

Scammel, G. V. *The World Encompassed: The First European Maritime Empires.* Berkeley and Los Angeles: University of California Press, 1981.

Schuman, Frederick L. *International Politics: An Introduction to the Western State System.* 2d ed. New York: McGraw-Hill, 1937.

Shaw, Stanford J. *History of the Ottoman Empire and Modern Turkey.* 2 vols. Cambridge: Cambridge University Press, 1976.

Silberner, Edmund. *The Problem of War in Nineteenth Century Economic Thought.* Translated by Alexander H. Krappe. Princeton: Princeton University Press, 1946.

Singer, J. David, ed. *The Correlates of War I: Research Origins and Rationale.* New York: Free Press, 1979.

———. *The Correlates of War II: Testing Some Realpolitik Models.* New York: Free Press, 1980.

Singer, J. David, et al., eds. *Explaining War.* Beverly Hills: Sage, 1979.

Singer, J. David, Stuart A. Bremer, and John Stuckey. "Capability Distribution, Uncertainty, and Major Power War, 1820-1965." In *Peace, War, and Numbers,* edited by Bruce M. Russett, pp. 19-48. Beverly Hills: Sage, 1972.

Singer, J. David, and Thomas Cusack. "Periodicity, Inexorability, and Steermanship in International War." In *From National Development to Global Community,* edited by Richard Merritt and Bruce M. Russett, pp. 404-22. London: Allen & Unwin, 1981.

Singer, J. David, and Melvin Small. "Alliance Aggregation and the Onset of War, 1815-1945." In *Quantitative International Politics,* edited by J. David Singer, pp. 247-86. New York: Free Press, 1968.

———. "Foreign Policy Indicators: Predictors of War in History and in the State of the World Message." *Policy Sciences* 5 (September 1974): 271-96.

———. *The Wages of War, 1816-1965: A Statistical Handbook.* New York: Wiley, 1972.

Siverson, Randolph M., and Joel King. "Alliances and the Expansion of War, 1815-1965." In *To Augur Well: The Design and Use of Early Warning Indicators in Inter-state Conflict,* edited by J. David Singer and Michael Wallace, pp. 37-49. Beverly Hills: Sage, 1979.

———. "Attributes of National Alliance Memberships and War Participation, 1815-1965." *American Journal of Political Science* 24 (February 1980):1-15.

Small, Melvin, and J. David Singer. *Resort to Arms: International and Civil Wars, 1816-1980.* Beverly Hills: Sage, 1982.

———. "Diplomatic Importance of States, 1816-1970: An Extension and Refinement of the Indicator." *World Politics* 25 (July 1973):577-99.

Smoke, Richard. *War: Controlling Escalation.* Cambridge, Mass.: Harvard University Press, 1977.

Snyder, Glenn H. *Deterrence and Defense.* Princeton: Princeton University Press, 1961.

Sorokin, Pitirim A. *Social and Cultural Dynamics.* 4 vols. New York: American Book Company, 1937.

Spiegel, Steven L. *Dominance and Diversity: The International Hierarchy.* Boston: Little, Brown, 1972.

Starr, Harvey, and Benjamin A. Most. "The Substance and Study of Borders in International Relations Research." *International Studies Quarterly* 20 (December 1976):581-620.

Stuckey, John, and Singer, J. David. "The Powerful and the Warprone: Ranking the Nations by Relative Capability and War Experience, 1820-1964." Mimeograph. Ann Arbor: University of Michigan, 1973.

Sumner, B. H. *Peter the Great and the Emergence of Russia.* New York: Collier, 1965.

Taylor, A. J. P. *The Struggle for Mastery in Europe, 1847-1918.* Oxford: Oxford University Press, 1971.

Thompson, William R. "Seapower in Global Politics, 1500-1945: Problems of Data Collection and Analysis." Paper delivered at annual meeting of International Studies Association/West, Los Angeles, 1980.

Thucydides. *The Peloponnesian War.* Translated by Rex Warner. Baltimore: Penguin, 1954.

Toynbee, Arnold Joseph. *A Study of History.* 12 vols. London: Oxford University Press, 1934-61.

Tufte, Edward R. *Data Analysis for Politics and Policy.* Englewood Cliffs, N.J.: Prentice-Hall, 1974.

Ulam, Adam. *Expansion and Coexistence: The History of Soviet Foreign Policy, 1917-1967.* New York: Praeger, 1968.

Vagts, Alfred. *A History of Militarism.* Rev. ed. New York: Free Press, 1959.

The Vietnam Hearings. New York: Vintage, 1966.

Wagner, R. Harrison. "The Decision to Divide Germany and the Origins of the Cold War." *International Studies Quarterly* 24 (June 1980):155-90

Wallace, Michael. *War and Rank among Nations.* Lexington, Mass.: Lexington Books, 1973.

Wallerstein, Immanuel. *The Modern World System.* 2 vols. New York: Academic Press, 1974 and 1980.

———. "The Rise and Future Demise of the World Capitalist System: Concepts for Comparative Analysis," *Comparative Studies in Society and History* 16 (September 1974):387-415.

———. "The Three Instances of Hegemony in the History of the Capitalist World-Economy." Paper delivered at III Conference of Europeanists, Washington, D.C., April 29-May 1, 1982.

Waltz, Kenneth N. *Man, the State and War.* New York: Columbia University Press, 1954.

———. *Theory of International Politics.* Reading, Mass.: Addison-Wesley, 1979.

Warth, Robert D. *The Allies and the Russian Revolution.* Durham, N.C.: Duke University Press, 1954.

Webster, Sir Charles. *The Congress of Vienna.* New York: Barnes & Noble, 1966.

Wedgwood, C. V. *The Thirty Years War.* New York: Doubleday Anchor, 1961.

Wei, William Wu-Shyong. "The Effect of Temporal Aggregation on Discrete Dynamic Time Series Models." Ph.D. dissertation, University of Wisconsin, 1974.

Wight, Martin. *Power Politics.* London: Royal Institute of International Affairs, 1946.

Wilcox, Walter F., ed. *International Migrations.* Vol. 2. New York: National Bureau of Economic Research, 1931.

Wilkinson, David. *Deadly Quarrels.* Berkeley and Los Angeles: University of California Press, 1980.

Wolf, John B. *Toward a European Balance of Power, 1620-1715.* (Chicago: Rand McNally, 1970.)

Wolfe, Thomas W. *Soviet Power and Europe, 1945-70.* Baltimore: Johns Hopkins Press, 1970.

Wolfers, Arnold. *Discord and Collaboration.* Baltimore: Johns Hopkins Press, 1962.

Wonnacott, Ronald J., and Thomas H. Wonnacott. *Regression.* New York: Wiley, 1981.

Woods, Frederick Adams, and Alexander Baltzly. *Is War Diminishing?* Boston: Houghton-Mifflin, 1915.

Wright, Quincy. *A Study of War.* 2d ed. Chicago: University of Chicago Press, 1965.

Yamamoto, Yoshinobu, and Stuart A. Bremer. "Wider Wars and Restless Nights: Major Power Intervention in Ongoing War." In *Correlates of War II,* edited by J. David Singer, pp. 199-232. New York: Free Press, 1980.

Yamane, Taro. *Statistics.* 3d ed. New York: Harper & Row, 1973.

Zellner, Arnold, and Claude Montmarquette. "A Study of Some Aspects of Temporal Aggregation Problems in Econometric Analysis." *Review of Economics and Statistics* 53 (November 1971):335–42.

Zinnes, Dina A. *Contemporary Research in International Relations.* New York: Free Press, 1976.

Index